Equity, Diversity, and Inclusion in Career Development

A Practical Handbook

Ifza Shakoor

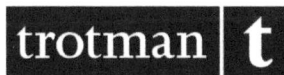

Equity, Diversity, and Inclusion in Career Development

This first edition published in 2025 by Trotman, an imprint of Trotman Indigo Publishing Ltd, 18e Charles Street, Bath BA1 1HX.

© Trotman Indigo Publishing Ltd 2025

Author: Ifza Shakoor

British Library Cataloguing in Publication Data
A catalogue record for this book is available from the British Library.

Paperback ISBN 978-1-911724-69-8
eISBN 978-1-911724-70-4

All rights reserved. This book is sold subject to the condition that it shall not, by way of trade or otherwise, be lent, resold, hired out or otherwise circulated without the publisher's prior written consent in any form of binding or cover other than that in which it is published and without a similar condition including this condition being imposed on the subsequent purchaser. No part of this publication may be reproduced, stored in a retrieval system or transmitted in any form or by any means, electronic and mechanical, photocopying, recording or otherwise without prior permission of Trotman Indigo Publishing.

Every effort has been made to trace copyright holders and to obtain their permission for the use of copyright material. The publisher apologises for any errors or omissions, and would be grateful to be notified of any corrections that should be incorporated in future editions of this book.

The authorised representative in the EEA is Easy Access System Europe Oü (EAS), Mustamäe tee 50, 10621 Tallinn, Estonia.

Printed and bound in the UK by CMP Ltd.

 All details in this book were correct at the time of going to press. To keep up to date with all the latest news and updates and to access the online resources that accompany this book, use this QR code or visit **www.trotman.co.uk/pages/equity-diversity-and-inclusion-in-career-development-resources**

Contents

Figures and tables	ix
About the author	xi
Acknowledgements	xv
Dedication	xvii
Foreword	xix
Introduction to the structure of this book	xxi
Glossary	xxiii

PART ONE
OVERVIEW OF EDI IN CAREER DEVELOPMENT — 1

Chapter 1 The need for EDI in career development — 2
- Author's rationale: Why this book? — 2
- Understanding the landscape — 4
- Understanding careers and EDI — 5
- Barriers — 6
- Sector level — 7
- Institutional level — 9
- Practitioner level — 10
- Client level — 11
- Enablers — 12
- Lived experiences — 14
- Where it all began: Centring practitioner voice — 15

Chapter 2 Introducing the TEDI framework — 17
- What is TEDI? — 18
- Sidenote on language — 21

Chapter 3 The TEDI framework practical toolkit — 23
- TEDI self-reflection prompts — 24
- Bias awareness map — 26
- TEDI toolkit self-audit — 27
- TEDI organisational reflection questions — 28
- Empowering clients through equity: A TEDI practice guide — 28

PART TWO
DEEP DIVE INTO KEY DIVERSITY INTERSECTIONS   31

Chapter 4   Understanding intersectionality in career development   33
Chapter roadmap   33
Author's voice   34
What is intersectionality?   35
The Intersectionality Wheel in careers practice   36
Reflecting on identity, power, and practice   37
Intersectionality barriers   39
Intersectionality enablers   40
What can I do next?   42
Embedding practice   42
Organisational toolkit   44
Practitioner voice as evidence: Why listening matters   45
Task   49
TEDI and intersectionality: How they intersect and why it matters   50

Chapter 5   Understanding ethnicity in career development   51
Chapter roadmap   51
Author's voice   52
What is ethnicity?   53
Understanding ethnic inequity in careers   54
Barriers   56
Enablers   58
Barriers and solutions   59
Practitioner toolkit: Surviving the system while shifting it   60
Reflection task: Auditing your organisation for ethnic equity   61
Organisational toolkit: Embedding ethnic equity into the system   62
Unpacking your voice: Reflections from the CDI Ethnicity Workshop   65
Thinking points and action grid   67

Chapter 6   Religion in career development   68
Chapter roadmap   68
Author's voice   69
Religious diversity defined   69
Understanding religion in the careers sector   70
Practitioner lived experiences   72
Client perspectives: When faith is part of the conversation   73
Barriers to inclusion   74
Enablers   76
Tools for reflection and practice review   78

Tools for practice	80
Organisational audit: Religion and belief inclusion	81
Unpacking religion: Reflective quotes for practice	83

Chapter 7 Gender equity in career development — 86

Chapter roadmap	86
Author's voice	86
What do we mean by gender?	88
Understanding gender inequity in the careers sector	89
Practitioner lived experiences	90
Barriers to gender equity	92
Enablers	96
Practitioner toolkit	97
Organisational toolkit: Structural change	99
Reflection task: Enablers	100
Reflective task: Unpacking gender quotes	101
Thinking grid	102

Chapter 8 Sexuality and sexual identity in the careers sector — 104

Chapter roadmap	104
Author's voice	104
What do we mean by sexuality and sexual identity?	106
Understanding sexuality and gender identity in career development	108
Practitioner lived experiences	109
Client perspectives	110
Barriers to inclusion	112
Enablers	113
Tools for practice	115
Organisational audit table	115
Reflective quotes	116

Chapter 9 Disability in career development — 119

Chapter roadmap	119
Author's voice	120
What do we mean by disability?	120
Understanding disability in the careers sector	122
Practitioner lived experiences	123
Barriers to inclusion	125
Enablers	127
Practitioner toolkit: Disability-inclusive practice	129
Organisational toolkit: Structural change	130
Thinking grid: Audit your practice	131
Reflective task: Unpacking disability quotes	132

Chapter 10 Neurodiversity in career development — 135
- Chapter roadmap — 135
- Author's voice — 136
- What do we mean by neurodiversity? — 137
- Neurodivergence in careers guidance — 138
- Practitioner lived experience — 139
- Client perspectives — 141
- Barriers — 142
- Enablers — 144
- Reflective quotes — 145
- Tools for practice — 147
- Practice reflection: Identifying barriers in your context — 148
- Organisational audit — 149

Chapter 11 Socio-economic status in the careers sector — 151
- Chapter roadmap — 151
- Author's voice — 151
- Socio-economic status definition — 152
- Lived experience and professional blind spots — 155
- Client perspectives — 156
- Barriers — 157
- Enablers — 159
- Reflective quotes — 161
- Tools for practice — 163

PART THREE
IMPLEMENTATION AND ACTION — 165

Chapter 12 Creating inclusive career guidance practices — 166
- Why implementation matters now — 166
- Principles of inclusive guidance — 167
- Building inclusive environments using the TEDI framework — 169
- From principles to practice — 171
- Common pitfalls and what to avoid — 172
- Case studies in inclusive practice — 174
- A step-by-step guide to embedding TEDI in careers work — 176
- From checklist to culture — 180
- Reflective practice grid — 181
- TEDI culture audit tool — 182

Chapter 13 Transforming practice through inclusion	**185**
Author's voice	185
Why is EDI important?	186
TEDI framework	187
Barriers to implementation and how to move through them	188
Recommendations	189
Tools for transformation: Practising equity through TEDI	190
TEDI self-assessment grid	191
Culture audit tool	192
Client's support and access form	192
Inclusive guidance checklist	193
Case study reflection prompts	193
TEDI implementation map	194
Leadership accountability matrix	194
Client voice integration tool	194
The ongoing TEDI journey	195
References	**197**

Online resources

To access the online resources that accompany this book, scan the QR code or visit the web address at the start of this book.

Figures and tables

Figures

1. The intersectionality wheel, © Sylvia Duckworth. (Reproduced with kind permission.) — 36

Tables

1. Bias awareness map — 26
2. What can I do next? — 42
3. Barriers and potential solutions — 60
4. Equity action plan — 62
5. Thinking points and action grid — 67
6. Barriers — 76
7. Practitioner reflection: Mapping barriers to faith inclusion — 78
8. Enablers and possibilities: Faith inclusion in careers work — 79
9. Organisational audit: Religion and belief inclusion — 82
10. Quotes — 95
11. Enablers — 100
12. Audit — 103
13. Tools for practice — 115
14. Organisational audit — 116
15. Barriers and implications — 127
16. Thinking grid: Audit your practice — 132
17. Practice reflection: Identifying barriers in your context — 148
18. Organisational audit — 149
19. Tools for practice — 163
20. Organisational audit — 164
21. Reflective practice grid — 181
22. TEDI self-assessment grid — 192
23. Inclusive guidance checklist — 193
24. TEDI implementation map — 194
25. Leadership accountability matrix — 194

About the author

Ifza Shakoor is an Equity, Diversity, and Inclusion (EDI) specialist, researcher, educator, and activist with over 10 years of teaching experience across schools, prisons, and alternative education settings. She is currently the EDI Associate at the Career Development Institute (CDI) – the first person to hold this national role – where she leads on anti-oppressive practice, structural inclusion, and equity-centred change in the careers sector.

One of the most transformative turning points in Ifza's career came when she joined the *Our Future Derby* project – a Department for Education Opportunity Area-funded programme designed to embed meaningful careers-related learning across 35 primary and secondary schools in the city. Working alongside Professor Deirdre Hughes OBE, who later became her mentor, Ifza helped steer the project into becoming the best-performing Opportunity Area-funded programme in England. This success was driven by her unwavering focus on making careers education fun, accessible, and relevant – particularly for students from underrepresented communities. It was this experience that sparked her deep interest in careers education and eventually led to her being awarded a PhD scholarship at the University of Derby, where she now conducts research through iCeGS (the International Centre for Guidance Studies) under the supervision and guidance of Professor Siobhan Neary, Professor Charlotte Chadderton and Dr Dominic Jackson-Cole.

She is currently pursuing her PhD at the University of Derby, researching EDI in the career development sector in England and the underrepresentation of ethnically diverse practitioners. She also served as Chair of the Postgraduate Research (PGR) Committee and EDI Chair, shaping institutional approaches to research culture, inclusion, and structural equity. In 2023, she was awarded the University's 3-Minute Thesis title, recognised for her ability to communicate systemic injustice with clarity and impact.

Ifza is an experienced educator, having completed teaching at secondary level in a religious school setting in England, while now transitioning back to her roots in primary education in an international setting in the Middle East. Her teaching journey spans diverse contexts, including working as a tutor for NEET and hard-to-reach students, which equipped her with a deep bank of alternative strategies and trauma-informed practices. She believes education must meet students where they are – not where systems expect them to be – and her work consistently reflects that ethos.

In 2024, Ifza was appointed the first-ever Reading Lead at a Category B male prison, where she developed a whole-prison literacy strategy. Although her time in the role was cut short due to parenting responsibilities, the experience further cemented her commitment to dismantling the structural inequalities that funnel so many young people – particularly from marginalised communities – into exclusion and incarceration. She often speaks about the need for accessible, flexible workplaces, especially for neurodivergent and parenting professionals, and continues to challenge employment models that overlook care responsibilities.

Ifza is neurodiverse, having been diagnosed with ADHD during the first year of her PhD – a discovery that offered long-awaited answers and strengthened her resolve to advocate for access, energy-sensitive working, and systems of belonging. She is known for her forthright voice on LinkedIn and her blog, where she writes on justice, hypocrisy, structural exclusion, and building systems with integrity.

She is also the founder of *A Career in Careers*, a global interview series highlighting diverse voices within the sector, which organically evolved into an international platform for practitioner storytelling and visibility.

A mother of three, Ifza became a young mum herself, and has always fiercely advocated for women – especially mothers – to continue education and pursue meaningful careers wherever possible. Her own journey through motherhood, higher education, and professional life has shaped her firm belief that care and ambition are not in conflict – and that structural reform is essential to make this a lived reality for more women.

She is currently developing two major ventures: *Rizq Jobs*, a diversity-led job board focused on inclusive recruitment and employment equity, and *Al-Firdous Waqf*, a Muslim charitable trust she is co-founding with her business partner, Mohammed Hakeem, to transform access to community funeral services, death committees, and burial provision.

Ifza also served as a school governor and was the first-ever Muslim board member of *YMCA Derbyshire*, where she helped steer the organisation's EDI approach and bring community-rooted perspectives into strategic decision-making.

Her work is lived, layered, and unapologetically practical. This book weaves together her journey as an educator, scholar, mother, and social justice practitioner – offering an honest, grounded, and action-focused guide to equity in careers work and beyond.

About the Author

A personal note from Ifza

Dear friends, readers, colleagues, and developing TEDI experts,

This is not just theory. This is lived. And I'm taking you with me on this journey. Knowledge should never be hoarded in the ivory tower. I am inviting you all to become experts in embedding TEDI.

With humility and an open hand
Your friend,
Ifza

Acknowledgements

This book would not have been possible without the encouragement, collaboration, and unwavering belief of many people.

To Dr Oliver Jenkin – thank you for planting the seed. Your vision and suggestion to turn this work into a book gave me the confidence to begin.

To Alexandra Price – your editorial guidance, patience, and professionalism brought clarity and coherence to every page. Thank you for trusting the voice and vision behind this work.

To all the webinar participants and speakers who contributed to the CDI EDI Lunchtime Series – your honesty, lived experiences, and courage to speak truthfully helped shape the tone, themes, and soul of this book. You created space for others simply by showing up.

To the Career Development Institute (CDI) and to David Morgan – thank you for appointing me as the first-ever EDI Associate. This role gave me the platform to embed systemic change, and it has been one of the most meaningful professional chapters of my life.

To Mohammed Hakeem – your critical feedback, generosity with your time, and encouragement to keep going meant more than you know. You reminded me why this work matters, especially when the process felt heavy. Thank you.

To Sylvia Duckworth – thank you for granting permission to include your powerful visual summary of intersectionality. Your work has helped countless people understand complex ideas more accessibly.

To Professor Deirdre Hughes OBE – thank you for always being just a phone call away. You believed in me before I did and chose me as your mentee, saying you saw yourself in me. I will never forget your overnight letter of recommendation for the PhD studentship that changed the course of my life. Thank you for your belief, your mentorship, and for holding space for me to grow.

To my colleagues and community at iCeGS (the International Centre for Guidance Studies) – thank you for shaping my thinking and offering intellectual and emotional solidarity. Special thanks to Professor Siobhan Neary, who not only supported my PhD journey but encouraged me to apply for the CDI EDI Associate role in the first place.

To the University of Derby – thank you for awarding me the studentship that opened this door. It gave me the time, space, and support to explore the structural inequities that underpin this work.

To the many educators, practitioners, and EDI professionals who have messaged, encouraged, challenged, or cheered me on over the years – your words, whether public or private, helped me push forward with purpose.

To my parents, siblings, and family – thank you for understanding the late nights, intense deadlines, and the many missed calls. Your belief in me held everything up. Thank you for instilling these values in me, where I cannot stay silent to injustice.

To my children, thank you for putting up with a workaholic mother. I hope I make you proud. One day, may you see my name and your faces light up, saying, 'That's my mama!'

And finally, to every reader of this book – thank you for choosing to walk this journey with me. May it be a resource, a provocation, and a companion in your work towards justice.

Thank you, I see you, and I appreciate every single one of you.

Ifza

Dedication

To Amma and Nana, my maternal Grandparents –
who came to England as economic migrants, seeking opportunity in a land that was often cold, unwelcoming, and far too racist. The prejudice you endured, alongside others whose skin carried more melanin, was relentless. Yet you persevered. You arrived with little more than the clothes on your backs, barely out of teenagerhood, shared homes with strangers, worked long hours on trains and in factories, and faced barriers at every turn. Still, you laid the foundations for everything we now have.

The opportunities falling at your grandchildren's feet today exist because of your sacrifice.
Through determination and courage, you paved pathway after pathway for us to walk. I carry your journey with me. I carry the weight of my ancestors – whose lands were colonised, whose languages were silenced, whose cultures were forced to adapt.
But today, your daughter does not conform.
I resist.
I recognise my power and privilege because of you, and I wield it in service of justice.
This book stands on your shoulders.

To everyone who ever felt different –
who didn't quite fit in,
who was told they were too much,
or not enough,
who felt unseen in the spaces that were supposed to welcome them.
I see you.
I hear you.
I am you.
This book is for us.

To my babies – Esa, Zayaan, and Ayla,
who remind me every day that love, learning, and justice must coexist.
May you grow into a world more equitable than the one we inherited.

And to the educators, changemakers, policymakers, and quiet and not-so-quiet disruptors –
this book is for you too.
You are the engineers of better futures – a world which meets people exactly where they are, and fights for true social justice for all.
We move beyond words into action.

– Ifza

Foreword

That equity, diversity, and inclusion (EDI) should be relevant to career development work will come as little surprise to most readers of this book. After all, EDI is one of the main points of the CDI's code of ethics, which states that practitioners should actively 'work towards the removal of barriers to personal achievement resulting from prejudice, stereotyping and discrimination' (CDI, 2024). That said, it remains the case that in the UK, the career development profession itself remains remarkably lacking in diversity, with the CDI's own research (co-led by this book's author) finding it to be 'weighted towards older, White, middle-class females' (CDI, 2023, p.3).

This offers us the context for Ifza Shakoor's *EDI in Career Development*, since, despite the career development sector's long-standing humanistic and social justice-orientated focus, there is still much to do if we are to evolve the sector in a truly equitable and inclusive direction. As Shakoor points out, the ways in which bias and marginalisation feature in the sector are multivariate, ranging from unconscious bias occurring in 1:1 career guidance sessions (e.g. certain occupations not being addressed as appropriate for particular client groups), right through to institutional bias (e.g. the same social demographics and ethnic backgrounds being represented at management level in professional bodies and employers). As such, this book offers much material for reflection for practitioners, line managers, service commissioners, and policymakers alike.

To really engage with Shakoor's message will mean that the reader needs to lean into some uncomfortable truths sometimes, since lasting change will not be possible without the kind of deep self-reflection that this book advocates. Fortunately, the reader is supported through this process with structured self-reflection and action planning exercises included within each chapter. Ultimately, this is a practical book, not an inert theoretical treatise, and the ethic of continual self-reflection and revision it encourages is not only healthy but a way of allowing the reader to root their practice in social justice and see what this means in their workplaces.

This is an essential book – one that all career development practitioners (and those who commission their services) should read and return to, regularly. I recommend it to individuals working in all parts of the sector and to those responsible for drafting and shaping career development policy.

Dr Oliver Jenkin PGCE RCDP, NICEC Fellow.

CDI Senior Professional Development and Standards Manager, and Editor of the CDI's magazine, Career Matters.

July 2025

References

Career Development Institute (CDI). (2023). *Equity, diversity and inclusion strategy 2023–2026*. Stourbridge: Career Development Institute.

Career Development Institute (CDI). (2024). *CDI code of ethics*. thecdi.net/about-us/cdi-code-of-ethics

Introduction to the structure of this book

This book has been deliberately structured into three interconnected sections to support both reflective understanding and practical application. Each part builds upon the last – moving from insight to action – to ensure that Equity, Diversity, and Inclusion (EDI) is not just understood in theory but meaningfully embedded in everyday career development practice.

In not conforming to norms, we begin with the glossary. I have tried to make this as accessible as possible and to keep the language jargon-free.

Part One: Overview of EDI in career development

This section sets the stage by exploring the rationale for EDI in the career development sector. It offers a critical overview of why this work is urgent and necessary, introduces the TEDI framework as a tool for change, and outlines the foundations for understanding EDI through practical and conceptual lenses. These chapters create a shared language and vision, ensuring readers are equipped with a clear and confident starting point.

Part Two: Deep dive into key diversity intersections

The heart of the book lies in this section, which examines key aspects of identity and systemic inequality that shape career experiences. Each chapter follows a consistent structure, exploring barriers, enablers, and practical solutions across intersections such as ethnicity, religion, gender, disability, neurodiversity, and socio-economic background. Lived experiences and practitioner insights are woven throughout, offering honest, grounded perspectives. These chapters are designed to challenge assumptions and expand the reader's ability to see – and act upon – the full complexity of clients' lived realities.

Part Three: Implementation and action

Finally, the book moves into applied practice. These chapters focus on how to translate awareness into action, offering tools, templates, and strategic guidance for creating inclusive careers services and guidance systems. This section also offers a vision for the future – encouraging practitioners, policymakers, and educators to become lifelong learners and changemakers in this space. It is where intention meets action, and where structural equity begins to take root.

Glossary

Yes, I know glossaries usually sit at the back of the book – but this is not a usual book. This is an inclusive one. And in the spirit of inclusion, why leave definitions until the end? Everyone deserves to understand the language from the start.

Accessibility

More than ramps and lifts, it's about ensuring everyone can participate fully, whether that's in a conversation, a service, or a workplace. This includes physical, sensory, digital, emotional, and cognitive access.

Advocacy

Standing up, speaking out, and using your position to push for equity – even when it's uncomfortable. Advocacy isn't passive; it's active disruption in service of justice.

Allyship

A verb, not a badge. True allyship means ongoing action, learning, and solidarity – especially when no one's watching. It's about relinquishing power, not hoarding it.

Anti-oppressive practice

An approach that actively identifies, challenges, and dismantles systems of oppression in practice. It's not just about being non-discriminatory – it's about consciously disrupting inequality at every level.

Assimilation

The pressure to conform to dominant norms in order to gain access or acceptance is often at the cost of one's identity. Inclusion must never mean erasure.

Audit

A structured way to assess current practice – not just a tick-box exercise but a deep dive into what's working, what's missing, and what needs to shift.

Barriers

The visible and invisible walls people face when trying to access opportunities or inclusivity. These can be structural, cultural, interpersonal, or internalised – and they rarely exist in isolation.

Belonging

That powerful feeling of being seen, accepted, and valued – not despite your differences but because of them. Belonging is the end goal of inclusion.

Bias

The assumptions we carry – consciously or unconsciously – that shape how we treat, respond to, or value others. Bias isn't just personal; it shows up in policies, systems, and culture.

By design

When injustice isn't accidental. 'By design' means systems were built in ways that exclude, marginalise, or benefit some at the expense of others – intentionally or through sustained neglect. If inequity is by design, then justice must be by redesign.

Code-switching

The act of changing one's language, appearance, or behaviour to fit into dominant norms – often done for safety, survival, or acceptance. It's exhausting and rarely a choice free from consequences.

Colonialism

The violent process of control and exploitation – where land, labour, culture, and autonomy were taken under the guise of 'civilisation' or 'progress'. Its legacies are not historical footnotes; they're embedded in today's systems, from education to employment.

Coloniser

Not just a person but a role – one that imposed power, erased cultures, and extracted wealth. The term reminds us that privilege and systemic inequality didn't emerge by accident – they were built.

Critical Race Theory (CRT)

A framework that explores how racism is embedded in systems, not just in individuals. CRT names injustice, highlights power dynamics, and insists on centring lived experience.

Cultural capital

The knowledge, behaviours, and connections that are valued by dominant systems – often unconsciously. Those who 'fit' are rewarded, while others are expected to adapt. Cultural capital shapes who is seen as 'professional', 'capable', or 'ready'.

Culture

The shared values, behaviours, customs, and ways of being that shape how people live, interact, and make meaning. Culture isn't fixed – it evolves. And it influences everything from how careers are perceived to how inclusion is experienced.

Decolonisation

Not a metaphor. Decolonisation means actively dismantling colonial power structures and returning voice, value, and autonomy to those historically erased. In careers work, it asks us to question whose knowledge counts and whose aspirations are legitimised.

Diversity

The range of visible and invisible differences between people – but it's not just about who is in the room. It's also about who feels safe to speak, be heard, and shape the space.

EDI (Equity, Diversity, and Inclusion)

Not a trend. Not a tick-box. A commitment to justice, fairness, and meaningful belonging across systems. Each letter matters – and they must work together.

Emotional labour

The hidden work of managing feelings, reactions, and responses – especially for marginalised individuals navigating oppressive environments. Often expected but rarely recognised or compensated.

Enablers

The people, tools, attitudes, and structures that make equity possible. Enablers shift the system closer to justice.

Equity

Fairness in action. Equity means recognising that people start from different places and adjusting systems so that outcomes can be just. It's not the same as equality.

Ethnically diverse

Used in place of terms like 'minority', 'BAME', or other othering language. Ethnically diverse centres people's identities without reducing them to statistics or margins. It affirms difference without deficit – and challenges the default whiteness often assumed in professional spaces.

Framework

A structured way of thinking or working that helps guide action. A good framework offers clarity, without being rigid.

Gaslighting

A form of psychological manipulation where someone is made to doubt their reality. In institutional settings, it's often used to deny lived experiences of discrimination or inequality.

In-group/out-group

Who is seen as 'us' versus 'them' – these dynamics shape who gets access, empathy, and influence. In-group favouritism often goes unacknowledged but drives exclusion.

Inclusion

The act of creating spaces where everyone feels valued, respected, and able to contribute. It's not about adding people in – it's about redesigning systems so nobody's left out.

Intersectionality

Coined by Kimberlé Crenshaw, this is about how different aspects of identity (race, gender, class, disability, etc.) intersect to shape lived experience – often creating compounding disadvantage.

Intervention

A deliberate action or strategy to shift the dial towards equity. Not always dramatic but always intentional.

Justice

The bigger picture. Justice is what we're working towards – beyond diversity statistics or training sessions. It's about fair systems, righting historical wrongs, and sustainable inclusion.

Liberation

The end goal – where systems are rebuilt to centre justice, dignity, and self-determination. Liberation isn't offered – it's claimed.

Lived experience

The expertise people hold from having actually navigated systems of oppression or exclusion – not studied from afar but lived, felt, and survived.

Marginalised

A term for individuals or communities pushed to the edges of decision-making, visibility, and power – not by accident but by design.

Microaggressions

Everyday slights, comments, or behaviours – often unintentional – that reinforce marginalisation. They may seem 'small', but their cumulative effect is deep and damaging.

Neurodiversity

The natural variation in how human brains work. It includes ADHD, autism, dyslexia, and more – and challenges the idea of one 'normal' way of thinking or processing.

Othering

The process of marking someone as different, deviant, or outside the norm. It reduces identity to stereotype and reinforces exclusion.

Power

Not just about authority or seniority – power is the ability to influence outcomes, set norms, or withhold access. It can be visible or hidden, earned or inherited. Naming power is the first step in redistributing it.

Practice

Not theory, not performance – practice is what we *actually do*. It's how values show up in real time. In the EDI space, practice means embedding equity into everyday decisions, systems, and relationships.

Practitioner

Anyone working directly with people in support, guidance, education, or advocacy roles. Practitioners are at the frontline of inclusion.

Privilege

Unearned advantage that operates invisibly unless named. Privilege isn't something to feel guilty about – but it must be used to uplift others.

Racism

A system, not just a slur. Racism lives in policies, practices, institutions, and cultures – and impacts outcomes in everything from health to employment.

Reflection

A critical pause. Reflection means stepping back to examine our own assumptions, choices, and impact – not for guilt but for growth. It's where insight is born and where better practice begins.

Representation

Ask yourself who is seen, who is heard, and who is missing? True representation goes beyond optics – it's about meaningful inclusion and influence at every level.

Resilience

Often celebrated, but too frequently weaponised. Resilience is the strength people show in the face of adversity – but the goal should be systems that don't demand it so relentlessly.

Social justice

The movement and mindset behind this work. It's about shifting the entire system to centre equity, fairness, and dignity for all – not just for some.

Systemic (or structural) inequality

The way injustice is baked into the very fabric of society – from education to healthcare to employment. It's not about one bad apple; it's about the whole tree.

TEDI

The Transforming Equity, Diversity, and Inclusion framework – created to support careers professionals in embedding justice and inclusion in practice. It's practical, reflective, and designed with lived experience in mind.

Tokenism

The performative act of including a minoritised person or identity for the appearance of diversity, without redistributing power or addressing the wider system.

Voice

Not just about speaking, but about being heard and having influence. Voice is power – and who gets to use it tells us a lot about who holds it.

White privilege

The societal advantages that benefit White people by default. It's not about individual intent but about systems that were built to benefit some while excluding others.

Whiteness

Not just about skin colour – whiteness refers to a dominant cultural framework that is often positioned as neutral, standard, or universal. It shapes norms, values, and structures, often invisibly.

> **Note on language**
>
> In this book, terms referring to racial identities such as Black and White are capitalised to acknowledge them as sociopolitical identities rather than colour descriptors. However, terms such as whiteness, white privilege, and white cultural norms remain in lower case, as they refer to systems or concepts rather than identities.

PART ONE
OVERVIEW OF EDI IN CAREER DEVELOPMENT

Part One lays the groundwork for understanding why Equity, Diversity, and Inclusion (EDI) is not an optional add-on, but a vital foundation of ethical, effective career development practice.

We begin by acknowledging the structural inequalities and everyday biases that shape access to opportunity – recognising that the world of work has never been a level playing field.

Chapter 1 – The need for EDI in career development – explores why EDI is necessary in our sector, particularly for those historically excluded or misrepresented in guidance systems.

Chapter 2 – Introducing the TEDI framework – introduces the TEDI framework – a model developed to help practitioners move beyond passive awareness towards intentional, embedded equity work. TEDI is built on four interconnected pillars: Transparency, Equity, Diversity, and Inclusion – and this section walks you through its origins, its purpose, and how it can support change at both individual and institutional levels.

Chapter 3 – The TEDI framework practical toolkit – then turns theory into tools, offering practical strategies and templates for applying the TEDI framework in your own setting. These include reflective prompts, workshop activities, and mapping tools to assess where your service is now – and where it needs to go.

Collectedly, these chapters create a shared language, offer a point of entry for those newer to EDI, and provide clarity for more experienced professionals looking to deepen their practice. Whether you're a careers adviser, manager, educator, or policymaker, Part One is your starting point – a place to pause, reflect, and build your foundations before stepping into the deeper, more complex terrain of identity and inequality in Part Two.

Chapter 1
The need for EDI in career development

Author's rationale: Why this book?

My journey into Equity, Diversity, and Inclusion (EDI) didn't begin in academia or through formal study – it began with lived experience. At the time, I was a Special Educational Needs and Disability (SEND)-specialist Primary School Teacher; I was constantly confronted with inequities – some blatant, others insidious – especially towards those who looked like me. I am a Muslim woman, born and raised in a socio-economically disadvantaged inner-city community in England, and the reality of that identity shaped everything I saw, felt, and experienced within the school system. I noticed how colourism influenced which pupils were 'favourites', how certain names were mispronounced while others were praised, how the voices of some were amplified while others – especially those perceived as disruptive or 'too much' – were silenced. I noticed how unconscious bias, covert racism, misogyny, and exclusion played out in the classroom, in the staffroom, and within policies that claimed to serve all.

It disturbed me deeply, not just as a teacher but as someone who had experienced these exclusions myself as a child. I kept asking myself, 'Where is the justice in all this?' And more importantly, 'What could be done to change it?' Frustrated by the limits of my role and the constraints of a system that felt more invested in preserving appearances than addressing root causes, I made the difficult decision to leave teaching. I entered the world of sales and marketing, and although I succeeded professionally, I felt a deep disconnect from any sense of purpose. Something was missing. It wasn't until I took on a Careers Coordinator role that I felt like I'd come home. For the first time, my skills, lived experience, and personal mission aligned. I was already doing this work in my own community – informally guiding, listening, and helping others find direction. Suddenly, it had a name: career development.

While completing my Master's in Education with a specialisation in Lifelong Learning, I became increasingly aware of how careers work in schools often reinforced the very exclusions they claimed to address. I saw how students who didn't fit the institutional mould – those with additional needs, those who challenged authority, those from less advantaged backgrounds – were strategically excluded from enrichment sessions during inspection weeks or careers fairs. These were the learners who needed that guidance most, yet they were the ones pushed out to preserve reputational polish. I channelled that frustration into my dissertation, which focused on widening access to outreach and enrichment for learners with SEND. I was awarded a distinction, and more importantly, my findings led to real change: the organisation I worked for reformed its outreach criteria based on my work. That was the moment I realised the power of applied research – when knowledge doesn't just sit in journals but shapes systems.

So, I leaned into that momentum and began a PhD at the University of Derby in 2021, focusing on Equity, Diversity, and Inclusion in the career development sector in England. I was fortunate to be awarded a full studentship and saw this as an opportunity not just to research but to reimagine the sector through the lens of those who've often been left out of the conversation. In June 2022, I stepped into a role that felt like a natural extension of this journey – becoming the first EDI Associate for the Career Development Institute (CDI). That role gave me insight into the systemic challenges from an organisational perspective. It pushed me to think beyond individual practice and look at how we shift cultures, structures, and policies at scale.

At the same time, I began grounding my work in transformative research principles, particularly those advocated by Donna Mertens. One line from her work has stayed with me: *'Everyone has a voice, but not everyone has the platform to be heard.'* That principle became my anchor. David Morgan, the Chief Executive of the CDI – and someone I've worked closely with throughout this journey – offered an additional lens. He said, *'Give people the platform to be heard, if they want it.'* That final clause – 'if they want it' – mattered deeply to me. It reminded me that not every person holding a marginalised identity wants to be a representative or token voice. We must create space without assumption. Offer platforms without expectation – always, always, centre consent. It was with this principle that we co-developed the CDI's EDI strategy. I said to David, *'You may be the CEO, and I may be a researcher and consultant – but what we both lack is lived experience of working in the sector. We cannot design an inclusive sector from the top-down.'* So we chose to step back and elevate the voices of those living this work – practitioners across the sector whose insights, if truly heard, could shape something far more authentic than any policy alone.

My own compass throughout this work is grounded in faith. A verse that continues to guide me is this: *'Stand out firmly for justice, as witnesses to Allah, even though it be against yourselves, or your parents, or your kin . . .' (Qur'an 4:135).* This verse is a reminder that justice isn't conditional. It isn't selective or circumstantial. It is a moral obligation – and for me, this book is a form of witness. A documentation not just of theory or research, but of real stories, grounded experience, and tools to create meaningful change. It was conceived long before it was formally commissioned and carries a sense of purpose that's never left me: to build something that empowers transformation, not just in rhetoric but in real, everyday careers practice. That commitment later gave rise to the Transformative Equity Diversity Inclusion (TEDI) framework – an approach rooted in justice, shaped by lived experience, and built to serve those who've long been unheard.

Understanding the landscape

The career development sector in England is historically fragmented and underfunded. Since the disbanding of Connexions in 2013, the field has lacked the structural coherence seen in other parts of the UK, such as Scotland and Wales, where more centralised and coordinated systems remain intact. In England, provision varies widely depending on postcode, provider, and population served – resulting in what many rightly call a postcode lottery of access and quality. The inconsistency doesn't just affect service users; it also influences the development, recruitment, and progression of those working within the sector.

The workforce continues to be understood – both anecdotally and through emerging data – as predominantly White, female, middle-class, and ageing (Neary, 2020; Neary, Hanson and Cotterill, 2017). This stands in sharp contrast to the diverse communities the sector is meant to support. But this is not just a demographic observation. The issue goes deeper. It is not simply about who is in the room or who is missing; it is about how the sector has been built, whose values have shaped its foundations, and which worldviews continue to be centred in its systems, assumptions, and frameworks. These are not surface-level gaps – they are structural. In my PhD, I explore how colonial legacies, institutional power structures, and the dominance of Western career development theories have led to the ongoing marginalisation of ethnically diverse practitioners. This marginalisation is not isolated to one point in the pipeline. It occurs at every level: access, progression, recognition, and influence. These patterns are not anomalies; they are baked into the system. Naming this openly matters. But naming alone is not enough. This book does not just set out to describe what's wrong. It offers a shift in worldview – one that refuses to reproduce the very structures it critiques. That worldview is heavily informed by the work of Donna Mertens, whose transformative research paradigm calls us to centre equity, social justice, and voice – not as an afterthought but from the very start. Mertens reminds us that epistemology matters. In plain terms, epistemology refers to how we know what we know – whose truths are considered valid, whose stories are documented, and whose experiences are centred or dismissed. Her work invites us to ask: Whose knowledge counts? And why? Traditional approaches, even when well-intentioned, often sideline or silence those at the margins. A transformative approach insists we do the opposite: we co-create with those who live the realities we claim to address.

This way of thinking laid the groundwork for the TEDI framework, which I introduce later in the chapter. TEDI wasn't born from a desire to have another acronym or model. It emerged from a very real need to go beyond performative diversity and into transformational change. It asks us to rethink not just what we're doing but how, why, and for whom. TEDI is about shifting power. It's about reimagining who holds knowledge, whose voice is amplified, and how systems can evolve to be more equitable from the inside out. Grounded in lived experience, informed by critical research, and designed for practical use in real-world careers work, this book draws on conceptual frameworks like Crenshaw's intersectionality, the transformative paradigm of Mertens, and the everyday realities shared by those within the sector. It offers an approach that is both human-centred and systems-focused. The goal here isn't to raise awareness for the sake of it, or to create another short-lived EDI project that dies with a funding cycle. The goal is sustainable culture change – where equity isn't an add-on, but the starting point.

Understanding careers and EDI

Equity, Diversity, and Inclusion (EDI) is no longer an optional component in career development – it is a fundamental necessity. Within the context of career guidance, EDI refers to the fair treatment, access, opportunity, and advancement for all individuals, while striving to identify and eliminate barriers that have historically prevented the full participation of certain groups. Career development professionals occupy a critical position in shaping equitable pathways for clients from a wide array of backgrounds. However, without conscious and embedded EDI integration, the risk of replicating existing inequalities remains high – no matter how well-intentioned the practice. Historically, access to education, employment, and progression opportunities has been unequally distributed, with many marginalised groups systemically excluded or overlooked. Ethnically diverse individuals, disabled people, those from working-class backgrounds, LGBTQIA+ communities, and others with visible or invisible diverse characteristics often find themselves navigating systems that were never built with them in mind. These are not isolated or accidental oversights – they are symptoms of long-standing, biased structures. The career development sector must confront its complicity in these structures, interrogate how it upholds inequity, and respond with intention and accountability. This book stands as both a reflection and a response: a compilation of practice, insight, and research taking place across the careers space, and a practical toolkit to amplify and embed inclusive careers practice at every level.

Barriers

Barriers to inclusive career development exist at multiple, interlocking levels – and each chapter in this book will explore these in greater depth, focusing on the specific intersections where they are most visible and most harmful. But before we delve into those layered complexities, it's essential to pause and name the roots of these patterns. This isn't just about presenting abstract data or theoretical concepts. It's about grounding the work in real conversations, real stories, and the journey of how these insights emerged – often painfully but with clarity and purpose.

In the year leading up to the launch of the CDI's Equity, Diversity and Inclusion Strategy in October 2023, I facilitated a series of intentional, meaningful conversations across the careers sector. These were not tokenistic consultations designed to tick boxes. They were designed with care to centre voices that had too often been silenced or sidelined. I listened deeply, asked challenging questions, and prioritised spaces where people could speak truth without fear of judgement or consequence. These conversations happened in many forms: one-to-one listening sessions with practitioners across England; sector-wide workshops co-hosted with David Morgan, the CDI's Chief Executive; anonymous surveys through the CDI's annual Big Listen survey; live lunchtime webinars; and informal drop-in spaces that allowed for more open and spontaneous reflection. These dialogues were never about extracting information. They were about co-creating understanding. At the heart of every conversation, three simple but powerful questions kept surfacing – questions that would ultimately form the spine of our EDI strategy, and which still guide my research, consultancy, and day-to-day reflections:

1. What are the barriers?
2. What are the enablers?
3. What can the CDI do to create a culture of inclusion?

These weren't just prompts – they became the anchor points that structured every draft of the strategy, and continue to shape the tools, workshops, and frameworks I use in my work today. What emerged from these conversations was sobering: the barriers are not isolated or incidental. They are layered, systemic, and often go unchallenged because they've been normalised in both policy and practice. What I heard was a sector grappling with discomfort, uncertainty, and fear. Barriers showed up in how careers support is structured, who gets to access it, and who gets left behind. They were present in the rigidity of funding models, in outdated one-size-fits-all approaches to guidance, and in the nervousness practitioners feel when navigating identity and difference. I heard from professionals who felt unseen, from clients who were misjudged or misrepresented, and from leaders who genuinely wanted to do better but didn't know where to start. Most critically, I heard over and over again how much these issues intersect – how race, class, disability, gender, and faith don't exist in silos, and how solutions must be rooted in this complexity.

This chapter begins the process of unpacking those barriers – at sectoral, institutional, practitioner, and client levels. But I want to be clear: these aren't abstract categories on a page. They are lived realities. They are emotional burdens. They are structural disadvantages. They are also opportunities – if we are willing to see them as such – for collective action, courage, and change. My aim throughout this book is not simply to describe or categorise these issues but to offer tools, language, and frameworks to dismantle them. The TEDI framework, along with the lived experiences shared throughout this book, was born from these early conversations. Together, they serve not only as a lens to examine the landscape of careers provision but as a call to move beyond theory – into real, grounded, and sustainable action. What follows is not a diagnosis. It's a blueprint for transformation.

Sector level

The career development sector in England continues to suffer from a deep lack of meaningful representation – particularly at senior, strategic, and decision-making levels. The workforce remains predominantly White, female, middle-class, and ageing, as highlighted by Neary (2020), and this demographic profile fails to reflect the rich ethnic, generational, gendered, and socio-economic diversity of the clients it serves across schools, colleges, universities, prisons, job centres, and third-sector organisations. This disconnect is more than just a demographic mismatch; it exposes a structural imbalance between those shaping services and those relying on them. When leadership does not reflect the realities of its communities, the risk of developing policies and practices that overlook or exclude lived experiences becomes inevitable.

Practitioners from ethnically diverse backgrounds, disabled communities, and neurodivergent identities remain significantly underrepresented throughout the sector. Where representation does exist, it is often limited to entry-level, frontline, or fixed-term roles with little to no clear pathways into leadership or influence. This lack of progression creates a cycle of stagnation, where visibility without voice leads to burnout, and diversity without power reinforces tokenism. The absence of diverse perspectives in policy development and strategic planning further narrows the worldview through which services are designed, delivered, and evaluated. Careers guidance, at its best, is meant to open doors. But when the sector itself lacks open pathways, it sends a contradictory message to those it aims to empower.

Beyond ethnic and cultural disparities, other intersecting inequalities persist. Age and generational divides manifest in tensions between a younger, more diverse client base and an older, less diverse practitioner workforce. Cultural mismatches can lead to miscommunication, misunderstanding, and a failure to create psychologically safe environments for disclosure and guidance. Socio-economic barriers, both for those entering the profession and those accessing its services, also play a significant role. The sector's low pay, coupled with the cost of required qualifications such as the Level 6 Diploma in Career Guidance and Development, or the Qualification in Career Development (QCD), makes it inaccessible to many – especially those from working-class backgrounds. Gendered assumptions continue to influence not only who becomes a careers adviser but also the advice clients receive, often reinforcing outdated occupational stereotypes instead of challenging them.

Recruitment into the sector remains largely informal, opaque, and reliant on insular professional networks. There is a serious lack of targeted outreach, funded support, or culturally relevant mentorship programmes designed to widen access for underrepresented groups. For those who do manage to enter the field, retention is often hindered by a lack of progression opportunities, poor visibility of the profession in wider society, and persistent perceptions that career development is a low-status, low-impact field. These factors combine to dissuade new talent, especially those from marginalised backgrounds, from pursuing or sustaining a career in this space.

Where equity and inclusion initiatives do exist, they are often reactive – driven by external funding pressures, diversity audits, or national policy shifts. Rarely are they embedded into organisational culture or long-term strategy. Instead, responsibility for driving EDI work is disproportionately placed on marginalised individuals themselves – often without formal recognition, resources, or institutional backing. This not only results in emotional exhaustion but also reinforces a dynamic where inclusion becomes an individual burden rather than a collective responsibility.

Until leadership in the sector is truly diversified, until intersectional workforce data is gathered, shared, and acted upon transparently, and until EDI becomes a strategic priority integrated into every aspect of organisational life, the sector will continue to fall short of its potential. Representation matters – but it must be meaningful, supported, and accompanied by systems that allow representation to flourish. A workforce that does not reflect the communities it serves, and does not take steps to understand them, will – however unintentionally – continue to perpetuate harm.

This book seeks to confront these systemic imbalances head-on. Through each chater, we will examine these intersections in depth – exploring ethnicity, gender, disability, neurodiversity, religion and faith, socio-economic status, and LGBTQIA+ inclusion. These are not just themes – they are people's lived realities. What follows is not only an analysis but a call to action, offering tangible strategies and a roadmap for systemic transformation across the career development profession.

Institutional level

At the institutional level, careers services across many settings continue to operate within a framework that privileges standardisation over responsiveness. The *'one-size-fits-all'* model remains dominant – relying on rigid processes, outcome-focused metrics, and narrow assumptions about what constitutes a successful career. These systems may offer a sense of efficiency and structure, but they often fail to reflect the multifaceted realities of the people who rely on them. Rather than embracing complexity, institutions frequently simplify, streamline, and standardise in ways that marginalise those who do not fit the dominant mould. This issue came into sharp focus during the national workshops I facilitated in January 2023 as part of shaping the CDI's Equity, Diversity and Inclusion Strategy. A powerful theme emerged: both practitioners and clients repeatedly voiced their frustration at being reduced to labels. Individuals with protected characteristics – whether related to ethnicity, gender, disability, faith, or any other aspect of identity – shared how exhausting and alienating it feels to be pigeonholed or tokenised in the name of inclusion. What they wanted was simple but radical in its implications: to be seen as whole people, not defined by a single strand of their identity or used to tick a diversity box.

Yet, institutions often struggle – or fail entirely – to make space for this nuance. Careers provision is still largely shaped around majority norms: dominant communication styles, westernised interpretations of professionalism, assumed access to financial resources or family support, and linear pathways that do not account for the lived experiences of those navigating systemic disadvantage. When adjustments are made, they are typically surface-level gestures: a translated leaflet here, a renamed workshop there, or a one-off diversity event during a designated calendar month. These are not the hallmarks of transformational inclusion. They are examples of performative accommodation – changes that appear inclusive on the surface but leave the underlying structures intact.

There is also an entrenched discomfort among some careers staff when it comes to talking about identity with care and confidence. Without regular training, space for critical reflection, or permission to make mistakes and learn, institutions often lean on impersonal policies instead of courageous conversation. The default becomes professional neutrality – an unwillingness to *'get political'* or delve into difference. But in an unequal system, neutrality is not neutral. It is complicity. It reinforces the status quo and silences those most affected by exclusion. The problem extends beyond advice sessions to the design of the curriculum, the allocation of enrichment opportunities, and the criteria used to select clients for employer engagement or prestigious programmes. When decisions are filtered through reputational risk frameworks, those deemed *'too difficult'*, *'off-brand'*, or *'unpredictable'* are systematically excluded. This disproportionately impacts learners who are ethnically diverse, neurodivergent, living with SEND, or who challenge normative expectations of behaviour, dress, or language. Instead of being seen as bringing vital perspective and potential, they are often written off – sometimes without even knowing they were being judged.

Institutions must move beyond blanket policies and begin embedding culturally responsive, reflexive, and human-centred approaches. Identity should be embraced as a strength, not managed as a complication. True equity in careers practice is not about treating everyone the same – it is about understanding where people are starting from, what barriers they face, and what support they need to thrive. It is about designing systems that work for the margins first, knowing that in doing so, we lift the centre too. Thriving must replace surviving as the ultimate goal.

Practitioner level

At the practitioner level, barriers to embedding EDI often arise not from resistance but from uncertainty, discomfort, and fear. Many careers professionals express a lack of confidence when engaging with EDI work, particularly when navigating identity, privilege, or systemic bias within their everyday practice. The desire to avoid saying the wrong thing or causing offence can quickly become silence – and that silence, though understandable, is not neutral. In fact, inaction can do just as much harm as overt exclusion when it leads to avoidance or maintains the status quo. While good intentions are often present, they are not enough. A reluctance to engage can prevent the kinds of meaningful reflection, dialogue, and disruption that EDI work demands. I witnessed this directly during my time with the CDI. One interaction stands out: David Morgan, the CDI's Chief Executive, shared that a White practitioner had asked him, *'Are White people being excluded from the sector now?'* The question, though rooted in concern, reflected a common misunderstanding that inclusion for some must mean exclusion for others. David, aware of the significance of such sentiments, turned to me for guidance. My response was grounded in both truth and compassion: *'No, we're not kicking anyone out or replacing anyone – we're plugging the gaps. This sector is big enough for all of us.'* That moment stayed with me because it captured the need to reframe inclusion as an expansion, not a threat. Inclusion is not about taking space away from those already present; it's about making room for those who have long been excluded, overlooked, or underestimated. The careers profession needs White practitioners, just as it needs ethnically diverse, disabled, neurodivergent, LGBTQIA+, working-class, and faith-informed practitioners. Everyone brings value. What we must avoid is disengagement, especially when conversations become challenging or uncomfortable.

Yet despite this understanding, many practitioners remain underprepared to engage critically with equity issues. Reflective questions such as *'What assumptions am I bringing into this session?'* or *'Whose worldview is being centred here?'* are rarely embedded into routine practice. Often, reflective practice is focused on process rather than positionality – it asks us what we did, but not who we were or what frameworks we unconsciously relied upon. In a profession so deeply influenced by identity, culture, and power, this lack of critical reflection leaves a significant gap. Practitioners may shy away from discussing race, class, or gender because they fear getting it wrong, but avoidance only maintains the invisibility of these issues. Without ongoing support, training, and encouragement, many understandably default to neutrality – but in an unequal system, neutrality becomes complicity. To move forward, the sector must invest in transformative Continuing Professional Development (CPD) that goes beyond tick-box compliance and into deeper, messier, more human territory. We need spaces that are safe enough to be vulnerable in and brave enough to hold discomfort without judgement. We need leadership that is willing to model imperfection and continual learning, rather than perfection and defensiveness. EDI is not about guilt – it is about responsibility. If we are to support every client fairly, we must start by examining the tools, frameworks, and assumptions we carry into our work. As gatekeepers, facilitators, and sometimes the first point of contact for those navigating unequal systems, careers professionals hold enormous influence. That influence can either widen opportunity or reinforce exclusion. The choice – every day, in every session – is ours.

Client level

At the client level, the most transformative impact of a diverse, equity-informed careers workforce is felt directly by those on the receiving end of guidance – particularly individuals from marginalised or underserved communities. Yet, despite the values that underpin the sector, many clients continue to report being misunderstood, stereotyped, or offered limited pathways shaped more by practitioner bias than client potential. These aren't isolated experiences; they are indicative of broader, systemic tendencies to reduce people to categories rather than engage with them as whole individuals. Ethnically diverse clients, for instance, are often assumed to be navigating their career choices primarily through the lens of family pressure or cultural expectations, when in reality, their motivations may be just as varied, personal, and complex as any other client's. Similarly, clients from working-class backgrounds frequently find themselves steered towards vocational options, regardless of their academic strengths or career aspirations, while neurodivergent or disabled clients are often told – implicitly or explicitly – to lower their expectations, rather than being supported to explore what is truly possible. These assumptions may not always be voiced aloud, but they seep into body language, tone, the questions we ask – or fail to ask – and the options we highlight.

Unconscious bias, alongside a lack of cultural humility and structural awareness, plays a significant role in this. Rather than practising genuinely person-centred guidance, some practitioners fall back on shortcuts – making inferences based on surnames, accents, clothes, or perceived confidence. When we do this, we close doors before they've even been opened. Yet, the foundation of ethical, impactful careers work is simple: we must not assume – we must ask. A career conversation should be led by curiosity, not judgement. Every client should be given the space to define success on their own terms and feel safe enough to articulate their lived reality, free from the fear of being misunderstood or dismissed. Clients don't want to be 'managed'; they want to be met – with respect, attentiveness, and genuine belief in their potential. This is where representation in the workforce matters deeply. A diverse careers workforce, when equipped with critical training and the confidence to hold identity with nuance, can bring more than relatability – it brings validation. But representation alone is not enough. It must be accompanied by empathy, critical awareness, and the skills to explore identity in a way that is neither invasive nor superficial. When these elements align, careers guidance becomes not only informative but transformational – it affirms identity, expands possibility, and challenges limitations imposed by systems, not clients themselves.

Enablers

Despite the systemic challenges explored throughout this chapter, there are equally powerful enablers that have the potential to reshape the career development sector into one that is truly inclusive and equitable. These enablers are not theoretical – they are already emerging in pockets of good practice across England and beyond, offering a glimpse of what is possible when equity is taken seriously and embedded with intention.

A growing shift towards culturally responsive and trauma-informed guidance models has brought fresh energy into the field. These models recognise that effective careers support cannot be neutral – it must be rooted in an understanding of people's lived realities, the impact of trauma, and the sociocultural context in which clients make decisions. Cultural sensitivity and emotional intelligence are not optional extras; they are essential components of meaningful guidance. When we acknowledge the full humanity of those we support, we move beyond box-ticking and begin to offer services that feel relevant, affirming, and safe.

Representation and visibility also remain critical enablers. When diverse practitioners are present – not just in delivery roles but also within leadership teams, boards, and curriculum design panels – the entire system benefits. These voices challenge dominant narratives, introduce fresh insights, and ensure that services reflect the communities they aim to serve. But representation must be more than symbolic. It must be resourced, respected, and coupled with power to influence decision-making. When people see themselves reflected across a sector, they are more likely to trust it, engage with it, and pursue careers within it.

Alongside representation, there is a pressing need for structured professional development and mentorship that goes beyond surface-level awareness. True inclusion work is ongoing – it requires consistent spaces for critical reflection, access to mentors who understand systemic barriers, and the courage to interrogate one's own assumptions. One-off training sessions and generic CPD cannot sustain this; we need transformative development that invites dialogue, self-inquiry, and growth. Practitioners must be supported not only to learn but to unlearn – the habits, narratives, and practices that no longer serve a diverse client base.

Leadership, too, plays a pivotal role. Institutions must model the values they expect their staff to uphold. This includes collecting and analysing disaggregated data, reviewing who gets access to services and who progresses through them, and being accountable for visible, measurable change. Equity must become a strategic priority, not a side project assigned to a lone staff member or diversity champion. When leadership steps up, the ripple effect is felt throughout the organisation.

Central to this book is the TEDI framework – Transformative Equity, Diversity, and Inclusion – which I developed through years of consultancy and research. TEDI is more than a checklist or a tool; it is a mindset and a model for change. It challenges us to move from compliance to transformation, from gestures to systems thinking. TEDI invites us to interrogate our practices, question our cultures, and reimagine inclusion as a core value – not an afterthought. The four pillars of TEDI will weave through each chapter: transformative practice that resists the status quo, equitable systems where fairness is embedded rather than enforced, diverse representation that is sustainable and meaningful, and inclusive practices that centre access, voice, and belonging. These principles underpin every tool, case study, and reflection in this book. My hope is that TEDI offers you not just a framework but a compass – one that can help steer your work, your institution, and ultimately, your impact, towards a future where equity isn't aspirational but expected.

Lived experiences

Real stories illuminate the lived realities behind systemic inequity in a way that data cannot. One Black male career development practitioner told me he didn't know a single other Black man in the sector. He worked in East London – a region known for its diversity – yet he felt like he was the only one representing an entire demographic. The weight of visibility, of being the sole figure young Black men could relate to, was exhausting. His experience wasn't isolated. It echoed stories I've encountered again and again through my work with the CDI, in prisons, alternative provisions, and with NEET students. The common thread is stark: when children and young people aren't recognised or supported in ways that meet their lived experiences – whether in education, careers guidance, or the home – they drift through systems that were never built for them. In that drift, they often internalise the idea that failure is their own fault, rather than the system's.

One man I met in prison shared how he'd moved from job to job with no real direction. No one had ever taken the time to ask him the right questions, to see past assumptions, or take into account his intersecting identity as a mixed-race, Black-perceived man from a low-income background. He described a lifetime of feeling invisible. The first time anyone genuinely tried to help him make sense of his future was from inside a prison cell. That moment has stayed with me; that is what happens when career development is offered through a narrow lens – when we reduce people to stereotypes, when we offer advice without understanding identity, history, or the structural barriers clients carry into every appointment. When people are told to *'aspire'* without being seen or heard first, that guidance does more harm than good. When people are not seen as whole, they are failed altogether.

What becomes clear through these stories is that lived experience must be central – not peripheral – to how we design, deliver, and reflect on career guidance. We cannot detach identity from this work. We cannot pretend that career decisions exist in a vacuum, untouched by race, class, gender, disability, trauma, or faith. I haven't written this chapter from an academic pedestal but from lived reality – from the classroom that didn't see me, to the boardroom that needed translating, to the prison wing where I sat across from people who sounded like me but had been failed by systems their whole lives. This chapter might begin with my own experiences, but it ends with a truth many of us hold: when systems are designed without us in mind, they often fail us completely. I've laid the foundations here. We've explored the systemic barriers in the careers sector, the ways institutions rely on outdated and exclusive models, and how practitioners – despite good intentions

– often don't have the tools or confidence to engage in this work fully. Clients continue to be mislabelled, misunderstood, and left behind. But there is also hope. There are enablers – practices and approaches that are already making a difference in pockets across the country. Culturally responsive guidance, meaningful representation, intentional leadership, and practitioners willing to do the work – they exist. It's from that place of possibility that the TEDI framework was born.

TEDI – Transformative Equity, Diversity and Inclusion – isn't a tick-box. It's not a buzzword or an exercise in compliance. It's a shift in mindset, practice, and culture. It's about challenging the idea that inclusion is an add-on, something we *'do'* occasionally, or something we outsource. Instead, TEDI is about embedding inclusion into the core of who we are and how we work – every day. I created this framework because the sector needed something practical, reflective, and rooted in lived experience. Something that would move us beyond awareness and into action.

This book is designed as a living toolkit – something you can pick up, apply, return to, and grow with. Whether you're a practitioner, teacher, leader, policymaker, or someone committed to working better with people – this book is for you. It isn't filled with jargon or inaccessible theory. It's grounded in real-life stories, tangible tools, and a call to reflect deeply, act bravely, and lead with intention.

In the chapters that follow, we'll explore key intersections – race, gender, social class, faith, sexuality, gender, disability, neurodiversity – not as isolated categories, but as interwoven aspects of who people are. We'll consider how we, as professionals, show up in this work and how systems can be reshaped to serve everyone more justly. Chapter 1 gave us the 'why'. Chapter 2 introduces the TEDI framework. Chapter 3 and beyond offer practical tools you can use in your own context – whether that's a school, prison, boardroom, or something in between. These aren't checklists. They're provocations, reflections, and starting points. This isn't the end of the conversation – it's the beginning. You are warmly invited in.

Where it all began: Centring practitioner voice

This book was never meant to be written in isolation – and it isn't. It's grounded in the voices, reflections, and lived experiences shared during the January 2023 EDI strategy workshops. That moment, in many ways, became the catalyst. What started as a one-off conversation quickly revealed itself to be something much deeper: a sector-wide hunger for honesty, accountability, and structural change. Those workshops became the springboard. They shaped the foundations of the TEDI framework, informed the CDI's EDI strategy, inspired the monthly lunchtime webinar series, and planted the first seeds of this book. Over the course of those sessions, practitioners from across the country shared not only what wasn't working – but also what was and what could. Their contributions weren't just powerful – they were essential. Their words now echo throughout every chapter. Rather than repeating where this all started in every section, let me say it clearly here: this book is built on practitioner voice. Not as token inclusion, but as critical expertise. You'll see their words throughout, not boxed off as side quotes, but embedded into the thinking itself. This book isn't just about EDI – it's written with and through it. It's about shifting from performative gestures to purposeful practice. That shift began in January 2023. Let this serve as your foundation for the road ahead. The voices that started this journey are the ones carrying it forward.

Chapter 2
Introducing the
TEDI framework

I often get told that Equity, Diversity, and Inclusion can often feel like overwhelming work – something abstract, complex, and easy to get wrong. But it doesn't have to be. This chapter is about shifting from theory to action, from hesitation to intention. Before diving into practical tools, we need to ground ourselves in mindset – and that's where the TEDI framework comes in. TEDI stands for Transformative Equity, Diversity, and Inclusion, and it's not just another acronym or model – it's a mindset. It asks you to lead with curiosity, take responsibility, and build inclusion into the very foundations of your work, not just bolt it on after the fact. TEDI encourages you to move beyond surface-level allyship and into practice that is honest, embedded, and human.

This framework wasn't something I sat down and created on a whim. TEDI was born out of lived experience, deep-rooted frustration, and the repeated realisation that what we were doing simply wasn't working. It grew organically – from my PhD research, yes – but more so from the endless conversations, consultations, and contradictions I encountered while working in classrooms, community centres, prisons, policy spaces, and boardrooms. Again and again, I saw organisations rush to set up working groups, publish vision statements, or book in 'unconscious bias' training – only to watch nothing fundamentally change. The same hierarchies remained, the same people made the decisions, and those with lived experience were thanked for their time but not trusted with leadership. Performative EDI was everywhere. People – especially those of us on the margins – were tired of watching equity be reduced to marketing straplines and occasional calendar events.

For me, transformative isn't just a word – it's non-negotiable. It means deep, structural, cultural change. It means shaking things at their roots. I saw what this looked like early on in my roles as a teacher and Careers Coordinator. The schools that truly moved forward didn't just publish diversity statements or tweak their policies – they embedded equity into how they made decisions, how they engaged with students, and how they built relationships. You could feel it. Inclusion wasn't an initiative; it was a way of being. TEDI is my response to that possibility. A refusal to accept equity as optional. A way to move inclusion out of committee rooms and into everyday culture.

TEDI has been shaped and tested across many spaces – through my consultancy work, my role as EDI Chair at the University of Derby, as part of the Interfaith Group at the Multi-Faith Centre, and through national roles such as my work with the CDI and YMCA. It's grounded in reality, not just theory. What I've learned is this: inclusion doesn't happen just because someone writes it into a strategy. It happens when people make it real – through relationships, reflection, and a readiness to change. TEDI gives structure to that process, offering a language, a set of pillars, and a way forward that is both values-driven and action-focused.

This chapter is the first time I'm sharing TEDI publicly – and I don't do so lightly. It isn't a polished product or a static checklist. TEDI is a living, breathing approach for people who want to do EDI work with authenticity and depth. For those who are tired of being stuck in the same cycles and who are ready to move past performative gestures into meaningful, sustainable change. TEDI is for those who understand that inclusion isn't an event – it's a culture. Cultures don't shift overnight. They shift when people are willing to hold the mirror up, stay with the discomfort, and do the work together. TEDI isn't just another framework. It's a call to action. A call to stop outsourcing the responsibility of equity and start leading it ourselves – from wherever we stand. Whether you're in a leadership position or just starting out, whether you're running a national service or delivering one-to-one guidance, TEDI is here to help you think, reflect, act, and grow. This is your invitation. Not to tick boxes – but to do better. Not perfectly, but intentionally; that's where real change begins.

What is TEDI?

The TEDI framework

Transformative Equity, Diversity, and Inclusion

TEDI isn't just another acronym – it's a practical, grounded framework for meaningful change. Designed with real-world settings in mind, TEDI helps you embed equity into your practice, policies, and everyday decisions. It's built around four interlocking pillars that support a cycle of reflection, action, and accountability.

T – Transformative assessment

You can't fix what you haven't fully seen.

This pillar focuses on critically assessing where you are now in terms of equity, diversity, and inclusion. That means asking the hard questions, gathering honest feedback, and digging beneath surface-level representation. The goal? To build a clear picture of your current landscape so change is rooted in reality – not assumption.

Key tools: Audits, surveys, lived experience data, deep listening.

E – Equitable initiatives

Equity requires intention.

This pillar is about developing and implementing initiatives that actively centre equity – and co-creating them with the very people most affected. From inclusive recruitment to anti-discrimination policy – this is where strategy meets solidarity.

Key tools: Stakeholder engagement, safe spaces, inclusive policy development, leadership representation.

D – Diversifying the culture

Culture isn't static – it can be shaped.

Here, the focus is on fostering a working environment where all identities are respected, all contributions are valued, and everyone feels they belong. This means more than token gestures. It means embedding diversity into the very culture of your organisation or practice.

Key tools: Training, reflective leadership, mentoring, dismantling exclusionary norms.

I – Inclusive practices

Equity in action.

This pillar is where inclusion is made tangible. It's about designing systems that actually work for the people they're meant to serve – especially those traditionally excluded. It's about embedding accessibility, adaptability, and reflection into everyday practice.

Key tools: Inclusive communications, flexible processes, reflective audits, accountability structures.

Together, these four pillars form a continuous cycle: assess, design, embed, evaluate – and repeat. TEDI is not a one-off project. It's a commitment to sustained, systemic transformation.

TEDI is not a checklist. It isn't a one-off initiative or a fashionable phrase to drop into reports. It's a mindset – a lens that should sit at the heart of everything you do, whether you're working directly with clients, leading a team, writing policy, or reflecting on your own role in this work. TEDI is rooted in the belief that inclusion isn't something we *'add in'* – it's something we build from. It came together from all corners of my journey – teaching in underfunded schools, designing strategy with national organisations, sitting with clients in prison wings, delivering training to exhausted staff, and researching what equity should really look like. It weaves together academic theory and grassroots experience, offering a framework that holds space for honesty, growth, and tangible change. TEDI doesn't give you all the answers – it gives you a way to ask better questions and a structure to start doing this work differently. At its core, TEDI is built around four interconnected pillars. These aren't steps to tick off or phases to complete. They're ongoing, evolving, and constantly influencing one another. Together, they create the conditions for truly inclusive and equity-driven practice.

The pillars are described in more detail below:

- Transformative practice and policies – this is about pushing beyond surface-level tweaks and interrogating the systems that uphold inequality in the first place. It asks you to challenge the status quo, examine where power sits, and centre lived experience as a form of valid, necessary expertise. It invites you to move from saying the right things to doing them – to ask yourself: Where have I shifted practice, not just language?
- Equitable cultures – this is where we talk a lot about equality, but equity requires us to acknowledge that different people have different needs. It's not about giving everyone the same – it's about recognising that people start from different places and need different forms of support to truly thrive. Equity is about proactively adjusting systems, expectations, and environments so that nobody is left behind trying to fit into a model never built for them in the first place. It's about cultivating spaces where everyone – not just the majority – can flourish.
- Diverse representation – this pillar goes beyond optics and asks the harder questions: Who's in the room? Who's shaping the conversation? Who gets heard, who gets overlooked, and why? True representation means recognising how multiple identities – across race, class, gender, disability, neurodivergence, age, and faith – intersect, and ensuring that those with lived experience aren't just brought to the table but are supported to lead. It's about dismantling gatekeeping and actively

creating space for underrepresented voices to direct policy, shape services, and define what inclusion looks like on their terms.

- Inclusion at the core – this means that inclusion can't be a bolt-on; it must be embedded into the language, leadership, policies, and everyday practices of your setting. Everyone in the organisation – staff, clients, leadership – should feel like they belong, like they matter, and like they have a role to play. If inclusion isn't built in, then people are being left out. TEDI reminds us that calling people in, not calling them out, is where the real work starts. Inclusion is not performance – it's presence, safety, and authenticity. It's the opposite of ticking a box and walking away. It's about creating space where people can show up as themselves and not feel like they have to leave parts of their identity at the door to be accepted.

So, why TEDI you may be wondering? We're surrounded by statements that promise equity, but far fewer systems that deliver it. TEDI is a response to the fatigue of tokenism. It's a refusal to settle for surface-level change. It offers a way to ground your practice in values, not fear; to build confidence in uncomfortable conversations; to embed self-reflection into your daily habits; and to move power – not just language. It doesn't ask you to be an EDI expert. It asks you to be honest, curious, and willing to act. TEDI is about rejecting performance in favour of presence. It's about doing the work – not perfectly, but with purpose. Now that you've been introduced to TEDI, the next chapter offers you tools you can actually use. Reflective prompts, self-audit templates, bias mapping, group discussion guides – real, practical resources you can take into your own context. These aren't about overhauling everything overnight. They're about beginning somewhere – with care, with courage, and with the knowledge that meaningful change always starts small but never stays that way.

Sidenote on language

You may have noticed by now – I don't use the term *'equality'* in this book. That's deliberate. I've long believed that striving for equality – treating everyone the same – misses the point when we're talking about real people with real, lived differences. Even in our own families, we intuitively know that fairness doesn't always mean sameness. One child might need extra support; another might need space to grow independently. One colleague might benefit from structured mentoring, while another needs flexibility to manage caring responsibilities or mental health. That's equity – meeting people where they are, and responding to their actual needs, not where we wish they were or where the system assumes they'll fit. I also choose my words carefully when talking about people. Terms like *'minority'* or *'BAME'* have become shorthand in many EDI conversations, but they often flatten rich and varied identities into boxes that feel reductive at best, harmful at worst. The term *'minority'* itself is a misnomer. The communities often referred to in the UK or US as minorities are in fact the global majority. When we use that kind of language uncritically, we unconsciously centre whiteness and marginalise everyone else. That's not just semantics; it's structure. Instead, I use terms like *'ethnically diverse communities'*, *'underrepresented groups'*, and *'individuals with intersectional identities'*. It's not about jargon. It's about clarity. It's about dignity. Language shapes how we see others – and how we see ourselves. It shapes what's possible and what's permitted. Throughout this book, I've chosen my words with intention, not perfection. I've thought deeply about the power they carry and the impact they leave behind. I invite you to do the same. Whether you're speaking in a classroom, a boardroom, or over a coffee with a colleague – language either opens doors or closes them. Let's choose words that open doors and invite people in, not exclude them.

Chapter 3
The TEDI framework practical toolkit

This chapter introduces a set of foundational tools to support you in building inclusive, equity-driven careers practice. These aren't checklists or one-off exercises. They're here to help you reflect, act, and sustain real change. At the heart of this practical approach lies the TEDI framework – Transformative Equity, Diversity, and Inclusion. TEDI isn't a project or a policy; it's a culture shift. It's a way of thinking, behaving, and leading that makes inclusion part of everything we do – not an extra we remember when convenient. TEDI is grounded in lived experience, critical insight, and the understanding that change isn't linear – it's messy, reflective, and requires both courage and care. This framework emerged from years of frontline practice, policy work, and conversations with practitioners and clients who were tired of surface-level solutions. It reflects what I've seen across schools, prisons, alternative provisions, and national organisations: meaningful equity work only takes root when it's embedded in mindset, language, and systems. As we saw in Chapter 2, the TEDI framework rests on four interlinked principles. Transformative practice calls us to challenge the status quo, centre lived experience, and reflect critically on how we work. Equitable cultures remind us that fairness isn't sameness – it's recognising different starting points and meeting people where they are, not where we wish they'd be. Diverse representation is about power – about who is visible, who shapes the agenda, and whose realities are reflected in our services. Inclusion at the core means just that: it's not a bolt-on or branding – it's built in from the start, in everything from leadership behaviours to daily interactions with clients. These pillars aren't theoretical. They're a call to action. That's why I've developed tools that bring TEDI to life in your everyday practice. They're not about perfection. They're about intentionality. One of the simplest yet most powerful tools I use in my work is a set of five questions. These aren't just prompts – they're habits. Anchors for reflection. When asked regularly, they shift your practice over time.

Ask yourself:

1. Who is missing from my practice?
2. What assumptions am I making?
3. What lived experiences do I lack understanding of?
4. How is power operating in this setting?
5. How can I be accountable – not just aware?

These questions help move us from performative to transformative. They help us stay present to what matters – real people, real needs, real equity. They aren't about getting it all right; they're about not looking away. The following tools and templates in this chapter will help you take this reflection further and translate it into concrete, everyday action. Whether you're working in a school, a prison, a boardroom, or somewhere in between, this toolkit is here to support you. Use what works, adapt what doesn't, and return to it as often as you need. That's what TEDI is all about – starting where you are and growing from there. I often say – meet people where they are and build from there.

TEDI self-reflection prompts

Self-reflection is the foundation of transformative EDI practice. It's where we begin to do the real work – not by ticking boxes or attending one-off trainings, but by looking inward with honesty and courage. The TEDI framework calls on us to move beyond surface awareness and examine how our values, identities, power, and blind spots shape our practice. This process isn't about guilt or performance. It's about holding up a mirror and choosing to act with integrity. This reflection tool is designed to help you pause and assess. You can use it during supervision, CPD sessions, mentoring conversations, or planning meetings. Whether individually or as a team, returning to these prompts regularly keeps the work grounded and alive. These questions aren't rhetorical. They're meant to guide real growth. Aligned with TEDI's four pillars – transformative practice, equitable cultures, diverse representation, and inclusion at the core – these prompts encourage critical thinking and honest reflection.

Reflection prompts
Transformative practice

- When have I acted to challenge a biased assumption – my own or someone else's?
- Where in my current role am I still reinforcing the status quo, and what would it take to shift that?

Equitable cultures

- What does fairness actually look like in my context? Who is flourishing – and who is being left behind?
- What tools or adjustments have I used to meet people where they are, not where the system expects them to be?

Diverse representation

- Who is visible in my organisation's decision-making spaces – and who isn't?
- How might I use my position to mentor, sponsor, or amplify someone from an underrepresented group?

Inclusion at the core

- Is EDI embedded in how I think and work or something I approach as an add-on?
- When have I avoided or simplified difficult conversations – and why? What held me back?

Study questions for practice and team discussion

- What does equity mean beyond equality – and how is that reflected in our day-to-day interactions?
- How might our organisation unintentionally exclude certain clients, communities, or staff?
- What would it take for inclusion to be a lived value in our service delivery – not just a line in a policy?
- How are power and privilege shaping my practice – and how can I challenge this constructively?
- What changes would make our work genuinely inclusive – and what support do we need to get there?

These questions are not meant to be asked once and forgotten. They're part of a reflective cycle that invites us to keep returning, revisiting, and realigning. Use them to create accountability, not criticism. Use them to build confidence in discomfort. TEDI isn't about perfection – it's about progress. Reflection is the first, and most ongoing, step.

Bias awareness map

This worksheet is designed to help you identify, understand, and begin to challenge your assumptions.

Use Table 1 to trace where your biases may come from, how they show up in your practice, and what you can do to interrupt them.

Table 1 Bias awareness map

Identity category	Where do your assumptions come from? (e.g. media, upbringing, schooling)
Race/ethnic identity	
Gender identity	
Social class/income	
Disability/neurodivergence	
Faith or belief system	
Family structure	
Other	

This is not about shame – it's about growth, honesty, and responsibility.

Reflection
What patterns are you noticing?

Where do you feel most confident – and where might you need more learning, listening, or support?

This sheet is designed to grow with you – my advice is to come back to it regularly.

TEDI toolkit self-audit

Transformative Equity, Diversity, and Inclusion

This self-audit is designed to support honest reflection on where you are, what's working, and where there is still room to grow. Use it during supervision, CPD, or as part of your ongoing reflective practice. Take time with each section – journal your responses with honesty, curiosity, and care.

Transformative practice

- In what ways am I challenging outdated or exclusionary practices?
- Where might I be maintaining the status quo – even without meaning to?
- How do I centre lived experience in the work I do?
- When was the last time I took a risk to advocate for equity?

Equitable cultures

- Who is thriving in my setting – and who is being left behind?
- Do I adapt my approach to meet individual needs, or do I rely on a 'one-size-fits-all' method?
- How do I typically respond when someone challenges inequity?
- What small, specific step could I take to make my practice fairer?

Diverse representation

- Whose voices are visible in my space – through materials, events, leadership, or decision-making?
- Do the people I work with see themselves reflected in what I offer?
- In what ways do I amplify underrepresented voices – such as mentoring, sponsorship, or sharing credit?
- When did I last stop to ask whose perspective might be missing?

Inclusion at the core

- Is inclusion something I add on – or is it embedded from the start?
- How do I model inclusive language, behaviours, and decisions?
- When have I avoided or oversimplified conversations about identity or difference – and why?
- What would help me feel more confident navigating these topics?

Final reflection

- What internal or external barriers might be holding back equity and inclusion in my practice?

- What's working well – what are my strengths, allies, or strategies that I can build on?
- What might I do differently to cultivate a deeper, more meaningful culture of inclusion?

TEDI organisational reflection questions

Use the prompts below to reflect on where your organisation currently stands and how you might begin – or deepen – a journey towards truly transformative, equitable, and inclusive practice.

What are the barriers?
- What systemic, structural, or cultural factors are preventing inclusion or equity from taking root? Think about internal policies, leadership representation, decision-making processes, language, accessibility, or embedded legacy systems that may be holding you back.

What is currently working – or what are the enablers?
- Where do you see signs of progress, strength, or momentum? Identify any initiatives, individuals, attitudes, or practices already contributing positively to a more inclusive culture.

What can my organisation do to create a culture of inclusivity?
- What tangible behaviours, actions, or shifts would help build an environment where all staff and clients feel seen, heard, and valued? Push beyond surface-level statements – what would it really mean to embed inclusion at the core of your ethos and everyday practice?

Empowering clients through equity: A TEDI practice guide

This toolkit is designed to support career development practitioners in embedding equity-driven, inclusive approaches into their client work. Drawing from the TEDI framework, each section offers simple, practical prompts to help clients reflect on their identity, context, and next steps with greater agency and self-awareness. These tools can be used in 1:1 sessions, group work, or as self-directed exercises.

Exploring identity and voice

Help clients connect with their multiple identities and consider how these shape their choices, confidence, and career goals.

Prompt: *What parts of your identity feel most visible in your life right now? Which parts feel overlooked or misunderstood?*

Recognising barriers and strengths
Support clients in identifying external barriers they may have encountered – without putting their experiences in a box which you label.

Prompt: *Have there been times when you've felt excluded or underestimated? What helped you keep going in those moments?*

Challenging assumptions and labels
Encourage clients to reflect on assumptions others may have made about them and how they choose to define themselves instead.

Prompt: *What's something people often get wrong about you? How do you want to be seen, and what would it take for that to happen?*

Reclaiming space and voice
Guide clients to notice when and where they shrink themselves or feel unable to speak up – and what conditions would help them thrive.

Prompt: *Where do you feel most confident and able to be yourself? What spaces or people support that version of you?*

Defining success on their terms
Invite clients to challenge narrow definitions of success and create their own vision based on their values.

Prompt: *What does success look like for you – not based on someone else's version, but your own?*

Planning inclusive next steps
Use the TEDI lens to help clients map next steps that honour their reality, capacity, and aspirations.

Prompt: *What is one step you can take that feels authentic to you? Who or what do you need around you to make it possible?*

These prompts are not prescriptive – they are conversation starters designed to centre identity, equity, and empowerment in career support. Use them with care, curiosity, and flexibility, adapting to the context and capacity of each client. The goal is not to *'fix'* people but to hold space for them to be seen, valued, and equipped to lead their own journeys.

PART TWO
DEEP DIVE INTO KEY DIVERSITY INTERSECTIONS

This part of the book forms its analytical and emotional core – taking you deeper into the critical diversity intersections that shape career development experiences and outcomes. Each chapter explores a specific area of identity and inequality, offering a balance of theory, real-world insight, and applied strategies to help practitioners embed EDI with both confidence and compassion.

Part Two is split into the following chapters:

- Chapter 4 – Understanding intersectionality in career development – explores how multiple systems of advantage and disadvantage interact to shape career access and experience. It offers a foundational lens through which all subsequent chapters should be read.
- Chapter 5 – Understanding ethnicity in career development – examines systemic racism, cultural identity, and racialised barriers in careers support, while offering anti-racist approaches for practice.
- Chapter 6 – Religion in career development – unpacks how faith, belief systems, and religious identity influence career decisions and access, especially in secular or misinformed environments.
- Chapter 7 – Gender equity in career development – explores the full spectrum of gender, from male underrepresentation to trans inclusion and challenging binary assumptions in careers support.
- Chapter 8 – Sexuality and sexual identity in the careers sector – engages with LGBTQIA+ inclusion, examining how sexuality and career expression intersect in both overt and hidden ways.
- Chapter 9 – Disability in career development – critically engages with ableism in the careers system and explores how inclusive, accessible, and disability-affirming guidance can be embedded.
- Chapter 10 – Neurodiversity in career development – discusses neurological difference beyond deficit models, offering strategies rooted in energy sensitivity, flexibility, and belonging.
- Chapter 11 – Socio-economic status in the careers sector – centres class, poverty, and social mobility, challenging practitioners to work beyond deficit narratives and address structural barriers in meaningful ways.

Each chapter in this section follows a consistent pattern: it introduces key terminology, outlines systemic barriers, shares case studies or practitioner reflections, and ends with tangible actions for change. Whether you're a frontline careers practitioner, a policy leader, or an educator, this section is designed to deepen your understanding and expand your toolkit for inclusive, equity-led practice. These chapters are designed not only to inform but to shift perspectives – ensuring EDI is understood in all its complexity.

Part Two aims to build the critical awareness needed to move from intention to transformation. By the end of Part Two, you'll be equipped with the tools, language, and understanding to support clients from all walks of life – with nuance, confidence, and care. We move from talking about the issues to pushing for real deep-seated action.

Chapter 4
Understanding intersectionality in career development

Chapter roadmap

This chapter lays the foundation for the rest of the book. Intersectionality isn't a preface – it's the lens through which all equity work must be understood. It shapes how power operates, how marginalisation is experienced, and how inclusion can be reimagined. Rather than offering a surface-level summary, this chapter grounds intersectionality in real-world practice, guided by practitioner voices, reflective prompts, and tools for change.

This chapter:

- Opens with an author's voice on why we centre intersectionality first – because without it, every other strand of EDI work risks being incomplete;
- Breaks down the meaning and origins of intersectionality, exploring Kimberlé Crenshaw's framework and how it applies in the context of careers guidance;
- Introduces the Intersectionality Wheel as a tool to map identity, power, and structural inequality – anchored in practical examples from careers settings;
- Spotlights the barriers and enablers of intersectional practice, based on lived experiences shared by practitioners across the sector;
- Offers dual toolkits: one for individuals embedding intersectionality into their practice, and one for organisations working to dismantle systemic inequity;
- Includes insights from the CDI EDI Intersectionality Webinar, placing practitioners' voices at the heart of the conversation;
- Closes with a reflection activity to move this work from understanding to action – because intersectionality is not theory to be admired, but practice to be lived.

Author's voice

Before engaging with any specific aspect of equity – whether it's ethnicity, gender, disability, or socio-economic class – it's essential to begin with intersectionality. For me, intersectionality is not a branch of inclusion work; it is the foundation upon which all authentic equity efforts rest. It offers a lens through which to understand the complexities of identity, power, and systemic inequality. We each embody a constellation of identities – some easily seen, others deeply held or rendered invisible by dominant narratives. These identities don't exist in silos; they intersect and interact in ways that profoundly shape our access, experiences, and sense of belonging. The more of these intersections a person holds – especially when they align with socially marginalised categories – the more likely they are to face layered forms of exclusion. Not because of who they are, but because our systems weren't designed with their full humanity in mind. Intersectionality provides the vocabulary and framework to examine how disadvantage is accumulated and experienced. It helps us move beyond box-ticking exercises or tokenistic representation, pushing us instead to explore the lived realities that emerge from the overlap of multiple identities. Without this lens, we risk reducing individuals to single categories that miss the nuance of their experience.

In the previous chapter, I discussed how ethnically diverse career development practitioners often feel burdened by the expectation to represent their entire community. That discomfort and resistance make sense when we understand intersectionality – because identity is never just one thing. To discuss race without acknowledging how it intersects with class, to speak about gender without recognising religious or cultural nuance, or to consider disability without exploring the role of societal norms is to fall short of meaningful inclusion. Throughout this book, I ask you to hold this intersectional frame. Let it influence how you read, how you reflect, and how you reconsider your role in shaping the careers landscape. Intersectionality is not the preamble to EDI – it is the essence of it. Each chapter is intentionally interconnected because real lives are interconnected. This work requires more than knowledge – it requires humility, intention, and the ability to sit with discomfort. The reflections shared in this chapter are drawn from the **CDI EDI Intersectionality Webinar** held in January 2025. These practitioner insights are not supplementary; they are central. They anchor the theoretical in the practical and remind us that this conversation is lived daily by those navigating, and challenging, the careers system from within.

What is intersectionality?

Intersectionality, a term introduced by legal scholar Kimberlé Crenshaw, describes how different elements of identity – such as race, gender, class, sexuality, disability, and others – intersect to shape distinct experiences of privilege and marginalisation. It is not simply a theory; it is a critical lens for understanding how systems of power and exclusion operate in tandem, often compounding the challenges faced by those situated at multiple margins. Within career development, intersectionality helps us reject the notion of a one-dimensional, *'average'* client. Instead, it recognises the layered and context-driven experiences that people carry into guidance spaces. I remember the way one practitioner shared it during the CDI Intersectionality Webinar: *'Unique experiences mean that people can face a variety of discriminations within their journey – not always visible, not always understood.'* Another said, *'Identities don't sit in neat boxes – they overlap, and sometimes they collide. You can't do this work properly unless you understand that.'* These comments struck a chord because they weren't just observations – they were lived truths. They brought to life what I already knew to be true: our work is not just about offering advice or ticking off outcomes; it's about sitting with complexity. We're not just helping someone with their CV or next step – we're navigating the weight of histories, identities, traumas, and hopes.

Intersectionality invites us to ask better questions. What happens when class and ethnicity interact? How does gender present when layered with neurodivergence? How do we hold space for those who carry identities that may be both visible and invisible? And how often do we, as practitioners, unknowingly filter our support through our own assumptions or comfort zones? One quote that has stayed with me ever since the webinar captures this beautifully: *'Intersectionality isn't a module. It's a mindset. It's how you sit with people and hold space for all the things they bring in – visible and invisible.'* This mindset is particularly relevant in the careers context, where there's often a temptation to simplify – to make guidance neat, measurable, and universal. But life isn't neat, and people aren't one-dimensional. Guidance that fails to engage with intersectionality risks missing the mark entirely. It's not just about meeting *'a client'* – it's about recognising the whole person behind that label. When we see intersectionality not as an extra, but as the baseline for how we work, we shift from surface-level inclusion to something far deeper and more transformative. That, to me, is what meaningful careers work should always strive to be.

The Intersectionality Wheel in careers practice

Visualising intersectionality allows us to move from abstract theory to something more grounded – something we can connect with in our everyday work. The Intersectionality Wheel (Figure 1), inspired by Crenshaw's original framing and developed further by practitioners, acts as a visual anchor. It helps us see what we might otherwise miss. Each coloured spoke of the wheel represents a distinct aspect of identity: race, ethnicity, gender identity, class, language, religion, ability, sexuality, mental health, age, education, and even attractiveness. These aspects do not operate in isolation – they blend, converge, and collide in ways that shape how people move through the world and how the world responds to them. As Crenshaw reminds us, intersectionality is *'a lens through which you can see where power comes and collides, where it locks and intersects'*. This quote sits at the heart of the diagram – not just as theory, but as reality. It is an invitation to acknowledge that our clients, colleagues, and even ourselves, live with overlapping identities that can either compound disadvantage or reveal privilege. The wheel doesn't simplify identity – it honours its complexity. For career development professionals, this means holding space for that complexity. As one practitioner in the CDI

Figure 1 The Intersectionality Wheel. © Sylvia Duckworth. (Reproduced with kind permission.)

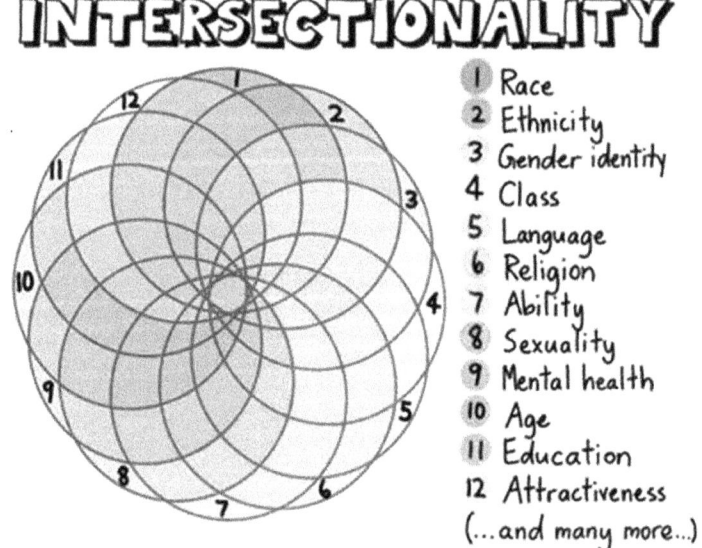

webinar put it: *'Clients don't come to us in pieces. They come as whole people – with stories, identities, traumas, and hopes.'* And our work should reflect that. Each intersection tells a story – of access, exclusion, resilience, and aspiration. A disabled care leaver applying to university, a Muslim woman returning to the workplace after raising children, a working-class Black boy labelled *'low ability'* by school systems – each of these journeys is layered. Each requires us to move beyond tick-box provision or assumptions about what support should look like. When we see people through just one lens, we miss the richness and the struggle that shapes their journey. In doing so, we risk replicating the same systems we claim we want to dismantle. This wheel – while simple in appearance – is deeply provocative. It pushes us to pause, to listen more carefully, and to ask: Whose story are we missing? Who are we failing to see in full colour? It invites us not just to reflect but to act – to step back from pre-written scripts and see people in their layered, lived realities. Intersectionality isn't an optional extra in careers practice. It is what gives that practice meaning, context, and truth.

Reflecting on identity, power, and practice

Intersectionality is not a theoretical add-on – it is a lens that fundamentally reshapes how we understand people, power, and systems. These reflection points are not checklist items to work through in a workshop or during CPD – they are provocations. They are intended to unsettle, to ask better questions, and to spark honest dialogue. In exploring the careers profession through a TEDI lens, I have been struck by the silences: the people and perspectives that are quietly omitted from dominant narratives – the stories that go untold, the systemic patterns that repeat, even when intentions are good. Practitioners I've spoken to have reflected candidly on how their own identities influence the support they offer. Many admitted that it's easier to relate to clients who mirror their own experiences, while others shared how unfamiliarity can lead to awkwardness, missteps, or oversights. One practitioner put it simply: *'Our own backgrounds lead us to make assumptions or lack awareness of how to talk to or understand perspectives of others we haven't had experience of.'* These reflections are not about blame – they are about growth. They echo the wider call for more critical, sustained reflexivity across the sector.

This self-examination is especially urgent in a profession that holds so much influence over people's futures. Career development is not a neutral space. Every interaction has the potential to either affirm someone's sense of possibility or reinforce the barriers they already face. Yet much of what is positioned as standard or universal within the system is in fact shaped by a dominant view of who the *'typical'* client is. As one participant asked: *'Career services are often shaped for the mainstream client. But who defines that? And what happens to those who never see themselves reflected in the system?'* Intersectionality offers a framework through which to understand why certain clients continue to be underserved. It makes visible the complex layering of identities – such as race, gender, class, disability, religion, and neurodiversity – and how these can combine to produce unique forms of exclusion or resilience. It helps us make sense of why one-size-fits-all provision not only fails but can do real harm, particularly when assumptions are left unexamined.

But intersectionality also raises uncomfortable questions for the structures and leadership of the careers profession itself. Who are we not designing for? Whose stories are absent from policy, strategy, and sector guidance? In conversations with practitioners, a pattern emerged: inclusion is often framed around representation – but far less often around transformation. Hiring a more diverse workforce is important. But so too is the harder work of reshaping the systems in which those staff are expected to operate. Without that deeper shift, diversity risks becoming a veneer. Practitioners also described the silences within their own settings – where intersectionality felt like a difficult or even unsafe conversation. Many expressed uncertainty about how to raise issues of race, disability, or class in teams that were predominantly White or middle-class. Some described feeling isolated. Others felt that their observations were dismissed as too political. Yet, nearly all recognised that naming these dynamics was essential. As one practitioner put it, *'We need to get comfortable with discomfort. That's where the growth is – for us and for the sector.'*

In gathering these insights, it became increasingly clear that careers professionals also bring their own identities into the room – and these inevitably shape practice. But these influences are rarely made explicit. Without space to reflect on how identity, power, and bias operate in our roles, even well-meaning interventions can reinforce harm. The TEDI framework invites us to look more closely – not just at the clients we serve, but at the systems we work within, and the assumptions we carry with us. Importantly, intersectionality affects everyone – but not equally. Some people sit at sharper intersections of marginalisation, experiencing layered barriers that remain invisible to others. A neurodivergent Black woman may be labelled *'difficult'* or *'intense'* due to intersecting biases around race, gender, and neurodivergence. A working-class White man may be perceived as *'unmotivated'* when the real issue is how classed expectations of aspiration are silently embedded in the system. A disabled Jewish student might be overlooked entirely due to the collision of ableism and antisemitism. These are not isolated examples – they reflect a systemic pattern. Unless our systems are intentionally designed to include, they will continue to exclude by default.

Representation matters deeply. But it is not just about who is visible in a service – it's about who feels safe, seen, and understood. Several participants reflected on how clients rarely see themselves reflected in the profession. This absence is not just symbolic; it has real consequences for trust, for access, and for the futures people are able to imagine. When people are perpetually positioned as outsiders, it becomes harder for them to believe they belong anywhere. Intersectionality asks us to notice who gets included in our vision of the future – and who gets left behind. In reflecting on all of this, I have found that intersectionality is not simply an academic concept or a policy term – it is an ethical stance. It demands attention, honesty, and the courage to act even when it feels uncomfortable. The Intersectionality Wheel is not just a tool – it is a mirror. It asks difficult but necessary questions: Which aspects of identity do we centre in our thinking? Which do we neglect? Who are we failing to see – not because they are invisible, but because our systems were never built to hold them in the first place?

These are questions for the profession to sit with. They are questions I carry with me, too – not as someone who holds all the answers, but as someone committed to challenging the gaps, amplifying the voices of those who live in the margins, and pushing the sector towards deeper transformation.

Intersectionality barriers

These barriers aren't new – and that's precisely the problem. They are entrenched, systemic, and quietly persistent, often going unnoticed unless someone is directly impacted by them. The discomfort they cause is usually borne by those at the sharpest ends of marginalisation, while those buffered by privilege are rarely required to notice, let alone act. Crucially, these issues don't stem from individual failings alone. They are symptoms of sector-wide inertia – an ongoing reluctance to interrogate the norms, policies, and practices that have shaped the careers profession for decades. When something has *'always been done this way'*, it becomes difficult to challenge without being perceived as disruptive or ungrateful. That culture of polite compliance continues to mask harm.

The silos that exist across the careers ecosystem – from schools to further education to adult employment support – reinforce narrow pipelines and discourage movement between sectors. These rigid boundaries not only restrict progression for practitioners but also reinforce an outdated view of who belongs where. In many school and college settings, trauma-informed or intersectional training is still not standard practice. This results in staff who are often underprepared to engage with the layered realities of the young people and adults they support. At best, this can lead to oversimplified guidance. At worst, it reinforces a deficit model – where individuals are blamed for systemic barriers.

Layered onto this are fixed mindsets held by some long-serving professionals who perceive EDI as a niche concern, or worse, as irrelevant to their role. These attitudes are not always overt, but they manifest in the quiet resistance to new approaches, the dismissive comments in team meetings, and the reluctance to engage in uncomfortable reflection. When coupled with pay inequality – particularly impacting those from working-class or marginalised backgrounds – it becomes clear how structural barriers are both economic and cultural. Opportunities for progression, recognition, or even stability are unevenly distributed. When those from underrepresented groups do break through, they often find themselves as the only one in the room, navigating imposter syndrome in environments not built with them in mind.

The visible absence of diverse leadership exacerbates this further. When leadership remains homogenous, it sends a powerful message – intended or not – that progression is conditional. To belong at the top, one must assimilate, dilute, or leave parts of themselves behind. This lack of representation doesn't just affect morale – it reinforces the status quo and limits what is imagined as possible within the profession. As one participant shared during an intersectionality workshop, *'The cycle of bias and prejudice gets embedded when training is inaccessible. If CPD isn't funded or required, most won't bother.'* This speaks volumes about how learning, development, and reflection are often treated as optional rather than essential. In a profession that shapes futures, this is not just short-sighted – it's harmful.

Mental health and wellbeing, too, are frequently approached in ways that overlook intersectional nuance. As another participant noted, *'Mental health and wellbeing support isn't aligned with intersectional realities. It's often too generic and misses the point entirely.'* When practitioners are expected to 'cope' within systems that ignore their identities, experiences, and needs, the result is quiet attrition. People leave not because they are incapable, but because they are exhausted by the cumulative weight of being unheard, unseen, and unsupported.

These barriers do not exist in isolation, nor do they impact clients alone. They shape the conditions under which careers practitioners work and live. When the profession fails to name and address them, it becomes complicit in reproducing the very inequalities it claims to challenge. To build a careers sector rooted in equity, we must do more than tinker at the edges. We must commit to systemic transformation – one that centres the realities of those who have long been pushed to the margins and reimagines what inclusive practice truly looks like from the ground up.

Intersectionality enablers

While the barriers within the careers profession are real and entrenched, there is also a quiet but determined momentum building – a collective push for change that isn't waiting for permission. These aren't token gestures or performative strategies handed down through policy directives. They are being led by practitioners on the ground who are tired of waiting and are choosing to do things differently. These enablers are hopeful. They are grounded in lived experience, informed by reflection, and most importantly, driven by care. Embedding intersectionality into continuous professional development is one of the most powerful levers for change. But it's not about delivering a one-off training module with a certificate at the end. True intersectional CPD is an ongoing, reflective journey – one that requires us to sit with discomfort, remain open to unlearning, and actively seek out perspectives we've been shielded from. It's about integrating equity into the very fabric of how practitioners see their roles and their responsibility to clients, to communities, and to each other.

Mentorship and peer networks are another significant force for change, particularly when these relationships are grounded in shared identity or cultural resonance. For practitioners who have spent years being 'the only one' in a team or service, these networks offer more than support – they offer validation. They act as informal sanctuaries where it's possible to exhale, to speak honestly, and to be understood without having to constantly explain or justify your lens. These spaces foster not only survival but growth. As one workshop participant explained, *'Safe spaces build confidence to speak about intersectionality. Without that, people stay silent – and that silence becomes culture.'* Another enabler lies in rejecting the notion that professionals always know best. The shift towards co-creation with clients and communities marks a turning point – where guidance is not imposed but shaped collaboratively. This doesn't mean surrendering expertise but rather repositioning it within a framework of shared power. Asking rather than assuming. Listening deeply and responding in ways that reflect people's actual lived realities. It's a movement away from standardisation and towards solidarity. Visible representation and inclusive leadership also play a vital role in sustaining momentum. Representation matters – not as optics or tokenism, but as a marker of possibility. When leadership reflects the communities being served, it disrupts long-standing narratives about who is 'suitable' or 'professional.' But it goes beyond demographics. It's about how those leaders lead. Are they modelling inclusive practice? Are they dismantling gatekeeping structures? Are they investing in the progression of others, or pulling the ladder up behind them? Trauma-informed approaches are increasingly being embraced too – not just as a technique but as a posture of practice. *'It's about more than language – it's about care, pace, and presence',* as one practitioner shared. This requires us to slow down, to reframe what success and engagement look like, and to recognise that our way of working must honour the trauma many clients – and indeed many practitioners – carry with them. This is where equity begins: not in policies, but in the micro-decisions we make every day to create safety, dignity, and trust.

None of this is theoretical. These practices are already alive in classrooms, youth services, careers hubs, and small grassroots initiatives. They exist quietly, often underfunded and unrecognised, but they exist. The challenge now is scale. How do we move from isolated examples to embedded norms? How do we ensure these enablers are not viewed as progressive extras, but as the gold standard for ethical, equitable careers work?

Thinking point:

- Which of these enablers have I witnessed or been part of in my own setting?
- What role am I already playing in this shift – and where could I lean in further?
- What would it take to move these from the margins of our practice to the centre?

What can I do next?

A reflection grid for practitioners, managers, and sector leaders.

Reading about barriers and enablers is important – but it is action that truly shifts culture. This grid offers a simple yet powerful way to pause, assess your current role, and take ownership of your sphere of influence (Table 2). Whether you're a practitioner working one-to-one with clients, a manager shaping service delivery, or a leader influencing policy and direction, this is your space to reflect with honesty and commit to one intentional step forward in each area.

Table 2 What can I do next?

Area	What's already happening in my practice or setting?	Where are the gaps or challenges?	What's one thing I will do next?

Embedding practice

Before we move on, I want to pause and say this clearly: none of this work is possible without the practitioner. You are often the first point of contact, the steady presence in someone's story, and the one holding space when everything else feels overwhelming. You're doing that while navigating your own identity, your own bias, and your own blind spots. This chapter isn't a set of rules or a list of everything you're doing wrong. It's an invitation – a practical, reflective, identity-conscious toolkit shaped to meet you where you are. This work requires intention, a willingness to sit with discomfort, and an understanding that change doesn't have to be loud or public to be real. Sometimes the most transformative shifts happen quietly – within ourselves.

Reflective practice

Embedding intersectionality into daily practice begins with reflection. This might involve journalling, peer debriefs, or even brief moments of intentional pause between clients. The key is to consistently ask: Who do I relate to easily – and why? Who challenges me – and what might that reveal about my assumptions? These are not surface-level reflections. They are foundational questions that open the door to deeper self-awareness. Techniques such as Clean Listening can support this process, helping you hold space without centring your own story or projecting assumptions. Reflective CPD sessions using real-world intersectional case studies can also offer insight into how identity, power, and professional guidance intersect in your everyday work.

Mentorship and peer learning

Mentorship plays a pivotal role in building both competence and confidence. But the most powerful mentoring isn't always top-down – it's relational, rooted in shared identity and lived experience. Peer learning networks, particularly those grounded in marginalised perspectives, foster a culture of mutual accountability and solidarity. Whether you connect through CDI initiatives or grassroots collectives, these networks provide space to challenge one another, share insights, and grow together in a sector where many still feel disconnected or isolated.

CPD engagement and development

Our approach to CPD must shift from generic to relevant. It's no longer enough to attend a broad-brush D&I session once a year. What practitioners are asking for is CPD that speaks to the complexity of their caseloads – training that is trauma-informed, culturally responsive, and grounded in the realities of guidance work. Resources like OpenLearn's D&I in the Workplace provide a starting point, but there is still a need for programmes built with and for marginalised practitioners. When CPD is rooted in lived reality rather than abstract policy, it becomes something practitioners can actually use – not just consume.

Mental health and identity

Mental health support must also be approached through an intersectional lens. Experiences of transition and marginalisation – being a care leaver, navigating a disability diagnosis, or living through systemic racism – are not separate from wellbeing. Practitioners are often the first to notice when something isn't quite right, yet many feel unprepared to respond. Integrating informal mental health check-ins, informed by an understanding of identity-based trauma, can help create safer, more attuned services. It's not about becoming a therapist – it's about being aware, responsive, and human.

Everyday advocacy

Advocacy doesn't require a platform – it begins in the everyday spaces you already inhabit. Whether it's raising a concern during a team meeting, sharing a lived experience at an internal training, or writing a reflective blog post, your voice has an impact. Participating in co-created projects or sector-wide forums helps break down barriers, but so do small, sustained actions. When practitioners speak truthfully from their position inside the system, they disrupt the silence that often shields inequality. You don't need to be loud to be powerful. You just need to speak – and keep speaking.

Organisational toolkit

Systemic change doesn't happen by chance – it happens by design. While the work of individual practitioners is crucial, lasting impact requires that organisational structures also evolve. This section is directed towards those with influence – whether you're leading a team, shaping policy, or building a service from the ground up. The responsibility of embedding intersectionality cannot rest solely on individual goodwill. It must be reflected in strategic decisions, everyday policies, and the culture that holds them. These aren't abstract aspirations. They are concrete, sector-informed actions backed by the lived experiences of practitioners who have long navigated the tensions between inclusion and institutional inertia. If your strategy claims that intersectionality matters, these are the steps that begin to prove it.

Strategic workforce development

We need to rethink how we bring people into the careers profession – and who we think it's for. That begins with disrupting narrow recruitment pipelines. Outreach must extend beyond traditional routes such as universities and school-based pathways. We need to tap into underrepresented communities, third-sector organisations, and adult learners. This includes using accessible explainer videos or infographics that demystify the profession, especially for those who don't see themselves reflected in current roles. Representation in leadership, on panels, and at sector events isn't a nice-to-have – it's a necessary signal of belonging, aspiration, and accountability.

CPD and training integration

Professional development should never treat equity, diversity, and inclusion as an isolated add-on. CPD must be interwoven with practice, not compartmentalised as a *'once-a-year'* topic. Sector-specific CPD is especially needed for those supporting adults, NEET groups, and community guidance – areas that often sit outside traditional school settings but face heightened complexity. Funding remains a barrier in many sectors, so offering subsidised or free CPD for practitioners in underfunded spaces is not just generous – it's just.

Mentoring infrastructure

We must reimagine mentoring beyond the old model of senior-to-junior. Identity-based mentoring that reflects lived experience is vital for meaningful development and retention. A CDI-led intersectional mentoring programme could radically shift who feels they belong in the sector. Pairing mentees not just with those who *'know the job'*, but with those who understand their background, challenges, and values – this is where mentorship becomes transformation.

Wellbeing and belonging

True inclusion is felt, not just declared. Wellbeing policies must reflect the real-world needs of marginalised staff. That could look like flexible working policies, access to culturally sensitive support, or safe spaces for processing workplace harm. But it must go further: regular feedback loops, such as anonymous pulse checks or reflection tools, allow us to hear what is often unspoken. Inclusion is not a static tick-box; it's a feeling of safety, recognition, and respect that must be measured and nurtured consistently.

Policy and culture shift

Words mean little without structural change. We must move from consultation to co-creation – embedding lived experience into policy development from the outset. That means avoiding tokenism and actively rewriting how recruitment, promotion, and leadership development work. Tools such as AdvanceHE's Intersectional EDI Framework can provide a practical foundation, but they must be adapted with honesty and context. Auditing inclusivity is not about shame – it's about seeing clearly, so we can act boldly. This toolkit doesn't claim to offer all the answers. But it begins to shift the burden from individuals quietly doing the work in isolation to systems designed to carry the responsibility of inclusion collectively.

Practitioner voice as evidence: Why listening matters

Equity work gets talked about a lot – in strategies, in policies, in neatly worded frameworks. But what's often missing are the voices of the people doing the work every day. Those navigating systems that weren't designed with them in mind. Those holding space for others while rarely being given space themselves. In the careers sector especially, I've seen how easy it is to centre theory and lose sight of the real stories unfolding behind the scenes. Listening – deep, uncomfortable, intentional listening – is where meaningful change begins. In January 2023, I co-facilitated a CDI webinar on intersectionality alongside David Morgan. It wasn't about offering a perfect model or ticking an EDI box. It was about asking a room full of practitioners: What's really going on in your world? What barriers are you facing? What would make a difference? What followed was powerful. Honest. At times hard to hear. But exactly the kind of truth-telling we need if we're serious about building an inclusive sector.

This section captures that moment. I haven't reshaped these reflections to fit a pre-planned argument. Instead, I've grouped them around the key themes that came up – because they speak for themselves. These are not complaints or one-off incidents. They're insights from people who live this work every day, and who are trying to make it better. For me, they sit at the heart of why the TEDI framework exists in the first place. If we're going to ask who benefits, who's missing, and what needs to change across practice, policy, culture, and systems – then this is where we start. By listening differently. By treating lived experience as expertise. The TEDI framework asks us to assess who benefits, whose voices are missing, and how we embed equity across practice, policy, culture, and systems – this section is the evidence base for why that work is so urgently needed.

Insights from the EDI Webinar
'If we want to reimagine a sector built on inclusion, we must start by listening differently.'

This line grounded the Equity, Diversity and Inclusion (EDI) Intersectionality Webinar, co-facilitated by David Morgan and me on 27 January 2023, as part of our shared commitment to elevating practitioner voice and rooting abstract ideals in lived experience. The session wasn't designed to be performative. It was a call to listen – to really listen – to the experiences of those working at the coalface of the career development sector. What followed was not an exercise in surface-level reflection, but a raw, often uncomfortable series of insights that revealed both the entrenched systemic barriers and the radical hope practitioners still carry. These aren't academic theories or conceptual ideals. These are truths lived daily by people who continue to show up, even when the system doesn't always show up for them.

Visibility, representation, and workforce diversity
A recurring and powerful theme throughout the session was the absence of visible representation in leadership, workforce demographics, and even the promotional materials that shape the narrative of our sector. Visibility isn't just about ticking off a diversity metric – it's about belonging, trust, and aspiration. When marginalised practitioners and clients don't see themselves reflected in the profession, the message is subtle but clear: this space might not be for you. As one participant shared, *'More representation/visibility/ diversify the workforce so that people can see themselves within the career development*

sector.' Others noted the narrow framing of careers work in public discourse, which is too often skewed towards schools and higher education, neglecting the breadth of the profession and the diversity of those it ought to serve. A lack of representation not only deters new entrants into the field but stifles innovation and perpetuates exclusionary practices.

Mentorship and belonging

Another key enabler highlighted was the importance of mentorship grounded in lived experience. Participants made it clear that traditional models of mentoring – those based on hierarchy or years of service – often fall short in supporting those navigating marginalisation. Instead, what's needed is mentorship rooted in shared identity, cultural understanding, and emotional safety. *'Mentoring – not just from those more experienced in careers but also those who understand different communities'*, one person noted. This wasn't just about professional development; it was about survival. In settings where leadership lacked cultural competency, mentorship became a lifeline. It provided solidarity in spaces where many felt isolated, invisible, or misunderstood.

Reflective practice and bias awareness

Several attendees raised concerns about the unconscious biases we all carry – and the need for continuous reflective practice to surface and interrogate those assumptions. *'Some people don't recognise the issues because they haven't been personally affected'*, one reflection read. Another noted, *'Our own backgrounds lead us to make assumptions or lack awareness of how to understand others.'* This level of honesty matters. It moves the conversation away from blame and towards growth. The practice of Clean Listening was named as a vital strategy – ensuring that practitioners are listening to clients without filtering their stories through our own lenses or lived experience. Reflection, then, is not a passive act. It is an active, necessary discipline to ensure we don't replicate the very barriers we aim to dismantle.

CPD and sector development

Professional development came under sharp scrutiny during the session. Participants expressed frustration that EDI training is often framed as an optional extra, rather than core to good practice. *'Embedding EDI throughout CPD – not as a separate module'*, was a consistent plea. Too often, access to meaningful training depends on where one works. Some organisations invest in trauma-informed, intersectional approaches; others offer little more than generic online modules. This inconsistency creates an uneven playing field – one where clients receive vastly different levels of inclusive support, simply based on postcode or budget. The message was clear: the CDI and wider sector must do more to standardise, subsidise, and prioritise CPD that meets practitioners where they are – and where their clients truly need them to be.

Trauma-informed and holistic approaches

Linked to this was a strong call for more trauma-informed guidance. Practitioners shared how many of their clients – especially those with refugee backgrounds, care-experienced journeys, or mental health challenges – need more than employability tips. They need to be seen in their full humanity. *'Trauma-informed practice helps us support clients better'*, said one attendee. *'Limited access to mental health support aligned with identity'* was another concern raised. These statements point to a wider truth: our clients don't leave their lived experiences at the door. The career development process must be holistic, compassionate, and sensitive to the intersecting challenges that shape how people navigate choice, change, and employment.

Systemic barriers and cultural disconnect

The webinar didn't shy away from naming the difficult truths. Practitioners voiced frustration at low pay, lack of progression, and institutional resistance. *'Pay scale is not attractive enough. Men can't afford to sustain their families'*, one participant reflected – highlighting how gendered expectations intersect with financial inequity. Others raised concerns that the sector is seen as 'support work' rather than as a professional field, which undermines its influence and investment. There was also a cultural disconnect: collectivist values, often held by clients from non-Western backgrounds, were described as being at odds with individualistic careers frameworks. This cultural mismatch can affect career decisions, mental health, and client-practitioner trust.

Practitioner-led solutions and structural change

Despite these challenges, participants didn't just name problems – they offered solutions. Practical, grounded, and sector-informed suggestions included creating infographic-style explainer videos to demystify the profession, encouraging employers to fund CPD, and embedding inclusive leadership development. *'Could the CDI provide infographic-style YouTube videos on intersectionality?'* one asked. Another said, *'Encourage employers to fund CPD. If it's not required, staff won't engage.'* These ideas weren't about fixing individuals; they were about reshaping systems so that people could thrive within them.

Co-creation and psychological safety

Perhaps the most urgent call was for co-creation and psychological safety – for practitioners as well as clients. *'Elevating voices from marginalised communities must be a sector priority'*, one attendee said. Another added, *'We need spaces to talk about the impact of intersectionality safely'*. This isn't just about inviting people to the table – it's about rebuilding the table, together. Practitioners were not asking for rescue. They were asking for respect, inclusion, and structures that reflect the complexity of the lives they support. When psychological safety is present, honesty becomes possible. When honesty is possible, real change can begin.

Task

The quotes below were shared during the CDI Intersectionality Webinar and offer powerful entry points for reflection. They're not just comments – they're lived experiences that invite us to pause, question, and respond. Whether you're working through these alone, with a colleague, or as part of a wider team conversation, this activity is a space to listen differently and begin to turn insight into practice.

How to use this

Choose any three quotes that speak to you – or challenge you. For each one, take time to reflect on:

- What does this raise for me or my setting?
- What assumptions does it prompt me to rethink?
- What one small step could I take in response?

This isn't about solving everything. It's about noticing what lands, what stirs discomfort, and what it might take to shift something, even slightly.

Quotes to reflect on

'Mentoring – not just from those more experienced in careers, but from those who understand different communities.'

'Our own backgrounds lead us to make assumptions.'

'Embedding EDI throughout CPD – not as a separate module.'

'More representation is needed so people can see themselves in the sector.'

'Career services are viewed as a luxury, not a necessity.'

'Some people don't see the issues because they've never had to.'

'Belonging is lost when working remotely without team connection.'

'Elevating the voices of marginalised groups must be a priority.'

You might use this in a journal, as a team reflection, or in a peer discussion. Some have found the think-pair-share method helpful – others prefer a quiet moment with pen and paper. However you approach it, make it honest, make it yours.

TEDI and intersectionality: How they intersect and why it matters

At the heart of the TEDI framework is a commitment to systemic change – change that doesn't just tinker around the edges but interrogates the very structures, policies, and practices that exclude. Intersectionality, as coined by Kimberlé Crenshaw, is about recognising how different aspects of identity – such as race, gender, disability, class, faith, sexuality – interact to shape lived experience. It's not a buzzword. It's a lens for seeing what is often made invisible in dominant narratives.

The TEDI framework is intentionally designed to hold space for this complexity. Each pillar of TEDI – Transformative Assessment, Equitable Policies, Diverse Culture, and Inclusive Practices – asks us to examine not just what we're doing but who we're doing it for. Intersectionality threads through all of this, not as a standalone concept, but as a principle that must shape how we assess systems, craft policies, build culture, and embed inclusion in daily practice.

- Transformative Assessment invites us to ask: Who is being served by our current structures – and who is being left out? Whose voices are being amplified in our audits and evaluations, and whose are still missing?
- Equitable Policies challenge us to move beyond performative equality statements to policies that recognise the specific barriers faced by marginalised groups – and work to dismantle them.
- Diverse Culture reminds us that a visibly diverse workforce is not enough. True diversity means cultural shift: ensuring that individuals from intersecting identities feel seen, heard, and able to thrive – not just survive.
- Inclusive Practices grounds it all in the everyday – because it's in the day-to-day interactions, decisions, and behaviours that inclusion is either felt or fractured.

Intersectionality is not a side conversation – it is the conversation. TEDI provides a structured, actionable way to embed that conversation across all levels of an organisation. It's not enough to say we care about equity. We have to build the infrastructure to show it. TEDI is that infrastructure. Intersectionality is the lens that makes sure no one is erased in the process. It offers a route forward – not just for individual reflection but for systemic transformation. While intersectionality is powerful on its own, without a framework, it can remain fragmented. TEDI makes it deliberate, structured, and actionable.

Chapter 5
Understanding ethnicity in career development

Chapter roadmap

This chapter takes an honest look at how ethnicity shapes the experience of career development – both for those receiving support and those delivering it. It moves beyond surface-level diversity talk to confront systemic barriers, power dynamics, and what meaningful representation really looks like in practice.

This chapter:

- Begins with an author's voice on why we centre ethnicity in this work – not as a trend, but as a necessity grounded in justice;
- Defines ethnicity in the context of careers guidance and explores how it intersects with identity, opportunity, and perception;
- Unpacks ethnic inequity – what it looks like in the careers sector, where it shows up, and how it impacts both clients and practitioners;
- Explores the structural, cultural, and interpersonal barriers that marginalised groups face, including gatekeeping, racialised expectations, and lack of progression;
- Shares enablers – practical strategies, culturally responsive approaches, and what good practice looks like when inclusion is more than a statement;
- Provides a dual toolkit: one for practitioners navigating these issues daily, and another for organisations ready to move from statements to systems change;
- Revisits reflections from the CDI's Ethnicity Workshop – not as static insight, but as part of a wider collective push for action;
- Ends with a reflection task and action grid to help you move from awareness to accountability.

Author's voice

When people think of Equity, Diversity, and Inclusion, ethnicity is often the strand that makes them shift in their seats. For me, though, it's central – because it's the identity I move through the world with. I don't approach this as an abstract theme, but as a lived experience. Language matters here. I choose the term *ethnically diverse*, not *minority*; how we name people either affirms their presence or reduces them to absence. It's not semantics – it's structural. One participant at the January 2023 CDI Ethnicity Workshop captured it clearly: *'Terminology matters. Using it properly shows you've done the work. It's about respect.'* And yet, time and again, when conversations around ethnicity and race are introduced, they are met not with engagement but with silence – a silence that speaks louder than resistance. I've seen the hesitation, the discomfort, the eagerness to move on. But that silence is not neutral. It's a barrier. This chapter, like the workshop that informed it, is about naming that barrier – and pushing through it.

Ethnicity is often the first strand of EDI to be erased when the conversation gets uncomfortable. It's too political, too complex, too risky; it's buried under umbrella acronyms like BAME, referring to Black, Asian, Minority Ethnic, or erased entirely through colour-blind approaches that pretend not to see difference, while quietly reproducing inequality. These aren't acts of inclusion – they're acts of erasure. They maintain the illusion that careers work is neutral when, in fact, it is always shaped by the identities we carry and the systems we navigate. Ethnicity matters because people matter. People bring with them culture, language, migration, trauma, joy, and resilience into every career space they enter. That can't be ignored or flattened. If guidance is to be ethical, it must be relational. It must reflect the lived realities of the people it seeks to support.

Ethnicity itself is relational and fluid. Unlike race, which is often imposed from the outside, ethnicity is something we identify with, based on shared ancestry, culture, language, and belonging. It's not just about skin tone – it's about heritage and context. It's about who we are, where we come from, and how that's read by others. Yet even with this nuance, the careers sector has too often misused, misunderstood, or overlooked it altogether. As one participant stated during the workshop: *'Careers theory doesn't speak to ethnicity or class.'* That's not just an academic oversight. It's a structural failure that shapes how guidance is developed, delivered, and experienced.

When we fail to name ethnicity, we also fail to name the cultural dissonance that can exist between clients and practitioners. We ignore the historical weight of colonialism, immigration, racism, and exclusion that many people carry into the room. We miss the fact that the frameworks we work within are not neutral – they are often built around the assumption of whiteness as the default. That assumption seeps into guidance, recruitment, leadership, and policy. It shapes who gets listened to, who gets opportunities, and who is treated as a 'fit'. And when clients from ethnically diverse backgrounds encounter that bias – whether overt or subtle – it affects not just their choices but their confidence, their sense of belonging, and their futures.

If we don't understand how ethnicity operates – how it intersects with faith, gender, class, immigration status, and lived experience – then our guidance becomes surface-level. If you're advising a Muslim young woman from a refugee background without acknowledging how these layers shape her reality, you're not offering meaningful guidance. You're offering a generic script. One that may sound supportive but fails to reach her.

This chapter is not about tick-boxes or token gestures. It is about resistance. It centres on the knowledge and voices of those who are so often expected to drive change while being excluded from decision-making tables. It listens to the voices of practitioners who said, *'We do not reflect the population'*. That isn't a passing comment – it's a call to action. Another practitioner said, *'If your policies don't change outcomes, they're just decoration'*. That isn't a critique – it's a truth.

The quotes you'll find here are not illustrative fluff. They are the heartbeat of this conversation. They move us from abstract policy to lived impact. They are the evidence the sector too often avoids. There are no simple answers ahead – but there are honest ones. If we are serious about equity, then ethnicity cannot be the strand we drop when things get uncomfortable. It must be the place we begin.

What is ethnicity?

Ethnicity is often mistaken for race, but they are not the same. Ethnicity refers to a person's identification with a social group based on shared ancestry, cultural heritage, language, traditions, and sometimes religion (Modood and Ahmad, 2007). It is self-defined, relational, and rooted in belonging – often shaped by migration, memory, and the complex ties between identity and community. Where race is externally imposed and rooted in binary thinking, ethnicity is fluid, evolving, and intersectional. It tells us not only where someone comes from, but how they carry that story, how they are read by others, and how that experience interacts with systems, power, and belonging.

Despite this, within the careers sector, ethnicity remains one of the most misunderstood, misused, or altogether ignored elements of identity. It is often absorbed into acronyms, avoided in data collection, or treated as politically inconvenient. As one practitioner at the January 2023 CDI

Ethnicity Workshop observed, *'Careers theory doesn't speak to ethnicity or class'*. That isn't just a theoretical omission – it's a structural failure. It affects how guidance is conceptualised, taught, and delivered. It reveals a wider issue: a sector hesitant to confront how whiteness operates as a default, how colonial histories echo in practice, and how the silence around ethnicity isn't neutral – it's protective of the status quo.

When we fail to name ethnicity, we fail to see the dissonance between clients and practitioners. We overlook the cultural mismatch that can impact trust, understanding, and relevance. We ignore how language, religion, migration stories, and cultural knowledge shape the career journey – and how those factors are often marginalised within the frameworks we claim are universal. Ethnicity affects how clients are perceived, how they are listened to, and what options are deemed appropriate or realistic for them. It intersects with faith, gender, socio-economic background, and immigration status. If a practitioner is offering advice to a Muslim young woman from a refugee background without understanding how ethnicity shapes her lived reality, then that advice is not guidance – it's a generic, surface-level script that risks erasure.

This work demands more than conceptual definitions. It requires honesty about where the sector has fallen short and what needs to change. One practitioner reflected, *'When you try and have conversations around ethnicity and race, it can be met with silence.'* But silence is never neutral. It upholds the myth of neutrality in careers guidance, masking how certain voices are always heard more loudly, and others are consistently sidelined. That silence protects comfort rather than fostering justice. It avoids accountability while claiming inclusion. That's precisely what this chapter – and this book – refuse to do. This section is not just to define. It's a mirror held up to the profession. It asks: Whose stories are missing? Whose frameworks are shaping the work – and at whose expense? What would it mean to centre ethnically diverse voices, not as an afterthought, but as foundational to how we understand and deliver ethical, equitable career development? These are not rhetorical questions. They are calls to action. If we continue to ignore the realities of ethnicity, we continue to offer a model of guidance that works best for those already well represented, while leaving others to navigate systemic barriers alone. Equity requires more. It begins here – with a willingness to listen, to unlearn, and to reimagine.

Understanding ethnic inequity in careers

Let's start by dismantling a myth the sector still clings to – the idea that careers work is neutral. It isn't. No profession operates in a vacuum, untouched by history, culture, or power. Yet, the careers sector has long positioned itself as offering impartial advice, as though impartiality somehow equates to objectivity. But objectivity, in a system shaped by colonial legacies, white middle-class norms, and systemic racism, is a fallacy. Impartiality becomes a smokescreen – one that conceals the ways our assumptions, language, and structures reinforce inequity. When that supposed neutrality is left unexamined, it doesn't level the playing field – it cements the existing one. Dr Oliver Jenkin reminded me that it is important to note that 'impartial' in guidance is usually framed as a practitioner being careful not to favour one option over another, and to bracket their views and assumptions when working with a client. So, to that extent, 'neutrality' is something striven for in a pragmatic sense. This doesn't mean that the sector is 'neutral', however, as I illustrate many examples of how structural neutrality/impartiality is not yet integral to the sector later in the book.

Too often, careers provision defaults to equality over equity. Equality assumes everyone starts in the same place and needs the same tools. But equity acknowledges that people arrive with vastly different experiences, barriers, and access to opportunity. It challenges us to ask: Who are we centring in our work? Whose experiences are shaping the frameworks we use? Uniformity is not fairness. Real fairness requires context, nuance, and an active commitment to dismantling structural barriers. Careers guidance can only be equitable when it meets people where they are – understanding how their culture, family structures, language, and lived realities influence the decisions they make. We cannot keep pretending that one-size-fits-all support is good enough. It never was. It never will be.

Ethnic inequity is not a fringe issue. It is embedded in the very fabric of our sector – in who gets hired, who gets promoted, who sits on panels, and who is expected to stay silent. The January 2023 CDI Ethnicity Workshop brought this reality into sharp focus. One practitioner reflected, *'We recruit in our own image. Panels are mostly White. That needs to change.'* That isn't an isolated critique – it's a pattern, echoed across the sector. Another added, *'If you're not from the right background, you don't even hear about these roles.'* That's more than just a visibility problem – it's an infrastructure problem. It's about access, power, and the stories we tell ourselves about merit, fit, and professionalism. When a practitioner said, *'I didn't see anyone like me. That's why I never considered this career'*, they weren't talking about optics – they were talking about exclusion, about the erasure that happens when institutions fail to reflect the communities they serve.

The profession isn't just lacking diversity – it's reproducing sameness. Another workshop participant pointed out, *'Most panels are White and recruit in their own image'*. That cycle doesn't break on its own. It must be disrupted. Yet time and again, ethnic inequity is met with deflection. *'People don't realise they're being exclusive because the default culture is white, middle-class'*, one attendee observed. That 'default' shows up everywhere: in our CPD offerings, our guidance resources, our definitions of success. It shapes how we interpret ambition, how we assess potential, and how we judge credibility. Left unchallenged, it sets the standard – and everyone outside of it becomes an exception to be managed, not a norm to be welcomed.

Ethnic inequity isn't accidental. It's designed. It's sustained through tradition, habit, and silence. It will continue unless we move beyond performative inclusion and take responsibility for structural change. This isn't about 'diversity' initiatives that leave systems untouched. It's about reimagining those systems entirely. If the careers profession is serious about inclusion, then ethnic equity can't remain a side topic – it must become central to how we think, act, and lead. This is not a call for representation alone – it's a call for reparation, for redistribution of voice, power, and possibility.

Barriers

We do not need more glossy reports or generic statistics to tell us what many of us already know from lived experience. The careers sector has an equity problem, and ethnicity remains one of the most avoided, diluted, or discomfort-inducing strands. It's the part of EDI that gets softened into safer language or only addressed when someone is bold enough to name the unspoken. But practitioners – particularly those from ethnically diverse backgrounds – have always been naming it. Quietly, sometimes loudly, but persistently. In January 2023, during the CDI Ethnicity Workshop, those voices came through with clarity, courage, and conviction. This section is not a neat summary – it's a refusal to sanitise what was said. These barriers weren't framed as theory. They were described as daily realities. They demand more than performative action. They require structural transformation.

The lack of representation is an issue so visible it barely needs explanation. Yet, it continues to be minimised. When leadership teams, boards, and advisory groups don't reflect the communities they serve, that absence sends a loud message about who belongs and who doesn't. Visibility is more than optics – it's about pathways, credibility, and cultural safety. *'We do not reflect the population'*, said one attendee. Another was clear: *'BAME Careers Advisers are role models.'* Without those role models, future generations would never even imagine themselves here. It's not just about who is in the room – it's about who never made it to the door.

Biased recruitment and retention practices reinforce this invisibility. As one participant put it, *'We recruit in our own image'*. This simple sentence cuts to the core of how sameness gets reproduced in panels that are mostly White, middle-class, and female – no matter how well-meaning. The sameness isn't accidental. It's designed through informal networks, cultural fit assessments, and unspoken assumptions about professionalism. The pipeline myth? That people of colour *'just aren't applying'*? It falls apart when you look closely at who gets through each gate – and who built the gates in the first place.

Even when diversity is achieved at the entry level, it rarely translates into leadership. Decision-making remains largely untouched. *'More support is needed for BAME to get into management'*, one attendee shared, pushing back on the narrative that progression is only a matter of merit or ambition. It's not. It's about structures, sponsorship, and the courage to confront bias where it's most entrenched. The sector doesn't have a pipeline issue – it has a promotion issue, a pay issue, and a problem with power being hoarded rather than shared.

That pay issue runs deeper than affordability – it's an equity concern. Practitioners from working-class or racially minoritised backgrounds often can't afford to remain in the profession. For some, the sector wasn't even visible in the first place. *'Selling the sector – many aren't told what a Career Advisor does'*, one participant noted. Another was blunter: *'Pay is too low. That's why people of colour don't apply.'* These reflections are not about personal preference – they're about structural exclusion masked as economic inevitability.

Then there's bias. It doesn't always come in overt acts. Often, it's in the micro-messages: being described as *'too passionate'*, overlooked for projects, or pigeonholed into 'diversity' roles with no real influence. As one practitioner observed, *'Lack of cultural understanding and pigeonholing'* continues to shape how colleagues are perceived and valued. Others described how stereotyping and assumptions lead to a hostile environment – one where being present doesn't equate to being included. Representation without power is tokenism.

This exclusion extends into the theory and training that underpin the sector. When frameworks are built on white, middle-class norms, they become irrelevant – if not harmful – for clients whose realities differ. *'Careers theory doesn't speak to ethnicity or class'*, one participant stated. Another was sharper: *'Our theory is white, middle-class and outdated.'* When the foundational models of our work ignore the lived experience of a large portion of the population, they fail to offer real guidance. Theory isn't neutral – it's a product of the context in which it was created. When that context is monocultural, the results are exclusionary by default.

A recurring theme from the workshop was silence. Not the absence of awareness – but the refusal to engage. *'When you try and have conversations around ethnicity and race, it can be met with silence'*, said one attendee. That silence isn't passive – it's protective. It shields people from discomfort while leaving inequity intact. Others spoke about the fear of saying the wrong thing, leading to hollow gestures and *'performative actions'* that make the surface look inclusive without addressing the rot underneath. But silence, whether driven by fear or indifference, upholds the very dynamics we claim to oppose.

Mentorship and allyship were mentioned not as luxuries, but as lifelines. *'Mentoring changed everything. I saw someone like me, and that gave me a reason to stay.'* Allyship, however, must go beyond performative declarations. It means sponsorship – active advocacy at decision-making tables, not just quiet support behind the scenes. It means creating structures where progression isn't conditional on proximity to whiteness, but on recognising and valuing diverse leadership styles and contributions.

The profession's inaccessibility to those outside dominant cultural and socio-economic backgrounds isn't accidental either. *'If you're not from the right background, you don't even hear about these roles'*, one participant explained. Even when people do enter the profession, the absence of meaningful support means many leave. It's not enough to widen the door – we have to change the room.

And finally, the hardest truth: most EDI work in the sector is decorative. If your policies don't change outcomes, they are just branding exercises. If they don't redistribute power, they are not equity – they are optics. *'EDI training needs to be embedded, not bolted on.'* What's needed is not more slogans or pledges, but systemic change that is uncomfortable, disruptive, and deeply necessary. If the sector wants to move forward, it must be willing to name these barriers – not in whispers but in strategy, accountability, and action.

Enablers

The barriers within the careers sector are deep, but so is the potential for change. Amidst the realities of inequity, practitioners who attended the January 2023 CDI Ethnicity Workshop offered more than just critique – they shared practical, experience-driven strategies that can shift the profession from surface-level inclusion to meaningful structural change. These enablers aren't optional extras; they are essential if we are to build a sector that reflects and respects the diverse communities it serves.

Mentorship and sponsorship emerged as key levers for change. When done well, mentorship provides belonging, visibility, and the confidence to stay. When paired with sponsorship – where someone in power actively opens doors and advocates behind the scenes – it creates pathways that don't require assimilation. These forms of support must be intentional, identity-informed, and sustained – not tokenistic or short-lived.

Representation must move beyond superficial measures. It is not enough to have visual diversity at the front desk while decision-making spaces remain homogenous. True representation means ethnically diverse leaders in positions of influence, shaping policy, culture, and direction. Representation builds legitimacy, role modelling, and trust – not just for clients but for future professionals seeking to see themselves reflected in the sector. One practitioner said it plainly: *'BAME Careers Advisers = role models for students.'* That representation is powerful, but only if it's backed by real authority and opportunity.

Training, theory, and CPD must evolve. Frameworks built around white, middle-class norms exclude by default. Practitioners repeatedly call for reform that embeds equity, not as an add-on, but as a foundational thread throughout initial training, continuing development, and guidance models. One attendee noted, *'EDI must be part of IAG frameworks – not separate from it.'* Equity should not be seen as additional work – it is the work. We also need brave, supported spaces to have real conversations. Too often, race is avoided out of fear – of getting it wrong, of causing offence, or of uncovering truths that make us uncomfortable. But avoidance sustains inequity. Practitioners voice a need for space to talk openly, reflect honestly, and grow collectively. *'We need space to get it wrong, learn, and move forward.'* Creating space for these conversations is not a distraction from our work – it is part of the work.

Change will not happen by accident. It has to happen by design. It requires commitment, structure, and a willingness to challenge the norms we've grown used to. But as these enablers show, it is possible. It is already happening in corners of the sector where courage, care, and clarity are being prioritised. The task ahead is to scale that commitment – so that it becomes not the exception, but the expectation.

Barriers and solutions

Naming the barriers is only one part of the work – we must also be clear on how to dismantle them. Table 3 overleaf captures the key structural and cultural challenges raised by practitioners during the January 2023 CDI Ethnicity Workshop, paired with possible responses. These aren't theoretical fixes. They are grounded, practitioner-driven ideas that reflect the urgency and possibility of change. This isn't about waiting for permission. It's about getting on with the work, using the tools and influence we already have.

Table 3 Barriers and potential solutions

Barrier	Potential solution
Lack of representation	Set diversity targets across all levels. Audit and publish workforce data.
Biased recruitment and retention	Diversify panels. Use contextual recruitment. Train against in-group bias.
Lack of ethnic diversity in leadership	Create targeted development pipelines. Sponsor progression, not just access.
Poor pay and sector visibility	Campaign for fair sector wages. Promote careers work in ethnically diverse settings.
Unconscious bias and stereotyping	Embed cultural humility training across all CPD. Challenge pigeonholing publicly.
Exclusion in careers theory and training	Diversify curriculum content. Co-create training with ethnically diverse practitioners.
Silence and discomfort in conversations	Facilitate safe spaces. Train leaders to model vulnerability and discomfort.
Lack of mentorship and allyship	Build structured mentoring schemes that prioritise identity alignment.
Inaccessibility of the sector	Engage with grassroots and third-sector partners. Host outreach events in local spaces.
Tokenistic policies and decorative EDI	Tie EDI to KPIs. Evaluate by outcomes, not activity. Invest in long-term culture shift.

The truth is, change doesn't just live in strategy documents or policy briefings – it lives in what we choose to notice, name, and act on in our day-to-day practice. The enablers outlined above offer a direction, but direction alone isn't enough without the tools to walk it. That's where this next section comes in. Whether you're a frontline practitioner trying to shift your approach, or a leader shaping culture from the top, the following toolkits are here to help you move from intention to implementation. They're not exhaustive, and they won't fix everything overnight – but they do offer a starting point. A way to hold ourselves and our organisations accountable to the very equity we claim to value. This is where theory meets practice. Where discomfort meets action. Where change, however slow or messy, starts to become real.

Practitioner toolkit: Surviving the system while shifting it

Let's start with honesty. Many of us know what it feels like to be the only one in the room. To be asked – implicitly or directly – to represent an entire ethnic group. To be seen, but not really heard. To walk a line between surviving a system and trying to change it. This toolkit isn't a fix for that experience – but it is a strategy for navigating it with integrity, reflection, and power. It's about holding space for yourself, even as you push for something better.

Practical actions for practitioners

- **Reflect intentionally**
  Take time to journal or voice-note how your identity shapes the guidance you offer. Ask yourself: Who do I naturally connect with? Who feels unfamiliar or challenging – and why?

- **Listen differently**
  Practise clean learning. That means actively removing your assumptions and letting the client lead. Their lived experience doesn't need your edits – it needs your presence.

- **Build your circle**
  Find or create peer spaces with people who understand the weight you carry. Use these networks to reflect, vent, share, and strategise. Solidarity is a survival tool.

- **Mentor with identity in mind**
  Offer mentoring that isn't colour-blind or neutral. Acknowledge how identity, background, and barriers shape careers – and support from that place, not in spite of it.

- **Interrupt the defaults**
  Pay attention to patterns. Who's always in the room? Who's always left out? Start naming them. Even one voice can disrupt a cycle.

Reflection task: Auditing your organisation for ethnic equity

Inclusion often lives in our values – but equity lives in our systems. This reflection task invites you to audit your organisation with honesty, curiosity, and courage. It's not about finding fault for the sake of it – it's about uncovering what needs attention so we can build better.

Start by asking:

- Who is visible?
- Who is missing?
- Who is being heard?
- Who is safe?

Step 1: Identify the barriers
Use the ten barriers outlined earlier in this chapter. For each one, ask:

- Does this show up in my workplace?
- How do I know?
- Whose voices are excluded from the conversation?

Step 2: Name the impact
Where barriers exist, explore the consequences:

- Who is being excluded, overlooked, or unsupported?
- What opportunities are being denied?
- What client or staff stories are we not hearing?

Step 3: Create counteractions
Move from passive awareness to active response:

- What bold, practical steps could we take?
- What structures need adjusting or removing?
- How can we do better, not just feel better?

Step 4: Draft your equity action plan
Use Table 4 to translate reflection into strategy:

Table 4 Equity action plan

Barrier	What this looks like in our setting	Action we can take
Lack of representation	All managers are White	Review recruitment strategy. Partner with diverse orgs.
Biased recruitment	Homogenous shortlists and interview panels	Diversify panels. Train recruiters on contextual practices.
Silence on race	No forum for difficult equity conversations	Set up safe, staff-led spaces to hold racial equity dialogue.

This isn't about blame. It's about responsibility. If you can influence change – even in one corner of your organisation – start there. Equity begins at your desk.

Organisational toolkit: Embedding ethnic equity into the system

Change isn't a happy accident. It comes from conscious decisions, held over time, by people who are willing to ask the uncomfortable questions. This toolkit isn't about tick-box training or one-off events. It's about embedding equity deep into how the organisation thinks, hires, supports, and leads.

Workforce representation

You can't meet the needs of communities you don't reflect. Homogeneity in staffing and leadership isn't just a missed opportunity – it's a replicator of harm.

'We recruit in our own image. Panels are mostly White.'

Actions:

- Audit who's in the building – and who isn't – across all levels.
- Set measurable, time-bound diversity targets.
- Work with specialist job boards and community partners to broaden your reach.

Recruitment and progression

Equity starts long before the job offer. It's shaped by who hears about the job, how they're assessed, and whether they feel like they belong once they arrive.

'Most interview panels are White, middle class, and female.'

'More support is needed for BAME to get into management.'

Actions:

- Diversify hiring panels and challenge in-group bias.
- Use anonymised and contextual recruitment methods.
- Establish clear, supported routes into leadership roles.

Pay equity and sector promotion

If salaries remain low, the profession becomes inaccessible to those from working-class and ethnically diverse backgrounds. That's not a budget issue – it's an equity issue.

'Pay is too low. That's why people of colour don't apply.'

'Selling the sector – many aren't told what a careers adviser does.'

Actions:

- Reassess pay through an equity lens.
- Promote the profession where it's not visible – in schools, youth hubs, and community spaces.
- Offer paid internships or shadowing to increase access.

Training, theory and curriculum reform

If your frameworks are built on assumptions of neutrality, they won't serve everyone equally. Theory must reflect lived realities – not just academic norms.

'Careers theory doesn't speak to ethnicity or class.'

'EDI must be part of IAG frameworks – not separate from it.'

Actions:

- Co-create training content with diverse practitioners.
- Embed anti-racist and culturally grounded knowledge in all CPD.
- Measure success by shifts in practice – not just hours completed.

Accountability, not opt-in

Equity work cannot sit on the edge of the organisation. It has to be owned, led, and funded.

'If your policies don't change outcomes, they're just decoration.'

Actions:

- Make EDI a board-level priority.
- Link inclusion to performance reviews, key performance indictors (KPIs), and funding decisions.
- Monitor and publish progress using real data.

Psychological safety and brave dialogue

Equity cannot grow in silence. Staff need spaces where naming injustice doesn't cost them their wellbeing or job.

'We need space to get it wrong, learn, and move forward.'

'Fear of saying the wrong thing leads to silence.'

Actions:

- Set up intentional, safe spaces for conversations about race and identity.
- Train leaders to hold space – not avoid it.
- Treat psychological safety as central to wellbeing and retention.

Unpacking your voice: Reflections from the CDI Ethnicity Workshop

These aren't case studies, and they're certainly not neat soundbites for the next CPD slide deck. These are lived truths – unfiltered reflections from careers practitioners who have navigated the discomfort, the silences, and the exhaustion of working in a sector that claims to be neutral but replicates inequality in plain sight. These words surfaced during the CDI Ethnicity Workshop in January 2023, an intentional space carved out to speak openly about ethnicity, identity, and injustice. They weren't shared for show. They were offered in vulnerability and with hope that someone would finally listen.

There's a habit in this sector to tidy things up, to take hard truths and soften them until they're palatable. But this section doesn't do that. It holds up a mirror – sometimes uncomfortably – so we can ask the harder questions. What is being allowed to persist? Who is being failed? What am I, what are we, willing to do about it? Don't read these as detached examples. Sit with them. Let them linger. Let them challenge your assumptions.

Visibility and belonging
'I didn't see anyone like me. That's why I never considered this career.'

'Advisers often don't reflect the clients. That affects trust.'

Representation is never just about optics – it's about belonging. When ethnically diverse practitioners and clients see no one like them in roles of influence or visibility, the message is loud: this space wasn't built with you in mind. It becomes harder to trust a system that doesn't reflect you, let alone one that assumes neutrality while upholding white, middle-class norms.

Access and awareness
'If you're not from the right background, you don't even hear about these roles.'

'Selling the sector – many aren't told what a careers adviser does.'

A lack of outreach breeds invisibility. If careers work is not promoted in diverse communities, then how are people meant to find their way into the sector? Access begins long before recruitment – it starts with awareness, storytelling, and disrupting who hears about what. A sector that's invisible to those it claims to serve is a sector cutting itself off from the talent it desperately needs.

Recruitment and gatekeeping
'We recruit in our own image. Panels are mostly White.'

'Bias in recruitment processes and access to mentors.'

This is where structural racism shows up: homogeneous panels, biased ideas of what 'professionalism' looks like hidden rules, and unwritten codes that reward familiarity over fairness. Even when someone makes it through the door, the support to thrive isn't guaranteed. Without access to mentorship or sponsorship, diverse practitioners are left to navigate alone – expected to assimilate rather than be celebrated for their difference.

Silence and discomfort
'When you try and have conversations around ethnicity and race, it can be met with silence.'

'Fear of saying the wrong thing leads to avoidance.'

This silence isn't benign – it's an active form of resistance. Discomfort is often avoided to protect the status quo. Yet the unwillingness to talk about race doesn't make inequity disappear. It deepens it. Practitioners spoke of feeling shut down, dismissed, or burdened with the sole responsibility of holding these conversations. Until discomfort is normalised and shared, meaningful change remains out of reach.

Systemic barriers and cynicism
'If your policies don't change outcomes, they're just decoration.'

'EDI is seen as a tick-box – until something bad happens.'

This isn't about a lack of knowledge – it's about a lack of action. Performative EDI work does more harm than good. It creates disillusionment, especially when policies promise inclusion but protect power. Practitioners can tell when EDI is performative. They know when it's reactive instead of proactive. The call here is not for more statements, but for actual structural change. For accountability that lives beyond a crisis.

Reflection prompt: Unpick and apply
Choose three of the quotes above and ask yourself:

- What truth does this reveal about your workplace?
- What systems or behaviours allow this to continue?
- What would it take to interrupt the cycle?

Use this as a journalling task, a team CPD discussion, or a moment of honest pause. You don't need to fix it all at once – but you do need to start listening differently.

Thinking points and action grid

This isn't a worksheet to tick through and forget. It's a conversation starter, a self-audit, a space to ask: where are we complicit, and where can we do better? If you've made it to this point, you're already past awareness. This is where change begins – not with perfection, but with persistence. Fill in Table 5 not for a policy review, not for an external audit, but for the communities, colleagues, and clients you serve. Make it count.

Table 5 Thinking points and action grid

Area	What's in place now?	Where are the gaps?	What will I do next?
Representation			
Recruitment			
Pay equity			
Mentorship			
Cultural competence			
CPD integration			
Safe conversations			

Take your time. There are no perfect answers – only honest ones. Commit to one small but significant action in each category. Maybe it's a piece of training, a conversation you've avoided, or a change in how you lead your team. Write it down. Revisit it.

This is your invitation to step into practice. The real measure of impact is what happens after the page is turned.

Chapter 6
Religion in career development

Chapter roadmap

This chapter explores how religion, belief, and spirituality shape identity, purpose, and belonging in career development – yet are often sidelined in equity conversations. It unpacks the silence that surrounds faith in professional spaces and offers tools to make inclusion more than a legal tick-box.

This chapter:

- Begins by exploring why religion, belief, and spirituality matter in careers work, and why they must be seen as more than personal, private concerns;
- Unpacks the disconnect between legal protection and lived reality – where practitioners of faith are protected on paper but often made invisible in practice;
- Examines how silence, discomfort, and calls for 'neutrality' can create exclusion, and how these dynamics show up in guidance spaces;
- Centres the lived experiences of practitioners and clients who face faith-based marginalisation in careers contexts, including how microaggressions, assumptions, or erasure manifest;
- Analyses the structural, cultural, and interpersonal barriers that block full inclusion – from uniform policies to the pathologising of religious values;
- Offers practical enablers, including inclusive language, culturally responsive practice, and faith-informed allyship. We end with tools to reflect, audit practice, and act – ensuring religious inclusion becomes embedded, not exceptional.

Author's voice

Religion is often viewed as too private, too sensitive, or too controversial to address in professional settings. But the reality is, belief and spirituality shape values, decisions, career goals, and workplace culture – whether we name it or not. When we first set up the workshops, we split them into different strands of diversity and realised religion needed to be separate from ethnicity. A religious diversity chapter is needed because faith isn't a footnote – it's a core part of identity. Yet too often, it's treated as sensitive, niche, or worse – irrelevant. In the careers sector, we talk about being person-centred, but we frequently leave out one of the most defining elements of many people's lives. Faith influences values, career choices, family expectations, working hours, clothing, and the kinds of workplaces people feel safe in. If we don't make space for this, we're not really being inclusive – we're just being selective.

This chapter matters because religion is often the first aspect of identity to be silenced in professional spaces. It gets pushed aside in the name of neutrality or misunderstood through the lens of dominant narratives. The result? People of faith, particularly those from marginalised communities, are expected to assimilate or downplay who they are just to be seen as 'professional'. I've written this chapter to open the door to those conversations that are usually avoided. Not just to talk about faith in theory – but to talk about how it shows up in careers work, how it shapes aspirations, and how the system either makes space for it . . . or doesn't. Religious inclusion isn't just about awareness days and prayer spaces. It's about power, respect, and belonging. If we're serious about equity, we need to stop pretending faith is neutral ground. This chapter doesn't ask you to have all the answers. It asks you to stay open, to listen, and to reflect. Silence around religion isn't neutral – it privileges dominant faiths and marginalises everyone else. Careers professionals have a duty to acknowledge that. You don't need to be a theologian. But you do need cultural humility.

Religious diversity defined

Religion and belief are protected characteristics under the Equality Act 2010. This means that by law, no one should be discriminated against for their religious beliefs, their lack of belief, or the way they choose to practise (or not practise) their faith. But legal protection is the baseline – not the benchmark. Just because it's protected on paper doesn't mean it's respected in practice. In careers work, religion is often treated as off-limits. Too personal. Too controversial. Too risky. So it gets erased – either by silence, discomfort, or the false comfort of neutrality. But for many people, faith is foundational. It shapes values, family roles, career choices, and what success even looks like. When we ignore that, we're not being neutral – we're being selective.

We need to understand that religion isn't the same as culture, ethnicity, or even practice. Two people from the same faith background may live that faith in completely different ways. One may pray five times a day; another may not pray publicly – or at all. One might wear visible symbols; another may not. Religious identity sits on a spectrum – from formal, organised religion to individual expressions of spirituality. It's deeply personal, and there is no single way it shows up. As one participant noted, *'Religion is not the same for every person and it's personal to each individual'*. And in careers work, that diversity matters when we talk about values and purpose; we're already talking about belief systems – we just don't name them. One powerful quote puts it clearly: *'Religious or non-religious beliefs can shape the values, goals, and career aspirations of clients.'* For some, career decisions are deeply connected to moral or spiritual codes. For others, it's about how work fits into their wider life calling. If we miss that, we miss them.

Religion also doesn't exist in a vacuum. It intersects with race, class, gender, disability, migration, and more. Islamophobia, antisemitism, and religious stereotyping don't happen in isolation – they're embedded in structures. A practitioner might face bias because they wear a headscarf or a turban. A student might struggle to access work experience because their faith restricts certain environments. Another might be told their career goals aren't *'realistic'* simply because they put family or faith ahead of prestige or salary. These are not individual issues. They're systemic exclusions. Then there's the silence – the absence of faith-based discussion in training, policy, or practice. *'I never once heard a discussion of religion during my training'*, one practitioner shared. Another added, *'Faith is such a core part of identity for many yet is treated like a private hobby in careers work'*. That silence sends a message: bring your skills, bring your qualifications, but don't bring your full self.

Language matters too. The way we ask – or don't ask – about faith can shut people down before they've even begun to speak. One practitioner called for *'allowing space to be different without fear'*. That means making space for prayer, for religious holidays, for spiritual values – and doing it without clients or colleagues needing to justify, apologise, or self-edit. None of this means that practitioners need to become experts in theology. But it does mean we need to get comfortable with our own discomfort. We need to move from avoidance to awareness, and from politeness to practice. When someone hides their faith at work – or feels their values are invisible in a guidance session – that's not just a missed conversation. That's exclusion.

Understanding religion in the careers sector

Despite being a protected characteristic under the Equality Act, religion remains one of the most marginalised aspects of identity in careers work. Not because people don't have faith – but because the system doesn't make space for it. Instead, religious identity is often reduced to a risk, an exception, or a logistical inconvenience. The message isn't always explicit – but it's loud: leave your faith at the door. Many practitioners from religious minority backgrounds report that faith is treated as a private belief to be managed, not a valuable perspective to be integrated. One Padlet practitioner wrote: *'Faith is seen as a problem to be managed rather than a strength to be respected.'* This is echoed in the wider culture of careers work, where *'neutrality'* often becomes the code for secular normativity. Faith is either stripped out completely or only discussed through the lens of conflict, accommodation, or compromise.

This discomfort is rarely about bad intent. More often, it stems from a lack of training and exposure. Many careers professionals say they don't feel confident discussing religion with clients – so they don't. But silence is never neutral. As one practitioner explained: *'There's a real cultural illiteracy when it comes to understanding how faith can shape career values.'* In practice, this means advisers can miss vital cues about how faith influences decision-making. Belief systems may guide what jobs are considered acceptable, where someone is willing to work, what ethical boundaries they hold, or how they define success. Ignoring this can lead to advice that's well-meaning but misaligned. It can also deepen the sense of being misunderstood.

One practitioner asked directly: *'How can CDPs approach religion with clients in terms of work-based skills? If and when is it appropriate?'* It's a valid concern – but one that points to the real issue. We don't have consistent frameworks, CPD, or policy tools to support those conversations; the burden falls back on the individual practitioner to decide, in real time, what to say and what not to. Faith is also largely absent from leadership spaces in the profession. There are few visible role models from a range of faith backgrounds, and even fewer discussions about how personal belief informs strategic decisions, values-led leadership, or inclusive organisational culture. As one practitioner noted: *'Positive role models are needed.'*

The result? Practitioners from religious backgrounds often feel they have to hide parts of themselves to fit in. One colleague simply shared: *'Having to hide your religion in the workplace.'* Another stated: *'I stopped wearing my religious jewellery at work to avoid comments.'* These aren't trivial choices. They are daily acts of code-switching that impact confidence, belonging, and professional identity. I've worked across many sectors, but only one organisation ever genuinely considered my religion. On my very first day, they asked me if I belonged to a religion, whether I prayed during the day, and what reasonable adjustments might support me to practise my faith at work. It was such a simple gesture – but deeply powerful. No one had ever asked me that before; no one has since.

Gill Frigerio's work at the University of Warwick has been pivotal in starting to shift this narrative. Through her writing on careers and Christianity, and broader work on values-informed guidance, she has helped to normalise the idea that faith and professionalism are not opposites. They can coexist. They can inform one another. They can enrich our practice when approached with care and curiosity. There is no single way to do faith-inclusive guidance – but there are many ways to begin. That's what this chapter is about: helping you to notice where religion is missing and giving you the tools to put it back into view – not as a challenge to be solved, but as a reality to be understood.

Practitioner lived experiences

There's something uniquely heavy about having to edit yourself before you walk into work. To pause at your jewellery box and ask, *'Will this invite a comment?'* To keep your prayer routine quiet, your beliefs unspoken, your presence diluted – just to avoid being labelled as 'too much', 'too religious', or 'not professional enough'. These aren't abstract issues. They're real, lived moments for practitioners across the sector. They tell us everything we need to know about where inclusion ends and assimilation begins. One practitioner shared, *'I stopped wearing my religious jewellery at work to avoid comments'*. For me this one sentence says more than a whole report could. It's about self-censorship – removing visible symbols of identity because we've internalised that visibility invites scrutiny. That to be outwardly religious is to somehow step outside the boundaries of what's comfortable, acceptable, or neutral. Another practitioner shared:

'As a Muslim woman, I've been asked if I'm allowed to work.'

It's a jarring question. One that reveals both ignorance and stereotype. That question isn't just offensive – it's revealing. It tells us that despite decades of progress, there are still assumptions lurking beneath the surface. That religious women, particularly those from visibly Muslim backgrounds, are still being othered in spaces that claim to be inclusive.

Other voices spoke of the subtle silencing that comes with trying to *'fit in'*. One quote stayed with me about *'having to hide your religion in the workplace'*. Hiding doesn't always mean absence – it means calculation. It means choosing your words carefully. Avoiding religious holidays in conversation. Not speaking up when guidance sessions clash with prayer times. Feeling like your values, your motivations, your whole self have to be compartmentalised to be seen as competent. It's not about abandoning faith – it's about constantly weighing up whether to show it.

And yet, one quote captured offers both clarity and hope: *'I've worked across many sectors and the best place which considered my religion was one when I first joined and they asked if I belong to a religion, whether I pray and to make reasonable adjustments for this. I've never been asked before or since.'* That's what it looks like to build equity in – not as an afterthought, not as a box-tick, but as a starting point. The fact that this experience is described as the exception – not the rule – tells us how much work we have to do. Several practitioners called for active allyship: *'We need allies who understand we are not all coming from the same starting point.'* This is about more than 'supporting' colleagues of faith. It's about dismantling the idea that religious neutrality equals erasure. True allyship means asking better questions. It means making space before someone has to ask. It means recognising that faith isn't a barrier to professionalism – it's often the foundation of integrity, purpose, and care.

These lived experiences don't sit outside of our career development sector – they are within it. If we're not making space for them, then we are actively upholding a system where faith continues to be silenced, diluted, or boxed in. This section doesn't aim to speak for all people of faith, but it does aim to show you what happens when that part of someone's identity is overlooked. Inclusion without faith is not full inclusion. If people are hiding who they are just to be seen as 'neutral', then we've got to ask – neutral for whom?

Client perspectives: When faith is part of the conversation

It's not just practitioners navigating the silence around religion – clients feel it too. For many, it's not just a missed opportunity. It's a dismissal of something central to who they are. In careers meetings, clients are often told they're at the centre of the conversation. That it's their values, their choices, and their goals that matter most. But if that's true, we need to ask why faith is so rarely part of that conversation. For a lot of people, their religious identity isn't just background – it's central to how they define success, choose workplaces, or assess whether a career path aligns with their beliefs. Then there's the quieter exclusion – the kind that doesn't make headlines but chips away at your sense of belonging as one practitioner shared, *'I've had careers talks where nothing reflected my beliefs or values'*. It's a sentence that captures both invisibility and exclusion. When the frameworks we use to explore career choices assume a secular worldview, faith-based motivations become invisible. Clients who are driven by service, spiritual fulfilment, or religious calling are often viewed as *'hard to place'* or *'limiting their options'*. But the real limitation lies in our frameworks – not in their faith.

Imagine sitting through professional development, watching videos, reading case studies, and realising this space wasn't designed with you in mind. It's not just about seeing yourself in the content – it's about knowing the people who created that content didn't even think to ask what your worldview might be. Another quote captured the weight of this silence: *'Faith is never mentioned. It's like it doesn't exist unless I bring it up – and even then, it's often brushed past.'* That's a heavy burden for a client to carry. When someone has to decide whether their faith will be received with respect, misunderstanding, or discomfort, they may choose not to bring it up at all. That means we're offering guidance on incomplete terms.

One practitioner reflected on the fear of *'getting it wrong'*, but clients notice when advisers avoid or deflect. That avoidance has an impact. It tells clients that only certain types of motivations are valid. That religion is personal – but not professional. That success means fitting into systems, not reshaping them. Let's be honest – some clients have learned not to expect inclusion at all. They've learned to keep their religious commitments off the form. To avoid mentioning dietary needs or prayer times. To not challenge suggestions that conflict with their beliefs. Not because they don't care – but because they've been told, directly or indirectly, that faith makes things complicated. But it doesn't have to be this way. Clients notice when advisers ask the right questions. When faith is approached with openness – not awkwardness. One idea from the Padlet stood out: *'How can CDPs approach religion with clients in terms of work-based skills? If and when is it appropriate?'* The answer is simple: it's appropriate when it's relevant – and it's relevant when the client brings it into the room. The work is in knowing how to make space for that possibility without assumptions, without overstepping, and without avoidance.

Asking a client *'Are there any personal or faith-based considerations you'd like me to keep in mind while we explore your options?'* can shift everything. It signals care. It tells them that all of them are welcome in this space. For many clients, being seen in their full identity – including their faith – is not just empowering. It's transformative.

Barriers to inclusion

Talking about religion in careers work still feels risky for many professionals – and that's a barrier in itself. The fear of saying the wrong thing often leads to saying nothing at all. But silence isn't neutral. It protects the status quo and places the burden back onto people of faith, who are left to navigate their identity without support or recognition. From the responses gathered across the sector, it's clear that this isn't an issue of irrelevance. Religious inclusion isn't avoided because it lacks importance – it's avoided because there's no roadmap. No shared vocabulary. No consistent training. So we're left with a professional landscape where faith is either ignored entirely or approached with unease, and both lead to exclusion.

One of the most entrenched barriers is the persistence of stereotypes. These aren't just frustrating – they shape workplace dynamics in profound ways. One practitioner shared, *'People assume I'm submissive or oppressed because I wear hijab.'* That one assumption can influence how someone is spoken to, whether their leadership is taken seriously, and how their ideas are received.

These narratives often go unchallenged, embedded deep in wider cultural biases that creep quietly into the structures of our institutions. Even when unspoken, they shape how safe and seen someone feels in their role.

The discomfort with openly acknowledging religious identity continues to show up in small but significant ways. Whether in team meetings, training settings, or during client interactions, many people of faith report feeling the need to hold back. As one person put it, *'I avoid faith-based conversations in team meetings'*. That's not an issue of personal preference – it's about self-protection. It reveals a professional culture where people have to second-guess whether it's safe to be fully themselves. That's not inclusion. That's conditional belonging. When people edit themselves just to fit in, the loss is collective – not just individual.

Another barrier is the dominance of secular norms in careers tools, guidance frameworks, and educational materials. When resources assume a secular worldview as the default, people of faith are forced to translate their beliefs into a language that doesn't reflect them. As one practitioner observed, *'Our materials assume religion isn't relevant.'* That's not just a gap in understanding – it's a quiet form of erasure. It tells clients and colleagues alike that their values, boundaries, and lived realities are outside the professional norm.

Underlying all of this is a serious lack of training. Most careers practitioners aren't given the tools or confidence to talk about religion with empathy, fluency, or curiosity. Instead, they're left to figure it out through trial and error – if they dare to approach it at all. *'There's no training on this – it's trial and error'*, said one practitioner. We would never accept that level of uncertainty when it comes to safeguarding, mental health, or SEND; why is faith treated differently? Why is it allowed to remain a blind spot?

One quote captures the challenge and the opportunity in one breath: *'People are scared to talk about religion in case they get it wrong.'* That fear is real, and it's understandable. But if we let fear guide us, we'll remain stuck in avoidance. Moving towards meaningful inclusion doesn't require us to be experts in every belief system. It requires us to be honest, open, and willing to learn – and that's a practice we can all commit to.

Barriers table

The recurring themes raised by practitioners aren't abstract – they're specific, tangible, and remarkably consistent across different roles and settings. When we pause to examine these barriers, they reveal more than just individual discomfort – they expose the structural silences and cultural defaults that have gone unquestioned for too long. Table 6 overleaf brings these themes into sharper focus, pairing direct quotes from practitioners with the wider implications they carry. These aren't isolated experiences.

They are patterns – clear signals that if we want truly inclusive careers practice, we need to address these foundations first.

Table 6 Barriers

Barrier	Quote	Implication
Stereotypes and assumptions	'People assume I'm submissive or oppressed because I wear hijab.'	Reinforces bias and limits client engagement
Discomfort with religious identity	'I avoid faith-based conversations in team meetings.'	Promotes self-censorship and workplace exclusion
Secular normativity	'Our materials assume religion isn't relevant.'	Ignores lived realities of clients and staff
Limited staff training	'There's no training on this – it's trial and error.'	Undermines confidence and cultural competency
Silence due to fear	'People are scared to talk about religion in case they get it wrong.'	Maintains inaccessibility and avoids meaningful inclusion

Enablers

It's tempting to centre conversations about religion solely around what's missing – but genuine progress begins when we recognise what's already working and intentionally build from there. The Padlet responses didn't just highlight the challenges; they also revealed practical actions, moments of hope, and strategies that practitioners are already testing in real time. These insights remind us that inclusion is not an abstract theory – it's built through consistent, often small, everyday choices. One of the most significant shifts we can make is to normalise religious identity within careers practice. Rather than spotlighting it as an anomaly or brushing it aside in the name of neutrality, we must embrace faith as a valid, everyday part of many people's lives. *'Faith-based motivation is valid and valuable'*, one practitioner affirmed. That statement alone offers a powerful counter to the idea that faith and professionalism are somehow incompatible. The goal is not mere tolerance but meaningful respect – acknowledging religion not as a problem to be managed but as a perspective that can deepen understanding, values, and purpose in career decision-making.

For this to become the norm rather than the exception, religion must be explicitly embedded into equity, diversity, and inclusion frameworks – not just mentioned in passing but reflected in policies, audits, data collection, staff training, and leadership development. Many organisations still leave religion off their data forms or EDI agendas, rendering it invisible in strategy and decision-making. Yet representation alone is not enough if it's not supported by structural change. Including questions about religious belief in onboarding processes, asking about prayer or fasting adjustments up front, and equipping managers with the confidence to navigate faith conversations are all small yet vital steps. One practitioner suggested creating a simple FAQ to cover how religion links with employability – something accessible, practical, and grounded in lived experience. These tools don't have to be complex, but they do have to be intentional and informed.

Representation at leadership levels was also raised as an ongoing gap. Practitioners from religious backgrounds repeatedly voiced the need for more visible role models – not as tokens, but as decision-makers whose lived experience could inform inclusive strategy. *'We need more positive role models to help break down barriers',* one practitioner explained, highlighting the importance of seeing faith not only accommodated but actively shaping the direction of services. Alongside leadership, storytelling emerged as a powerful enabler. While statistics provide one kind of evidence, narratives humanise policy. One Padlet post recommended a panel conversation with practitioners of different faiths sharing their career journeys – not to speak for entire communities, but to offer real insight into how faith shapes their values, decisions, and professional identities. These kinds of stories have the capacity to build empathy, break stereotypes, and open up new possibilities for guidance.

Allyship was another recurring theme – but with a clear caveat: it must be genuine, not performative. True allyship means more than attending an awareness session or posting a statement of support. It involves listening with humility, asking thoughtful questions, and actively creating space for faith-based perspectives. One quote captured this simply: *'Ask, don't assume.'* That act of curiosity – rooted in respect rather than fear – can be the foundation of inclusive relationships with both colleagues and clients. Sometimes, the changes that make the biggest difference are deceptively small. A practitioner shared how, during induction, they were asked whether they had any religious needs, including prayer times. *'I've never been asked before or since.'* That one moment of care stayed with them, not because it solved everything, but because it acknowledged their full identity from the outset. Inclusion doesn't need to be expensive or overly complicated – but it must be embedded with intention.

Inspiration from other sectors offers practical models to adapt. The Open University's reciprocal mentoring scheme, built on contact theory, was highlighted as a promising approach. By pairing individuals across difference, the initiative fosters empathy, mutual understanding, and the breakdown of unconscious bias through lived dialogue. This is the kind of intervention that doesn't just raise awareness – it changes relationships. These examples, tools, and mindsets are not aspirational – they're already happening. The question now is whether we are willing to move from scattered good practice to consistent systemic change. The tools are there. The voices are speaking. What remains is our collective commitment to act.

Tools for reflection and practice review

It is one thing to read about barriers and enablers in theory – but another entirely to sit with them, reflect on your own context, and begin shaping change. The purpose of the following tools is not to diagnose, criticise, or prescribe. Instead, they are designed as gentle but structured prompts for reflection. They offer a way to map where your practice or institution currently stands on religious inclusion and to consider what more could be done. These are starting points, not endpoints – meant to support honest self-assessment, stimulate team discussion, and help translate intention into meaningful action.

Practitioner reflection: Mapping barriers to faith inclusion

The first table (Table 7) focuses on *mapping barriers*. It asks you to consider whether common obstacles – such as lack of training, secular bias, or fear of getting it wrong – are present within your setting. By identifying examples, surfacing blind spots, and brainstorming potential solutions, you begin to move from vague discomfort to practical, informed improvement. The table is an invitation: to pause, to notice, and to think courageously about how inclusion is currently being enacted – or unintentionally undermined – within your space.

Table 7 Practitioner reflection: Mapping barriers to faith inclusion

Barrier	Does this exist in your organisation? (Y/N/Unsure)	Examples/evidence	Potential actions or solutions
Stereotypes and assumptions about religious identity			
Discomfort with religious expression in staff or clients			
Secular bias in careers resources or guidance approach			
Lack of visible religious role models or representation			
Limited training or CPD on religion and belief			
No process to ask about faith-based adjustments			
No visible faith inclusion in EDI strategy			
Fear of saying the wrong thing blocking conversations			

This table is designed to help careers professionals and leaders reflect on how well their institution is currently addressing barriers to religious inclusion, and to begin identifying specific, actionable steps forward.

Enablers and possibilities: Faith inclusion in careers work

The second table (Table 8) moves us into possibility. It summarises a series of enablers drawn from practitioner voices, alongside tangible ways these can be applied. Whether it's normalising religious identity in conversation, building faith into policy and training, or creating cross-cultural mentoring opportunities, these are not abstract aspirations – they're already in motion in parts of the sector. This tool invites you to consider what's already happening in your setting and what could be strengthened. You don't need to adopt everything at once. But choosing one action and embedding it with intention can begin to shift the culture of your practice, making space for more honest, inclusive engagement with faith.

Table 8 Enablers and possibilities: Faith inclusion in careers work

Enabler	Quote or insight	Application or action	Notes/reflection (your setting)
Normalising religious identity	Faith-based motivation is valid and valuable.	Mention faith explicitly in client values conversations. Acknowledge it as a career driver.	
Inclusion in EDI policy and training	FAQ to cover key points about how religion links with employability.	Add religion to internal audits, CPD sessions, and induction checklists.	
Representation in leadership	We need more positive role models to help break down barriers.	Actively recruit, profile, and platform staff of faith in leadership.	
Spiritual literacy and storytelling	Panel chat with careers advisers of a particular faith . . .	Share diverse practitioner stories in blogs, CPD, and events.	
Allyship rooted in curiosity	Ask, don't assume.	Train staff in how to open inclusive dialogue. Embed curiosity into coaching techniques.	
Proactive religious adjustments	I've never been asked before or since.	Build prayer, food, and holiday needs into standard onboarding processes.	
Cross-cultural empathy programmes	OU reciprocal mentoring scheme based on 'contact theory' . . .	Create staff pairing or mentoring schemes across difference to build empathy.	

This table summarises enablers that support religious inclusion in the careers sector, paired with practitioner insights and strategies for implementation.

These tables are not meant to be filled in once and forgotten. They're meant to be revisited – over coffee, in supervision, at team planning sessions. Their power lies in repetition and reflection; faith inclusion, like all equity work, is not a single act. It's a sustained, deliberate commitment to recognising and respecting the full humanity of those we work with.

Tools for practice

Having explored the barriers and enablers to religious inclusion and reflected on how these may show up in our own settings, the next step is to move from awareness into action. This section offers practical tools to help practitioners turn insight into impact. These are not prescriptive formulas or rigid frameworks, but adaptable resources designed to meet you where you are. Whether you're working one-to-one, facilitating groups, or shaping wider organisational strategy, these tools invite you to begin. They centre curiosity over certainty and intention over perfection. We don't need to be experts in theology to do this work well – we just need the confidence to start the conversation, to reflect with purpose, and to respond with care.

The following tools were developed in response to real practitioner needs – many voiced uncertainty about how to engage with faith-based topics meaningfully. These resources offer a starting point. They're grounded in TEDI values: transformative practice that questions assumptions, equitable policies that move beyond silence, diverse cultures that makes faith visible, and inclusive behaviours that validate belief as part of professional identity. Most of all, they are designed to make faith inclusion part of our everyday work – not a specialism, but a standard.

Faith literacy reflection task

Ask yourself: *'What do I know about belief systems in my client base?'* Begin by listing the major religions or belief systems represented in your community. Then, reflect on what you understand about each – and where there may be gaps. This isn't a task rooted in guilt, but in curiosity. Consider what assumptions you might be carrying, what voices you haven't heard, and where you might want to deepen your knowledge. This tool encourages self-awareness and positions learning as an ongoing part of equitable practice.

Career values inventory with a faith overlay

We often use values inventories to support clients in identifying what matters to them. Yet we rarely ask how those values are shaped. This tool invites you to explore that connection explicitly. Prompt clients with a question such as: *'Are there any personal, cultural, or faith-based principles that influence how you approach work or career choices?'* A simple question like this can create space for deeper meaning and honour the role that belief plays in shaping purpose and decision-making.

Inclusive session planning checklist
Small acts of consideration can make a significant difference. This checklist encourages you to review planned sessions or events for inclusivity. Do the dates clash with major religious festivals? Does the environment support religious observance – through dietary options, prayer space, or simple acknowledgement? Inclusion here isn't about overhauling everything. It's about being intentional, showing clients and colleagues that their beliefs are seen and respected.

Responding to faith-based career dilemmas
Sometimes, clients raise questions that touch directly on faith – concerns about working in a secular environment, navigating faith-based restrictions, or managing workplace expectations. Practitioners often hesitate, unsure how to respond. This tool provides a gentle scaffold: begin with open questions, resist the urge to fix or solve, and instead validate the client's worldview. Focus on values alignment, explore practical routes, and most importantly – listen. You may not have all the answers, but creating space for the question itself is a powerful act of inclusion.

Action planning template: Religion in your setting
This tool prompts wider reflection at the team or organisational level. Where does religion show up – and where is it absent? Do you collect data on religious identity? Is it named in your EDI strategy? Are staff trained in inclusive faith practice? Use this template to map current gaps and plan realistic next steps. This is about embedding change systemically – not as a reactive add-on, but as a proactive part of how we define equity in careers work.

Together, these tools offer a way forward – one rooted not in fear of getting it wrong, but in hope of getting it better. Start small but start when we make space for belief in our practice; we're not just including religion – we're recognising the whole person.

Organisational audit: Religion and belief inclusion

While individual reflection and practitioner tools are crucial starting points, systemic change also requires organisational accountability. Without examining structures, policies, and leadership practices, inclusion work risks becoming performative rather than transformative. This audit table (Table 9) is designed to support organisations – whether careers services, education providers, or employers – in identifying how religion and belief are currently embedded (or overlooked) across different operational areas. It helps move the conversation from intent to implementation.

Table 9 Organisational audit: Religion and belief inclusion

Area	Inclusive practice	Evidence needed	Actions
Representation	Are religious identities reflected in leadership and staff?	Staff demographic data, leadership bios	Review recruitment, promotion pipelines
Environment	Are workspaces and materials faith-friendly?	Visual cues, resource audits	Adapt spaces, review materials
Training	Is religion addressed in cultural competency CPD?	Training logs, feedback forms	Include faith in CPD sessions
Policy	Do policies explicitly include religion and belief?	EDI strategy, HR policies	Update language and implementation

This tool should be used collaboratively – perhaps in an EDI working group, leadership team, or CPD setting – to ask honest questions about institutional culture. Are religious identities represented in leadership? Do spaces and materials actively welcome people of faith? Is faith embedded in training and policy, or is it simply assumed? Each row prompts reflection on inclusive practice, evidence needed to back it up, and specific actions that could drive progress. It's not about scoring high – it's about spotting gaps and committing to change.

Reflection task: Enablers

Take a moment to pause – not just to notice what's missing, but to recognise what could be possible. Change doesn't begin with a strategy – it begins with attention. The enablers discussed earlier aren't abstract ideals. They're already happening in pockets of practice. The challenge is to embed them more widely, more intentionally, and more bravely.

Use the questions below to reflect personally or with your team:

- Which of the enablers listed earlier are already active in your setting – intentionally or informally?
- Which enabler is noticeably missing, and what barriers might be holding it back?
- What one step could you take – this month, this term, this year – to begin activating or deepening one of these enablers in your practice or policy?

This is not about overhauling everything overnight. It's about making one small, conscious shift. When we normalise conversations about faith, build tools around it, and centre it in EDI work, we begin to create a space where clients and colleagues don't have to fragment who they are to fit in.

You can return to Table 8: Enablers and possibilities as a working document – use it for self-reflection, strategic planning, or to spark dialogue with others. The work starts with a question: Where is faith in our practice – and where does it need to be?

Unpacking religion: Reflective quotes for practice

This section is your space to pause. To sit with complexity. To listen without rushing to fix. Each quote shared here emerged from real experiences – practitioners and clients alike. They are not abstract provocations. They are reflections of systems, silence, and survival. Use them not as evidence to be analysed, but as mirrors to your own setting. What do they stir in you? What might they reveal?

'Faith is seen as a problem to be managed rather than a strength to be respected.' This single sentence echoes across countless spaces, where religion is treated as a compliance issue or logistical challenge. But faith can also be a compass – a deep well of values, motivation, and resilience. What does your organisation communicate, implicitly or explicitly, about religion? Is it welcomed, tolerated, ignored – or genuinely respected? Too often, faith is positioned as an inconvenience rather than an insight. The real work lies in shifting that lens and embedding it into how we design, deliver, and discuss careers support.

'People are scared to talk about religion in case they get it wrong.' That fear isn't just a personal barrier – it's structural. When inclusion strategies sideline religion, they create a vacuum. Practitioners aren't equipped with the tools or confidence to engage, so silence becomes the default. But silence is not neutral. It sends a message; ask yourself: has fear led to avoidance in your own practice? What would it take to move from caution to curiosity? From silence to meaningful engagement? You don't need to have all the answers – but you do need the courage to keep asking better questions.

'I've had careers talks where nothing reflected my beliefs or values.' Inclusion isn't about visual diversity alone. It's about whose realities are woven into the content, language, and frameworks we use. Think about your workshops, your guidance sessions, your resources. Who is reflected – and who is missing? When career narratives exclude faith-based values, they tell some clients that

their motivations don't matter or don't belong. We need to stop asking clients to leave parts of themselves at the door just to be seen as employable.

'Ask, don't assume.' It sounds simple, but it takes practice. When was the last time you asked a client, openly and without judgement, whether their cultural, spiritual, or faith-based beliefs shaped their career goals? When did you last ask a colleague what inclusion looked like for them – not based on assumptions, but through their own words? Inclusion is not about having the perfect phrasing – it's about creating space for people to define their experience on their terms. Being person-centred means being willing to learn, to listen, and to sit with uncertainty.

'I've never been asked before or since if I had any religious needs.' This quote lands with a quiet power. It reminds us that inclusion doesn't have to be grand – it just has to be intentional. A simple question during onboarding or meeting planning – about prayer times, dietary needs, or religious holidays – can transform someone's experience of belonging. Yet this kind of acknowledgement remains rare. Why? Because our systems aren't built with faith in mind. But they could be. What would it mean to embed that intentionality into everyday practice – not as a favour, but as a standard?

'Religion is not the same for every person and it's personal to each individual.' Even when we do talk about religion, we often collapse complexity. But faith is not a monolith. Interpretations vary by denomination, culture, family, and personal conviction. It's not enough to say, *'we're inclusive of Muslims'* or *'we have a Christian network'*. We must ask: are we holding space for intra-faith diversity? Are we prepared to meet each person where they are, even when it doesn't align with our assumptions or frameworks?

This section isn't about finding definitive answers. It's about noticing what we've been missing when we avoid these conversations; we don't create safety – we create absence. Absence breeds mistrust. Religion is already in the room – shaping career decisions, informing values, influencing availability and priorities. But when we fail to acknowledge it, we risk alienating the very clients we claim to centre.

We often speak of neutrality as a virtue. But neutrality usually mirrors the dominant culture. If we never name faith, we default to norms that privilege the secular and marginalise the spiritual. In a sector rooted in person-centred practice, we cannot afford to erase a central part of so many people's lives. This is your challenge: go back to your policies, your onboarding questions, your CPD content, your assumptions. Ask yourself – honestly – where is faith? Not just as a protected characteristic listed on a form, but as a lived, nuanced, everyday reality.

We don't need perfection. We need openness. We need spaces where people can bring their whole selves, without fear of being othered. We need the courage to get it wrong if it means we're finally making space to get it right. Inclusion that doesn't include religion – especially for those who hold it close – isn't inclusion at all.

Chapter 7
Gender equity in career development

Chapter roadmap

Gender isn't a topic we've outgrown. It's one this chapter faces head-on – with honesty and intention. In a sector like careers, where identity, perception, and power shape everything from who gets in the room to who gets promoted, gender remains a critical conversation.

This chapter doesn't just explore gender as a concept – it examines how it's embedded in the structure of careers work. From pay gaps and panel decisions to job titles and expectations of care, it unpacks how gendered assumptions quietly shape the profession. It asks why the sector is still seen as *'women's work'*, and how that perception continues to harm, especially the women doing the work. More than that, it invites a move beyond symbolic equity into deeper questions about power, value, and voice.

Throughout, you'll hear from practitioners whose lived experiences bring these issues to life. Their words are not side notes – they are evidence, insight, and a call to action.

This chapter will:

- Define what gender means in the context of careers work;
- Unpack structural and cultural barriers that sustain inequity;
- Share lived experiences from across the profession;
- Offer enablers and tools for practice and leadership;
- Close with a reflective task and action grid to move from theory to practice.

Author's voice

Gender in the careers sector . . . we acknowledge it exists, we nod at representation, but we rarely sit with the realities. The truth is, gender shapes everything – from whose voice gets taken seriously to who's expected to smile more and ask for less. This isn't just about inclusion. It's about value; when a profession is overwhelmingly female and still underpaid, we have to ask: who is doing the work, and who is getting the recognition?

I've seen it. I've lived it. Many of you reading this have too. Careers work is still viewed by some as a *'soft option'*, a helping profession suited to *'nice little old ladies in cardigans'* – to borrow the phrase derived from the research by Neary et al. (2017). That stereotype may sound quaint, but its impact is far from harmless. It shapes how the profession is funded, how it's positioned, and how practitioners are perceived. While women dominate frontline roles, senior leadership often remains disproportionately male. Women are often seen in the front-facing roles, but look closer – behind the scenes, at the top in the career development sector sit a disproportionate number of men.

This gendered imbalance is compounded by a structural invisibility. As Neary et al. (2017) argue, the careers sector itself lacks a unified identity. Many practitioners *'fall into'* the role, often through non-linear routes. Add to that a sector still grappling with low visibility, and it becomes clear how gendered assumptions are allowed to persist unchecked.

When we ask why the sector struggles to attract male practitioners, we need to flip the question: what are we doing – or failing to do – that signals this is women's work and not a viable, respected career for all?

Practitioners at our CDI Gender Diversity webinar put it simply:

> *'Representation of all genders – you can't be what you can't see.'*
> *'Need diversity – because we work in a diverse community, and young people are more inspired by someone who looks like them.'*

Representation matters. Not on a surface level alone but as an impact. Young people look at us and decide whether this is a space where they can see themselves.

When that space is gendered, so is their aspiration.

Sit with this for a moment. This chapter is about naming what we've allowed to remain unspoken. It's about unlearning the idea that gender equity has been achieved and replacing it with real conversations, real data, and real structural change. Why? Because we can't fix what we're not willing to face.

If you're a man reading this, and you've ever tuned out of a conversation about menopause or gendered health because *'it doesn't apply to you'* or *'you're not the target audience'*, it's time to rethink that. You being in the room matters.

You not making a joke, not rolling your eyes, not quietly switching off during training – *that* matters. Supporting your female colleagues through things like menopause isn't a nice extra. It's the baseline of a respectful workplace. If you're in a position of leadership, it's your responsibility to model that understanding when men show up – really show up – to listen, to advocate, and to challenge the culture of silence or dismissal; they shift the atmosphere for everyone. It's not about guilt or shame. It's about maturity. Compassion. The kind of allyship that doesn't wait until it's trending to take action.

What do we mean by gender?

Before we can meaningfully discuss gender equity in the careers sector, we need to clarify what we mean by 'gender' and how it differs from 'sex'. Sex refers to the biological attributes that distinguish males, females, and intersex individuals – such as chromosomes, hormone levels, and reproductive organs (WHO, 2023). These characteristics are typically assigned at birth and are generally consistent across different societies.

Gender, on the other hand, encompasses the roles, behaviours, activities, and attributes that a given society considers appropriate for men, women, and people of diverse gender identities. According to the World Health Organisation, gender is a social construct that varies across cultures and over time (WHO, 2023). It influences how individuals perceive themselves and how they are perceived by others, affecting their opportunities and interactions in various aspects of life, including the workplace and education settings. According to Lindqvist et al. (2020), there is no single way to define gender. Their review outlines four common ways researchers conceptualise it:

1. Gender identity – how individuals internally identify.
2. Gender roles – behaviours, traits, and expectations assigned by society.
3. Gender as a relational category – how individuals position themselves in relation to others.
4. Gender as a social category – how people are grouped and treated based on perceived gender.

This complexity matters. In a sector like careers work – which is predominantly staffed by women – oversimplified notions of gender contribute to deep-rooted stereotypes about the profession. Gender roles are often assumed rather than questioned, and the labour is feminised to the point of devaluation.

As one practitioner observed that they would like *'More respect for the profession so it isn't seen as women's work.'* The association of careers work with femininity impacts pay, progression, and professional legitimacy. We can't ignore that gender doesn't operate in isolation. It intersects with race, class, disability, and more. A White cis woman and a trans Black woman will not experience the sector in the same way. Understanding how gender is constructed, coded, and applied is essential if we want to reshape the careers profession into one that's equitable, inclusive, and fit for the communities it serves.

As Neary et al. (2017) point out, the perception of the career development profession as a 'soft', feminised space has contributed to poor visibility, low pay, and a lack of strategic positioning. One practitioner echoed this directly: *'More respect for the profession so it isn't seen as women's work.'* This sentiment underscores the need to challenge and change the gendered perceptions that devalue the profession and limit its appeal to a more diverse workforce.

It's essential to recognise that gender does not operate in isolation. It intersects with other aspects of identity, such as race, socio-economic status, and sexual orientation, creating complex experiences of privilege and discrimination. For instance, a woman of colour in the careers sector may face different challenges than her White counterparts, influenced by both gender and racial dynamics. Understanding these nuances is crucial for developing inclusive practices and policies that address the multifaceted nature of identity and promote equity within the careers profession.

Understanding gender inequity in the careers sector

We need to stop pretending that gender equity is a given just because the sector is female-dominated. It isn't. If anything, the over-representation of women in frontline roles has been used to justify lower pay, undervaluation, and a lack of structural investment. There's a difference between presence and power. On paper, careers work might look inclusive – women are everywhere. But scratch beneath the surface and the cracks start to show. Leadership roles are still skewed. Sector visibility still leans towards certain voices. The assumptions underpinning who belongs in the profession haven't really shifted. The labour is feminised. The decision-making is not. Let's name what we see. There's a glass ceiling in the careers sector – but there's also a glass cliff where few women are seen at the top.

Women are not only underrepresented in leadership – but they're also often promoted into unstable or high-risk roles when organisations are struggling. They're expected to clean up the mess but not hold the pen on strategic reform.

Meanwhile, the echo chamber effect means leadership positions are often passed between the same networks, replicating the same patterns. One practitioner put it plainly: *'Awareness of unconscious positive discrimination that moves men into leadership positions more quickly.'* This can be interpreted as the perception that male competence continues to be rewarded – even in a field that relies so heavily on 'feminised' skills like empathy and care. Then there's the client-facing dynamic. Practitioners are not just navigating internal bias – they're dealing with gendered expectations from clients, schools, and even colleagues. A quote from one practitioner stays with me: *'Grammar schools prefer an adviser who is less mothering.'* Less mothering. I questioned myself here – what does that mean? Less nurturing? Less emotionally intelligent? Less visibly female? These coded expectations place women – particularly those who lead with care – in an impossible bind. Too warm and you're seen as unprofessional. Too firm and you're difficult. One practitioner captured this tension in a simple phrase: *'Careers advisers being more professional.'* But what does 'professional' look like – and who gets to decide?

We also need to address the ongoing imbalance in leadership roles. While women dominate practitioner-level positions, leadership tends to skew male – or, at the very least, rewards male-coded behaviours. The result? A profession that is over-associating femininity with delivery and masculinity with authority. When a sector is feminised and underpaid, it's not a coincidence. It's a hierarchy. This matters not just for the people working in the system – but for the clients we serve. If young people only ever see women in guidance roles and men in leadership, we're reproducing gender norms we should be disrupting.

The careers profession needs to ask itself hard questions. Not just about who is in the room – but about whose authority is assumed, whose presence is expected, and whose leadership is trusted. Until we address the patterns that are hidden in plain sight, equity will remain out of reach. We still don't have robust data on who makes up the sector. The CDI's data is the most complete we've got, but it's far from enough. Without clear, regular insights into who's in the profession, who's advancing, and who's being left behind – we're working in the dark. That's not a coincidence. Data gaps are equity gaps.

Practitioner lived experiences

The (limited) data we have about gender in the careers sector only scratches the surface. Numbers can't capture the texture of daily experiences – the microaggressions, the quiet assumptions, the emotional load. That's why in this chapter, as with those on intersectionality and ethnicity, I centre practitioner voice. Lived experience isn't an additional anecdote to tell a story – it's raw evidence.

This section draws on stories shared during the Gender Diversity in Careers webinar. These aren't isolated incidents. They're patterns – warning signals that something in our system is off-kilter. *'The expectation that as a female you will cope with whatever resources and skills you are given . . . when I left, I was replaced with two full-time members of staff.'* This quote hits hard because it's so familiar. Women in the careers sector are often expected to stretch themselves, to pick up the slack, to do *'just one more thing'* – until they quietly burn out. Only then does the organisation realise the scale of what they were holding. When two people are hired to replace one, it isn't a compliment. It's a reckoning. I've been in this position myself, where a colleague left an organisation, and I was asked to pick up on her role and continue mine. When I asked for a promotion, after proving my worth, I was given an empty title with the same pay but double the work. I graciously accepted, feeling very puzzled but needing the work, so the show went on. Similarly, a female practitioner shared that she *'Still felt a need to prove myself more than my male colleagues.'* Even in female-majority environments, men still benefit from a baseline of assumed competence. Women, meanwhile, often have to work twice as hard for the same credibility. That credibility is fragile – it can be undermined by tone, dress, assertiveness, or perceived lack thereof. The rules are unwritten, but the penalties are real.

Another colleague shared her experience of *'not being listened to because of how I look'*. Let's sit with this for a second. This isn't just gender; it's about how gender intersects with race, age, class, style, and body type. Professionalism is still coded in ways that exclude. If you don't match the image of what leadership *looks* like, you're often sidelined before you've even spoken. *'I'm still "too young" or "not experienced enough" – this is often assumed.'* The constant pressure to overperform, to prove yourself, to justify your place in the room – it's exhausting. I certainly felt this, and behind the scenes, I began applying for new jobs and feeling burned out. These assumptions don't just affect who gets promoted – they shape who sticks around.

We were told by another practitioner that she experienced, *'Sometimes being seen as the receptionist/administrator when you're the Careers Adviser.'* This is more than a simple mistake. It reflects deep, systemic assumptions about who holds power and who supports it. If women – particularly women of colour – are automatically read as admin staff, that's not about role confusion. That's about hierarchy, visibility, and embedded bias.

Female colleagues are often expected to take on a pastoral role – simply because of their gender. *'I'm expected to deal with the wellbeing issues as well as the careers advice – because I'm a woman.'* This quote exposes the emotional labour gap. Women in the profession are often expected to provide invisible care work – to be therapists, mediators, nurturers – without training, time, or thanks. It's not just draining. It's deprofessionalising. While empathy is essential in careers work, it shouldn't become a justification for overloading some and overlooking others. *'We are still told to be "professional" – but that often means silent, deferential, and self-sacrificing.'* This is one of the most dangerous barriers of all. The idea that being 'professional' means swallowing discomfort, avoiding conflict, and staying agreeable. But who gets to define professionalism? And who does that definition serve? Too often, it means that calling out inequity is seen as disruptive, while tolerating it is rewarded as mature. But professionalism should never be a muzzle. It should be a framework for fairness – not a disguise for submissiveness.

These quotes paint a stark picture. Not because they're extreme, but because they're common. They remind us that inequity doesn't just show up in pay gaps or promotion stats – it shows up in assumptions, in expectations, in how often someone is interrupted or ignored. If we really believe in equity, then we need to start believing the people who say *this isn't working*. We need to move from passive awareness to active change.

This section isn't here to offer token voices. It's here to hold up a mirror to the profession. If we're serious about equity, we need to ask:

- Why are so many women still expected to carry emotional labour with no support?
- What assumptions do I make about my colleagues – and who gets to lead?
- Who is expected to do the 'extra' work of support, care, or administration in my setting?
- When have I mistaken professionalism for silence?
- Why is professionalism still viewed through a narrow, gendered lens?
- Why do so many practitioners still feel like they're not seen, not heard, not fully valued?
- If there were more men in the sector, would the same pay disparities still be there?

The answers won't come from policy alone. They'll come from listening – and then acting on what we hear. Listening is only the first step. What matters is what we do next.

Barriers to gender equity

Despite its female-majority workforce, the careers sector continues to reproduce gender inequities – some visible, others deeply embedded. Structural and cultural barriers persist, from gendered assumptions to invisible promotion pathways. These are not isolated incidents but recurring themes – revealed through lived experiences shared by practitioners. The reflections gathered and shared above bring to light the systemic and cultural barriers that continue to limit gender equity in the profession.

A core challenge is the lack of visible gender diversity across the sector. Practitioners have pointed out that representation matters, not just symbolically but functionally. One practitioner wrote, *'Representation of all genders – you can't be what you can't see.'* As an aside, we must pay homage to Marian Wright Edelman, a Black American scholar, whose famous words, *'you can't be what you can't see'*, the career sector often uses without attributing to her. Without a range of gender identities being reflected in career roles, particularly in leadership, the field risks reinforcing the stereotype that it is a women's domain. This not only limits who enters and stays in the profession but also narrows how young people see their own potential futures.

Stereotyping also shapes how professionals are perceived. For instance, one adviser shared, *'Grammar schools where I work prefer an adviser who is less mothering'*. This comment underscores how traits associated with femininity – like warmth and nurturing – are often undervalued or even stigmatised in educational settings. These stereotypes subtly penalise those who exhibit such traits, suggesting that professionalism is still too often coded as neutral, assertive, and male.

Leadership pathways within the sector reflect these biases. Another practitioner commented on the *'unconscious positive discrimination that moves men into leadership positions more quickly'*. Even in a profession dominated numerically by women, men continue to rise through the ranks at a faster pace. This reveals a gendered double standard in how competence and authority are recognised and rewarded. Practitioners also described a familiar but often invisible burden: emotional labour. The assumption that women will pick up extra responsibilities without question is widespread but seldom acknowledged. This expectation of quiet endurance, without recognition or remuneration, leads to burnout and reinforces professional inequity.

The profession itself suffers from devaluation, linked directly to its gendered identity. When one practitioner called for *'more respect for the profession so it isn't seen as "women's work"'*, they pointed to a broader cultural issue. Sectors associated with care and guidance – often staffed by women – are frequently underfunded, underpaid, and undervalued. This perception is not just insulting; it's structurally damaging.

Compounding this is the issue of pay. Another Padlet entry noted, *'Increasing pay/set professional salary scales would attract more diversity.'* Low pay restricts access to the profession and pushes many out before they have a chance to grow. It is not simply a matter of economics but of equity. Without pay reform and professional recognition, the careers sector will continue to limit its potential workforce – and the quality of service it can offer.

Together, these barriers reveal a pattern of gendered expectations, inequitable progression, and institutional neglect. To address these issues meaningfully, we must look beyond surface-level inclusion and confront the structural and cultural foundations of the profession itself. Doing so will require brave conversations, policy change, and a collective commitment to rebuilding the sector with equity at its core.

Structural and cultural barriers

Alongside the individual experiences outlined above, broader systemic challenges continue to reinforce gender inequity in careers work. These include:

- The gender pay gap;
- Stereotyping and role assumptions;
- Lack of inclusive CPD (Continuing Professional Development);
- No visible representation at the top;
- Lack of targeted recruitment;
- Gender norms within schools;
- Careers advice is seen as 'supportive' rather than strategic.

These patterns are not accidental. They are products of long-standing norms that must be actively unlearned. These experiences aren't anomalies – they're patterns. The repetition of similar stories across different institutions and settings signals that these aren't just personal struggles but structural flaws in the careers sector. To support further reflection, Table 10 summarises key gender-related barriers reported by practitioners, alongside their original quotes and the broader implications they carry for the profession.

Use this as a mirror. This is a phrase I repeat throughout the book to make you reflect. Ask yourself:

- Do any of these quotes reflect your own experience or describe what happens in your organisation?
- What role might you be playing in upholding or dismantling these patterns?

Table 10 Quotes

Barrier	Quote	Implication
Assumption that careers is 'women's work'	'More respect for the profession so it isn't seen as "women's work"'	Sector devalued; progress stalled
Unconscious bias in leadership pathways	'Awareness of unconscious positive discrimination that moves men into leadership positions more quickly'	Uneven progression: leadership remains male-skewed
Gendered expectations around care	'Grammar schools where I work prefer an adviser who is less mothering'	Caring traits seen as unprofessional; stereotyping
Emotional overwork without support	'The expectation that as a female you will cope with whatever resources and skills you are given . . . when I left, I was replaced with 2 full-time members of staff'	Invisible labour burdens women disproportionately
Pay and progression inequity	'A suggested pay scale from CDI'	Low pay restricts diversity; limits retention and growth

These quotes are more than reflections. They are invitations – to reconsider assumptions, reframe leadership norms, and redesign the systems that continue to overlook or undervalue gendered experiences in careers work.

Take a moment to reflect:

- Where do these barriers show up in your context?
- Which of these quotes hits closest to home?
- What action, however small, could begin to shift one of these dynamics?

True equity begins not in abstract policy, but in honest self-examination and everyday practice.

Barrier	Do we see this here? (Y/N)	How does it show up?	What could we do differently?
Assumption that careers is 'women's work'			
Unconscious bias in leadership pathways			
Gendered expectations around care			
Emotional overwork without support			
Pay and progression inequity			

You may wish to complete this individually or as part of a team discussion. It can also be used during CPD, management reviews, or equality impact assessments. The goal is not perfection – it's progress. If CPD continues to reward visibility over reflection, confidence over collaboration, then we're still reinforcing the same masculine-coded models of success. Start where you are and begin building a more inclusive culture from within.

Enablers

While the barriers are deeply embedded, so too is the potential for change. Practitioners across the sector not only began identifying the problems – they also offered grounded solutions. These enablers offer hope, but more importantly, they offer strategy. If implemented collectively and courageously, they can shift the careers profession from a place of structural imbalance to one of genuine inclusion and equity.

One of the most powerful enablers is visible representation. One practitioner shares that a powerful intervention to help perception of the profession could be for *'An organisation that can attend careers fairs to show it as a possible career'*. Visibility isn't just about optics; it's about access and aspiration. When careers professionals attend schools, fairs, and community events, they help dismantle outdated stereotypes and open doors for those who may never have considered the sector. Another key strategy is mentorship and sponsorship. *'Establish mentorship and sponsorship programmes to support the professional development of individuals from underrepresented genders'* speaks to the power of both support and advocacy. While mentorship offers guidance, sponsorship brings opportunity – ensuring that talented individuals are not just supported but championed. This dual approach helps dismantle the informal networks that have historically favoured dominant groups.

Flexible working arrangements are also essential. As one practitioner noted, *'More flexible working opportunities that would support women with caring responsibilities'*, the rigid 9–5 model excludes many potential and current professionals. Flexibility should be a right, not a favour – an embedded aspect of inclusive practice that recognises the realities of modern life. Perhaps unsurprisingly, pay reform came up repeatedly. *'Increasing pay/set professional salary scales would attract more diversity'* speaks directly to the material barriers many face. Low pay disproportionately affects those already marginalised, and until this is addressed, the profession will struggle to retain a truly diverse workforce. Financial equity sends a message: this work matters, and those doing it are valued.

Leadership also matters – not just who gets there but how they lead. *'Mentorship – women who make it into leadership roles mentoring and supporting other women to rise up – and men . . . mentoring new recruits'* highlights the importance of gender-balanced leadership and recruitment panels. When leadership remains homogenous, so do the decisions made. Equitable leadership not only diversifies decision-making but also sets a precedent for the next generation of professionals. Beyond internal change, we must also consider how the profession is positioned externally. One comment urged the sector to *'Encourage Careers Education in schools . . . so students have a greater appreciation of the importance of the profession'*. This is about more than promotion – it's about reframing careers guidance as a respected, strategic, and vital field, not just a 'supportive add-on'.

These enablers are not abstract ideals. They are practical, actionable steps shared by those doing the work. The challenge now is to implement them – with intention, with urgency, and with accountability.

Practitioner toolkit

Gender-inclusive practice
This section is for you. Not the policymaker version of you. Not the formal job-title version of you. But the everyday practitioner – working in real settings, with real people, under real pressure. You.

Gender inclusion doesn't begin with a new policy or a training event. It begins with how we see, hear, and respond to each other. With the everyday choices we make. With the assumptions we don't question. With the language we use without thinking. This toolkit offers prompts and practical actions to help you reflect, reframe, and reimagine your practice – with gender inclusion at the centre.

Reflective questions
Take a few moments to ask yourself – honestly:

- What assumptions do I make about gender and leadership?
- Do I associate certain traits – like assertiveness, empathy, or professionalism – with specific genders?
- Who do I unconsciously defer to in meetings or discussions? Who do I expect to take on emotional labour?
- When a client shares something that challenges gender norms, how do I respond?
- Am I reinforcing traditional gender roles through advice – or through silence?

These questions aren't easy. But sitting with them is where change begins.

Noticing your own language and bias

Language is powerful. It reflects what we believe – and it shapes what others come to believe too.

- Are you using gendered job titles (e.g. *'chairman', 'policeman', 'businessman'*)? Switch to inclusive alternatives like *'chair', 'officer',* or *'businessperson'*.
- Do you default to *'he'* or *'she'* when a person's gender isn't known? Try *'they'* as a neutral default.
- Do you describe behaviours like confidence or emotion as either *'too much'* or *'not enough'*? Who defines what's *'enough'*?
- Are you more likely to compliment women for appearance and men for authority?

Paying attention to language is one of the quickest ways to surface hidden bias. No need for guilt – just be ready to adjust.

Building inclusive client guidance

Career guidance isn't just about CVs and interviews. It's about helping people imagine what's possible.

- Avoid inadvertently channelling clients into gender-stereotyped roles (e.g. *'You're nurturing – you'd be great in childcare'*). This is an extreme example, but it's to drill a point. A competent careers adviser would never be so directive. This is not to say that latent sexism doesn't happen in guidance – it definitely does – but it is probably more subtle than this.
- Use role models and stories that reflect a full range of gender identities and break stereotypes (e.g. male nurses, female engineers, non-binary entrepreneurs).
- Ask open, non-assumptive questions, which is something careers advisers are trained in, like *'What kind of working environment would energise you?'* instead of *'Do you want to work with people or things?'* This can avoid inadvertent sexism.
- Consider the impact of caring responsibilities, work–life balance, and confidence through a gender-aware lens – without making assumptions.

Inclusion isn't about perfection. It's about consistent curiosity, courage, and care. If you're in the room, you have power – the power to include, the power to question, and the power to make space. The more intentional you are with that power, the more this profession can truly serve everyone.

Organisational toolkit: Structural change

Shifting individual practice isn't enough. It must be matched by structural changes from those in leadership positions. Culture doesn't shift by accident. It shifts when leadership decides to stop replicating what's always been done – and starts building systems that actually reflect the people doing the work.

This section isn't about ticking boxes or generic HR templates. It's about structural moves that show your organisation is serious about gender equity – not just during awareness weeks, but in how it hires, promotes, listens, and leads. Here's the thing: gender equity doesn't only mean advocating for women. It also means asking why some men – particularly working-class men, disabled men, or men from racially minoritised backgrounds – aren't represented either. If your team is made up of women at the bottom and White men at the top, then yes, it's gendered. But it's not diverse. If we want meaningful inclusion, we have to look at all angles. Who isn't showing up in this space? And more importantly – what's stopping them?

Here are some starting points for leadership:

- Conduct a gender audit of promotions and pay: If you're not tracking who's progressing and who's plateauing, you're only seeing half the story. Break it down by gender identity *and* intersectional data – race, disability, class, and more.
- Sponsor women and non-binary staff – and underrepresented men: Mentorship helps people survive the system. Sponsorship helps them shift it. That means backing your staff behind closed doors, not just during performance reviews.
- Balance masculine and feminine-coded leadership traits: Still rewarding dominance and calling it *'confidence'*? Still calling emotional intelligence *'soft skills'*? Flip the narrative. The future of leadership is relational, not just transactional.
- Rethink what leadership looks like: If everyone in your leadership pipeline looks the same, ask why. Are you valuing style over substance? Visibility over impact? Challenge what you're calling 'potential' and who gets to define it.
- Design policies that reflect care roles, flexibility, and real life: If your leadership model assumes someone else is doing the school run, managing health appointments, or handling life administration – it's not inclusive; it's outdated. Rewrite it.
- Create visible pathways for underrepresented men: Don't just ask *'Why aren't more men applying?'* Ask: *'What's the image of this profession we're putting out there?'* Showcase diverse male role models. Be intentional about the narratives you platform.

Equity doesn't happen through intention alone. It happens through accountability, access, and redistribution of power. If you're in a leadership role, you are already shaping the culture – so the only question is, are you reinforcing inequality or helping dismantle it?

Reflection task: Enablers

Take a moment to consider the following:

- Which of the enablers in the table below are currently active in your setting?
- Which one is missing, and why?
- What could you personally do to introduce or strengthen that enabler in your team, organisation, or practice?

You can use Table 11 as a working document for self-reflection, team discussions, or strategic planning.

Table 11 Enablers

Enabler	Quote	Application
Visible representation at careers fairs	'An organisation that can attend careers fairs to show it as a possible career.'	Attend schools and community events to challenge stereotypes and raise visibility.
Mentorship and sponsorship programmes	'Establish mentorship and sponsorship programs to support the professional development.'	Develop internal mentorship schemes and align senior leaders as active sponsors.
Flexible working arrangements	'More flexible working opportunities that would support women with caring responsibilities.'	Introduce or embed flexible schedules into core organisational policy.
Pay reform and professional recognition	'Increasing pay/set professional salary scales would attract more diversity.'	Create structured, transparent pay scales tied to professional competencies.
Gender-balanced leadership and panels	'Mentorship – women in leadership mentoring other women – and men mentoring new recruits.'	Ensure recruitment and promotion panels reflect gender diversity and equity.
Careers education repositioning	'Encourage Careers Education in school so students have a greater appreciation.'	Deliver assemblies, workshops, and curriculum resources to shift external perceptions.

Reflective task: Unpacking gender quotes

These quotes weren't shared for decoration. They came from real people – practitioners who took the time to put words to what many of us have felt but haven't always said aloud. This section isn't about case studies or anonymous commentary. It's about naming what's happening so we can stop pretending it isn't.

What you're about to read is uncomfortable because it's true. The truth isn't there to make us feel guilty – it's there to move us. To help us listen better. Respond better. Do better.

Use these quotes as mirrors. Sit with them. Unpick them. Share them with your team if you're able to. But above all – ask yourself what you're going to do with what you now know.

'Representation of all genders – you can't be what you can't see.'

Visibility is not symbolic. It's structural. If people don't see themselves in the profession – or in leadership – they're less likely to enter, less likely to stay, and less likely to believe they'll ever belong. Representation shapes aspiration.

- What does this mean in my setting?
- Who is least visible, and why?
- How could I shift what visibility looks like around me?

'More respect for the profession so it isn't seen as "women's work."'

When work becomes gendered, it becomes devalued. When it's labelled *'women's work'*, it's often seen as emotional, easy, and low-paid. We need to stop accepting that and start asking why care-focused work is still positioned as lesser.

- How is careers work viewed in my organisation?
- Does the gender makeup of the team impact its value?
- What would a genuine shift in respect look like – structurally, not symbolically?

'Grammar schools where I work prefer an adviser who is less mothering.'

This isn't just about one school. It's about the language we use when we talk about professionalism. When *'mothering'* becomes shorthand for *'too emotional'* or *'not strategic'*, we reinforce the idea that emotional intelligence is a weakness. It's not.

- What do we really mean when we say someone is *'too caring'*?
- Whose traits get coded as professional – and whose don't?
- Am I rewarding empathy in practice, or just in theory?

'When I left, I was replaced with two full-time members of staff.'

This is what happens when emotional labour and invisible responsibilities go unrecognised. It's only when someone leaves that the scale of their contribution becomes visible. By then, it's too late.

- Who's carrying more than their job title suggests?
- Have I normalised overwork in the name of dedication?
- What would it look like to prevent burnout rather than respond to it?
- 'Awareness of unconscious positive discrimination that moves men into leadership positions more quickly.'

Even in a female-majority sector, leadership often remains male-dominated. That doesn't happen by accident. It's about who's seen as competent, who's fast-tracked, and who gets a second chance. That awareness isn't enough – we need action. If your organisation is serious about gender equity, ask how men are being equipped – not just to not harm – but to actively advocate, interrupt, and redistribute power.

- Who moves through the system with ease?
- What networks exist that quietly support some and not others?
- What can I do to make leadership progression more transparent and fairer?

Reflection
Use these quotes as your entry point. For each one, or for the ones that resonate most:

- What does this mean in my context?
- Who is most impacted by this?
- What small shift can I commit to?

This isn't about performative reflection. It's about real-world accountability. If we're serious about equity, we have to be serious about where we go from here.

Thinking grid

Audit your practice
This section isn't for performance – it's for progress. Table 12 is a space for you to step back, look honestly at your organisation or practice, and assess where gender equity is showing up – and where it's missing completely.

No jargon. No box-ticking. Just truth.

Table 12 Audit

Category	Current reality	What needs to shift?	First step
Leadership	Who holds power? Who is represented at decision-making levels?	Are gendered patterns present in progression and visibility?	Map out leadership demographics. Set goals for diversity.
CPD	Who accesses development opportunities – and who doesn't?	Are programmes inclusive and free from gender bias?	Audit CPD uptake by gender. Review content and facilitators.
Recruitment	Are job adverts, panels, and criteria gender-neutral?	Do any steps reinforce unconscious bias or exclusion?	Diversify panels. Use inclusive language in job specs.
Perception	How is the profession viewed within your organisation or externally?	Is it seen as *'soft'*, feminised, or low impact?	Start a dialogue. Reframe the narrative at senior levels.
Pay	Are salary bands transparent and equitable?	Do gendered pay gaps exist in roles or departments?	Conduct a pay audit. Push for structured scales.
Culture	What's normalised in your space – jokes, expectations, silence?	Who feels safe here? Who doesn't?	Run anonymous pulse checks. Build space for challenge.
Client-facing language	What assumptions do your materials or conversations make?	Do they reflect diverse gender identities and experiences?	Review wording across platforms. Pilot inclusive language.

How to use this grid

- Complete it individually, then bring it to a team discussion.
- Use it during EDI reviews or strategic planning.
- Revisit it quarterly. Change doesn't come from one workshop – it comes from consistent action.

Use this as a personal reflection, a team exercise, or part of an internal review. The point isn't to have all the answers. It's to stop pretending we don't know the questions.

Your answers may feel uncomfortable. Remember change was never designed to be comfortable. Equity isn't a destination, nor is a truly inclusive workforce – it's a daily discipline. This chapter is a beginning, not a checklist. What comes next is yours to shape.

Chapter 8
Sexuality and sexual identity in the careers sector

Chapter roadmap

This chapter explores sexuality and sexual identity in careers work, from both practitioner and client perspectives. Drawing on lived experiences, practitioner insights, and intersectional understanding, it will:

- Begin with an author narrative rooted in visible allyship and professional reflections;
- Define what we mean by sexuality and sexual identity;
- Examine how assumptions and barriers show up in everyday practice;
- Amplify the lived experiences of LGBTQIA+ clients and professionals;
- Identify systemic challenges and patterns of exclusion;
- Share practical tools, reflective prompts, and organisational strategies;
- Close with a values-based vision for authentic inclusion.

Author's voice

This chapter covers sexuality to support EDI in making the workplace culture equitable – not just for clients, but for those of us within the careers workforce too. It matters because we cannot talk about equity, diversity, and inclusion with any credibility if we sideline or dilute the experiences of LGBTQIA+ individuals. I've been in far too many rooms where the silence around sexuality was deafening. Where people wanted to say the right thing but instead said nothing. Where the fear of getting it wrong completely overshadowed the need to say anything at all. I've worked with countless practitioners who care deeply but feel paralysed by discomfort. I always say the same thing – silence causes more harm than a clumsy, well-intentioned mistake ever could. The goal isn't perfection. It's presence.

I've been a visible ally for years now, and I carry that responsibility seriously. It's not about token gestures. It's about noticing when heteronormativity creeps in through policies, examples, and *'neutral'* career guidance that only feels neutral to those at the centre. It's about challenging the assumptions that go unchecked – the default use of *'partner'* only in heterosexual contexts, the constant recycling of career case studies that never reflect the full spectrum of identities. One practitioner put it bluntly in a Padlet during a session: *'Slap a rainbow on it!'* That line hit me hard; they weren't being cynical – they were being honest. Too often, LGBTQIA+ inclusion is reduced to aesthetics. Rainbow logos, Pride month lanyards, and posters of smiling same-sex couples that disappear as quickly as they went up. Inclusion isn't seasonal. It's not symbolic. It's about creating genuine safety, all year round. It's about how people feel when the colours are gone, and the flag is packed away.

I've watched good people freeze because they're afraid to offend. *'I don't know what words to use.' 'What if I mess up?'* I've heard them all. But those of us in this sector – especially those of us with privilege – have to lean into the discomfort; the stakes are far higher for LGBTQIA+ clients. While we worry about phrasing, they're worrying whether they'll be safe in the building. Whether disclosing their identity will cost them a job, a placement, or a reference. That fear is real. Our discomfort can't be the thing that shuts down progress.

Gender identity and expression are part of this too, and I think we need to be more honest about how culture shapes our understanding. I've had more open and compassionate conversations about gender identity in Pakistan than I have in some UK professional spaces. The khusra community has existed for generations. It hasn't always been accepted, but it has been seen, named, and recognised. There's something powerful in that sometimes what looks like progress in policy doesn't translate to lived visibility. We can't keep congratulating ourselves for *'inclusion'* if it's only safe in theory.

For those wondering what the khusra community is, below is a brief description. In South Asia, khusras include people who are transgender, intersex, and gender non-conforming. In countries like Pakistan, their presence is both historic and visible – yet their lives remain deeply marginalised. They've always been part of the social structure, present in ceremonies, cultural traditions, and communal life – but rarely protected, respected, or centred in mainstream narratives.

In recent years, under former prime minister Imran Khan's government, legal rights were extended to the khusra community – including recognition of a third gender and certain employment protections. On paper, this looked like progress. But lived reality tells a different story. Recognition doesn't always equal safety. Policy doesn't always translate into protection. And inclusion that only exists on forms or ID cards is not enough. The community still faces violence, poverty, and exclusion on a daily basis. So when we talk about *'progress'*, we have to ask: who is it really reaching? Because visibility without safety isn't justice – and rights without dignity aren't liberation.

This chapter isn't just about LGBTQIA+ inclusion – it's about belonging. It's about not having to choose between being visible and being safe. I've worked with students who've delayed job applications because they didn't want to go back into the closet. I've had clients who asked quietly, *'Do you think I can be out in that industry?'* and then hesitated, because they already knew the answer. I've sat with people who felt forced to edit their whole self to be employable. That's not inclusion. That's survival.

If we truly care about EDI, then we need to stop expecting people to split themselves in two. We can't claim to be person-centred if we only accept parts of the person. Our role isn't just to help people get through the door – it's to ask what happens once they're inside. Will they be respected? Supported? Will they be able to grow? Being 'included' doesn't mean being safe. Until we create cultures where people don't have to choose between authenticity and ambition, we still have work to do.

What do we mean by sexuality and sexual identity?

Sexuality and sexual identity refer to the emotional, romantic, and physical attraction we feel towards others – and how we understand and express that within ourselves. These identities include lesbian, gay, bisexual, queer, asexual, and pansexual people, as well as those who are still exploring. Throughout this chapter, I use LGBTQIA+ as an umbrella term, while recognising that each part of that acronym holds distinct, layered experiences that deserve more than a tokenistic grouping.

Although this chapter primarily centres on sexuality, I've chosen to include reflections on gender identity – not as a sideline, but because the stories, practitioner experiences, and Padlet contributions made it clear that these areas cannot be easily separated. In real life, people don't compartmentalise their identities in tidy silos. Clients don't arrive saying, *'This week is about sexuality, next week I'll explore gender'*. These parts of self are entangled – especially when navigating career decisions, workplace safety, and systems of inclusion or exclusion. Gender identity, which refers to someone's internal sense of being male, female, both, neither, or somewhere along the spectrum, is not the same as sexuality – but too often, in careers work, the two are collapsed or misunderstood. I've included more on gender identity here than originally planned because the stories I listened to demanded it.

The legal framework does recognise both. Under the Equality Act 2010, sexual orientation and gender reassignment are protected characteristics. Section 7 specifically protects those undergoing, having undergone, or perceived to be undergoing gender reassignment, while Section 12 addresses discrimination based on sexual orientation. These are vital benchmarks – but law alone doesn't equate to lived safety. Rights on paper can't shield someone from microaggressions, isolation, or the quiet but constant need to hide. The Stonewall 'LGBT in Britain – Work Report' (2018) revealed that over 60% of LGBTQIA+ individuals go 'back into the closet' after higher education – particularly when entering the workplace. That statistic continues to stay with me. It captures the gap between visibility and safety. Between being acknowledged and being welcomed. Between representation and real belonging.

To understand how someone navigates their own sexual identity over time, the CASS Model (Vivienne Cass, 1979) offers a helpful frame. It outlines six stages: confusion, comparison, tolerance, acceptance, pride, and synthesis. But as many practitioners will attest, these stages are not neat, linear, or time bound. One practitioner reflected, *'They may not feel ready to come out – there are six stages'*, capturing the emotional complexity and layered considerations behind disclosure. Especially in careers work, where identity, ambition, and environment intersect, the decision to be out – or not – is rarely a binary one. It's a daily calculation of risk, belonging, and survival.

What strikes me is how, in some contexts, conversations around gender identity and sexuality are more visible or culturally acknowledged than in so-called progressive Western spaces. In Pakistan, for example, the khusra community has long been recognised as a third gender, woven into cultural and even spiritual traditions. Their social positioning remains precarious, but their visibility is embedded in public consciousness. That, to me, is a powerful contradiction. In contrast, UK systems often claim equality while sometimes sidelining gender diversity through bureaucratic processes, vague policies, or tokenistic inclusion that doesn't translate into daily experience.

I've written this chapter with intention: not to conflate sexuality and gender identity, but to honour the reality that both often sit at the heart of how people navigate careers, identity, and inclusion. In the careers space, we are meant to guide individuals towards futures they can thrive in – but that means interrogating whether those futures are truly safe. Will they be seen, heard, and respected in those spaces? Or will they have to dim themselves just to fit in? Because if the answer is the latter, then that isn't a future worth pointing anyone towards. Inclusion must mean something deeper than surface visibility. It must offer safety, affirmation, and the freedom to exist fully.

Understanding sexuality and gender identity in career development

Careers work too often rests on the unspoken assumption of neutrality – yet that so-called *'neutral'* space is quietly constructed through the lens of heterosexual and cisgender norms. From the way career options are presented, to the assumptions embedded in employer brochures, to the language we use during interviews and CV workshops, the default setting is straight, cis, and conforming. Unless a client explicitly discloses their identity – and even then – that disclosure is not always met with affirmation, or even basic understanding. But identity enters the space whether we invite it or not. I've worked with clients who are constantly calculating: Will I need to suppress a part of myself to survive in this workplace? Will I be safe in this office, this industry, this country? These are not hypothetical questions – they are what one Padlet practitioner described as a *'psychological bottleneck'*, an internal traffic jam of fear and caution that delays or derails career exploration altogether.

Another practitioner wrote: *'Delay and emotional turmoil . . . this resonates and can be observed in practice.'* And it does. I've witnessed incredibly talented students withdraw from networking events, not because they lacked confidence, but because they weren't sure if it was safe to be themselves. I've spoken with clients who've ruled out entire sectors – law, finance, policing – based not on ability, but on fear of reputational harm and identity erasure. These aren't *'soft'* issues. They are structural barriers rooted in a lack of visible safety. What's needed is a shift in framing – from asking whether someone fits a job to asking whether the job fits who they are. I always return to one key question: *'Will I be safe and able to be authentic in this organisation?'* It's a question that surfaced time and again in the Padlet discussions. As one practitioner put it: *'Helping students consider . . . will I flourish here?'* That word – flourish – is so important. It moves us beyond mere survival and points us towards dignity, growth, and self-actualisation. Careers practitioners shouldn't be coaching clients to tolerate exclusionary systems – we should be helping them locate or build systems that embrace them.

For LGBTQIA+ clients considering international placements, the risks compound. Padlet reflections underscored how *'students [were] anxious about overseas placements, countries not being safe for LGBTQ+LGBTQIA+ people'.* These aren't imagined fears. They are rooted in real legislation, cultural hostility, and intergenerational trauma. So, we cannot champion global opportunities without also helping clients assess global safety. This means more than listing visa requirements – it means navigating geopolitics, human rights, and the ethics of recommending placements in spaces that may cause harm. Equally, we need to expand how we assess employers. The question should no longer be, *'Can I do this job?'* but *'Can I thrive in this space without having to fragment my identity?'* Padlet practitioners echoed this: *'Talk more about the culture of companies, not just the role.'* It's not enough to list inclusive policies; we must teach clients how to read the room – look for signs of belonging, analyse language, observe tone, and sense how leadership models inclusion or sidelines it.

Authenticity and belonging are not luxury extras – they are prerequisites for long-term career fulfilment. If clients feel they have to mute or mask their identities to be hired, something is broken. As one voice asked, *'Do people have to bring parts of themselves to work they would rather leave at home?'* That question is a powerful litmus test – one I've embedded into every identity-aware careers conversation. We need to be bold enough to ask it, even when it feels uncomfortable. When we speak of sexuality and gender in career development, we must go beyond policy tick-boxes and Pride month banners. It's about how we structure our guidance sessions, the space we make for dialogue, the relevance of the resources we choose, and the courage to ask deeper questions.

One practitioner said it perfectly: *'Time for some students – those who want to talk about how sexuality is impacting on choice – it's career counselling, not just information.'* Exactly that. This work isn't transactional. It's transformational. It's not just about helping someone take the next step – it's about ensuring the path ahead holds space for their whole self to walk freely.

Practitioner lived experiences

Across all the Padlet reflections, one message emerged with unmistakable clarity: the emotional labour of LGBTQIA+ professionals is both invisible and unsupported. Too often, that labour takes the shape of quietly carrying a dual burden – doing the job while simultaneously navigating an identity in a space that wasn't built with them in mind. I've spoken to practitioners who, once *'out'*, are automatically positioned as the go-to EDI lead – not because they chose to be, but because visibility is misread as consent. As one practitioner put it: *'Huge responsibility for the person who is marginalised themselves.'* That line stuck with me. I've seen this dynamic play out repeatedly – the same person being asked to speak on panels, deliver training, represent inclusion – without extra pay, without adequate support, and often without the safety to say no.

For many LGBTQIA+ professionals, workplace isolation compounds this burden. Being the only visible queer or trans person in the room doesn't just affect wellbeing – it redefines the terms of engagement. It becomes a calculation: Is it safe to speak up here? Will I be heard or tokenised? One practitioner's comment captured it perfectly: *'It's a lonely place when no one else shares your experience but assumes you'll speak for it anyway.'* That assumption – the expectation to speak for an entire community – can be as exhausting as it is reductive. Then there's the silence. Not the neutral kind, but the kind that suppresses rather than supports. Practitioners described how fear of saying the wrong thing leads to total disengagement, leaving LGBTQIA+ inclusion work to stagnate. One observed: *'People don't engage with sexuality or gender inclusion work because they're worried about causing offence . . . but that inaction causes harm too.'* Silence, as I often say, isn't safety. It's complicity, masked as caution.

Even empathy becomes its own burden. There's an unspoken idea that lived experience makes someone automatically responsible for all learning, translation, and emotional labour. The assumption that *'you're closer to this, so you'll understand it better'* becomes a lazy excuse for others to opt out. As one practitioner wrote: *'Always being the one to answer the awkward questions in staff training is exhausting.'* It's not just about being visible – it's about the weight of being expected to educate, challenge, and reassure all at once. The result? Practitioners are left holding everyone else's discomfort while trying to safeguard their own wellbeing.

This is where boundaries begin to blur. How does one remain visible, hold space for students, and still maintain emotional safety? One practitioner expressed it honestly: *'I feel torn between wanting to be a role model and needing to protect myself from emotional fatigue.'* That tension is real. I've heard it time and time again. We don't talk enough about the emotional cost of representation – especially in the careers sector, where practitioners are often asked to be both counsellor and symbol. The weight of that expectation is unsustainable. Yet, so many carry it, knowing how much it can mean for a young person to see themselves reflected. This point interlinks with the CDI Code of Ethics in this context, particularly around self-care.

We also have to situate this within the broader organisational context. Too many careers services remain stuck in surface-level gestures instead of committing to structural change. One practitioner summed it up: *'There's an assumption that being out in a careers setting is easier now – but it depends entirely on who's in the room.'* Visibility may have increased, but vulnerability hasn't vanished. If the culture hasn't shifted, then the risk remains. That's why representation alone isn't enough. What's needed is a commitment to systems that recognise complexity, value lived experience without commodifying it, and distribute the labour of change; being the *'only one'* in the room should never mean being the only one expected to make the room safer.

Client perspectives

Many LGBTQIA+ clients navigate careers with a kind of quiet calculation that isn't always visible to practitioners. It's not just about whether a role aligns with their skills or interests – it's about whether they'll be safe. Whether they'll belong. Whether they'll have to trade authenticity for access. As a researcher working alongside CDPs, I've been fortunate to hear so many stories – honest, vulnerable reflections that lay bare the emotional labour behind career decision-making.

One such story was shared with me during a lunchtime webinar, where a CDP recounted supporting a thoughtful, ambitious graduate who had her heart set on a communications role in a global company. She had all the qualifications, but when she researched the regional office she would be applying to, she noticed a lack of any visible LGBTQIA+ inclusion. No pronoun use in bios, no employee resource groups, no reference to equality in leadership statements. *'I just don't know if I can be myself there'*, the student had said. So she paused. She didn't apply. Not because she wasn't capable – but because she wasn't convinced the organisation was capable of holding space for her. This is what I call the invisible tax – the emotional energy spent assessing every space for threat, microaggression, or silence. Some clients end up writing off entire sectors – tech, law, policing, media – because of reputations that haven't yet been earned back. They ask themselves: *'Is this an environment where I'll be tolerated, or one where I'll be celebrated?'* The answer shapes not only what they apply for, but how much of themselves they bring. The desire to *'bring my whole self to work'* is powerful – but it's not equally available. One quote from the Padlet resonated deeply: *'Loss of a place to belong.'* That's what many LGBTQIA+ clients feel when they can't see themselves reflected in leadership, or when their identity is left off every form, ignored in policy, or met with awkward silence in the room. Even something as small as a practitioner stumbling over pronouns or skimming past personal identity in a CV workshop can send a message: this space might not be for you.

We also have to hold space for those still exploring their identity – who may not yet have language, safety, or confidence to disclose. A client shouldn't have to *come out* in order to be understood. We need to be attentive to cues, gentle in our questions, and aware that disclosure is not a one-off event, but a constantly negotiated act. Sometimes it's verbal, sometimes it's withheld, sometimes it's in the pause between lines on a form. As practitioners and researchers, we must move beyond binary questions of *'out'* or *'not out'*. We must understand that visibility is not always the goal – belonging is. Belonging doesn't require someone to shout their identity; it requires a system that meets them with dignity, regardless. If we want to create truly inclusive careers spaces, we need to ask: *What futures are possible for this client not just professionally, but personally? What does it mean for them to thrive – not just survive – in the roles we help them explore?* That's where real careers guidance begins.

Barriers to inclusion

Every barrier we encounter isn't just a logistical challenge – it's a message. It signals to LGBTQIA+ clients and practitioners that some truths are still too inconvenient, some identities still too complex for the system to hold. These signals are often subtle, but their impact is lasting. If we don't name them directly, we risk entrenching a culture of surface-level inclusion, where only certain kinds of visibility are welcomed, and everything else is rendered invisible. This chapter doesn't claim to offer an exhaustive list – there are barriers that weren't raised in the Padlets, ones that are culturally specific, or too nuanced to capture neatly in a few lines. But what it does aim to do is offer a mirror. A starting point. A provocation for conversations we've too often avoided.

Tokenism remains one of the most corrosive patterns in the sector. The quote *'Slap a rainbow on it!'* speaks volumes. It names the discomfort practitioners feel when institutions opt for temporary visibility over permanent change. Pride month branding, for instance, without any substantive work behind the scenes – no policies reviewed, no behaviours challenged, no voices meaningfully included. It's not that visibility is the problem. It's when visibility is the only gesture, it becomes hollow; worse, it becomes harmful. LGBTQIA+ staff and clients are left feeling more alienated, not less, when their identities are reduced to seasonal campaigns instead of being woven into everyday practice. Performative allyship, without meaningful action, erodes trust and deepens disillusionment. Psychological safety is another foundational need that continues to be unmet. The practitioner who noted *'Students delay decisions due to fear'* captured a truth that resonates deeply across practice. Fear of being discriminated against. Fear of being outed. Fear of not being believed, or worse, of being pathologised. For LGBTQIA+ clients, career decisions aren't neutral steps – they're emotionally weighted negotiations with risk. When every opportunity is filtered through the question *'Will I be safe here?'* the pressure to assimilate becomes exhausting. When the choice becomes authenticity versus acceptance, we're no longer talking about ambition – we're talking about survival.

The lack of representation compounds this further. When LGBTQIA+ clients look around the careers profession and see no one who reflects their identity, it sends a silent but powerful message: this space may not be for you. One quote said it plainly: *'Lack of visible LGBTQ people in the careers profession.'* This isn't a call for token appointments – it's a call for mirrors. For models of success that affirm diverse identities and show that thriving is possible. When clients can't see anyone like them in the roles they aspire to, it creates a gap that no CV or qualification can fill. Representation doesn't solve everything, but its absence is always felt. Binary thinking is another barrier – subtle, insidious, and often unacknowledged. The assumption that LGBTQIA+ is a singular, homogenous group flattens complexity and erases lived experience. One practitioner named it clearly: *'LGBTQIA+ not being a homogenous group.'* Within that acronym lies a rich spectrum of intersecting identities shaped by race, class, culture, religion, disability, and more. When we treat inclusion as a checkbox exercise, we lose the ability to respond to that nuance. When we ignore intersectionality, we risk creating strategies that fail the very people they're meant to support. Inclusion that doesn't account for diversity within diversity will never be enough.

We must talk about the international context. For LGBTQIA+ clients, global opportunities don't come with global safety. The practitioner who noted *'HE students anxious about overseas placements'* as a significant issue for them highlighted an often-overlooked reality. Moving abroad isn't just a matter of visas and logistics – it can mean stepping into environments where being queer or trans is criminalised or culturally targeted. The excitement of international work is real, but so is the danger. As careers professionals, we can't gloss over these risks. It's not about scaring clients – it's about equipping them. Informed, values-based decision-making is part of our role, and that means talking honestly about where they can thrive, not just where they can go. These barriers remind us that inclusion isn't about being allowed in – it's about being able to exist fully once you're there. It's about agency, not just access. If LGBTQIA+ clients have to edit, conceal, or dilute themselves to feel safe in careers spaces, then those spaces are not inclusive by design. We have to stop inviting clients into systems that ask them to shrink in exchange for opportunity. Inclusion must mean that they can show up, speak up, and be supported as they are – not just tolerated, but genuinely valued. That's the work still to come.

Enablers

Throughout the Padlets, practitioners offered powerful glimpses into what meaningful, inclusive practice can look like. These weren't abstract ideals or distant aspirations – they were grounded, replicable actions that are already shifting the landscape of careers work for LGBTQIA+ individuals. They reminded me that the seeds of transformation are often small but intentional. What we need now is to water them.

One practitioner wrote about *'LGBTQIA+ mentoring – employers coming in to do this'*, and that line stayed with me; it's not just about guidance – it's about visibility. Mentorship rooted in shared experience makes the future feel more reachable, more real. When role models enter the room, everything shifts. Their presence alone becomes a mirror, offering clients a glimpse of what's possible when you don't have to split yourself to succeed. Visibility becomes safety, and safety becomes strategy.

The emergence of targeted platforms and events – like Student Pride Careers Fairs, myGwork, Human Libraries, and curated LinkedIn role model projects – is helping to shift the narrative entirely. These aren't just visibility exercises; they are spaces that empower clients to ask deeper, more critical questions: Who will see me? Who will stand with me? Who's already walked this path? They centre the full self, not just the CV. In these spaces, careers guidance isn't reduced to skills audits or job descriptions – it becomes identity-affirming, future-building work.

Another clear enabler was the creation of safe, exploratory spaces where clients don't have to seek permission to be themselves. As one practitioner said, *'It's about having the space to reflect, not just the pressure to decide'*. That line captures what good guidance can and should be. When identity isn't framed as a disclosure but embraced as part of career choice, the entire tone of the interaction changes. Clients begin to see that who they are is not a barrier to work, but a compass pointing towards it. Partnerships with community groups and local LGBTQIA+ organisations also emerged as a vital practice. These collaborations extend trust, expand reach, and signal to clients that their identities are not only acknowledged but respected through action. Careers services do not have to have all the answers, but they do need to build relationships with those who've been asking – and answering – the right questions for a long time. Inclusion isn't a solo practice. It's relational. It's collective.

Training also featured heavily as a key enabler – not as a tick-box CPD session but as an ongoing journey. One practitioner insightfully noted, *'It's not about solving – it's about listening, reflecting, and staying open'*. That shift in mindset – from fixing to witnessing – changes everything. It reframes discomfort not as something to avoid, but as something to learn from. Staff don't need to be experts in every identity. But they do need to be human, open, and willing to learn without putting the emotional labour back on those most impacted.

And at the heart of it all is allyship. True allyship is quiet, consistent, and accountable. It doesn't centre itself or demand applause. As one practitioner said, *'There's a difference between being supportive and expecting people to do the work for you'*. That distinction matters; allyship, done right, lifts without loading. It supports without spotlighting itself. It always remembers that the responsibility to create inclusive spaces should never fall solely on those already burdened by exclusion.

These enablers show us that we don't need to reinvent the wheel – we need to redistribute the labour. We need to invest in what already works, amplify what's already happening, and embed it so deeply into our practice that it becomes the default, not the exception. Inclusion doesn't start with rainbow lanyards or social media campaigns – it starts with relationships, reflection, and a relentless commitment to do better. When we get that right, we don't just serve LGBTQIA+ clients – we reshape the entire system for the better.

Tools for practice

If we want to move from intention to impact, we need tools that help us translate values into everyday practice. These aren't just checklists – they're conversation starters, accountability anchors, and ways of embedding inclusion into the core of what we do. The tools listed in Table 13 are designed to support practitioners, clients, and organisations in making equity real – not theoretical.

Table 13 Tools for practice

Tool	Description
LGBTQIA+ inclusive language guide	Offers accessible do/don't phrasing to build practitioner confidence and fluency. It helps staff avoid assumptions, use affirming language, and move away from deficit-based framing.
Reflection tool	Supports clients in evaluating values, safety, fit, and authenticity when exploring or applying for roles. Encourages holistic career thinking beyond salary and title.
Visibility mapping worksheet	Aids organisations in auditing where and how LGBTQIA+ inclusion is made visible – not just in symbols, but in stories, leadership, and lived culture. Enables targeted actions for greater visibility and belonging.

These tools aren't exhaustive, but they offer a starting point. They remind us that inclusion isn't something we do once – it's a lens we must keep adjusting, checking, and refining. They give us the scaffolding for more honest, more human, and ultimately more effective careers work.

Organisational audit table

Change doesn't start with good intentions – it starts with honest reflection. Table 14 is designed to help teams assess their current landscape, identify blind spots, and take meaningful steps towards lasting LGBTQIA+ inclusion. It's not a compliance tick-box. It's an opportunity to align our internal practices with the values we so often put on display.

Table 14 Organisational audit

Area	Current practice	What needs attention?	Actions
Visibility	Rainbow flag only during Pride	Seen as tokenistic	Year-round visual inclusion signals that affirm daily presence, not just seasonal awareness.
Representation	Few LGBTQIA+ staff in public-facing roles	Feeds isolation and invisibility	Develop staff spotlight stories that reflect diversity across roles and levels.
Training	Reactive EDI training only	Doesn't build deep confidence	Embed ongoing, proactive learning spaces with co-designed input from LGBTQIA+ communities.
Outreach	Few events with LGBTQIA+ organisations	Missed trust-building with communities	Partner with organisations like myGwork and local charities to co-create opportunities.

These columns are starting points, not end goals. The real work is what happens next – in team conversations, budget decisions, recruitment practices, and everyday culture. Inclusion must move off the posters and into the policies. It must be lived, not just declared.

Reflective quotes

This section invites readers to pause. To sit with discomfort, not rush past it. To ask not only but also. These quotes are not abstract – they are voices from the field, from those living the realities of marginalisation. Use them as a tool for self-inquiry, team discussion, or quiet reflection.

'Not wanting to say the wrong thing.' That fear is real – but so is its impact. When we let fear freeze us, inclusion becomes someone else's responsibility. Ask yourself: what's stopping me from engaging in LGBTQIA+ inclusion work? Is it truly lack of skill, or a discomfort I've avoided sitting with?

'Will I be able to be authentic?' This is a question clients carry silently. But do we ask it aloud? Do we go beyond job fit to explore identity affirmation? Or are we so focused on employment that we forget to ask whether the space will affirm who they are once they get there?

'Huge responsibility for the person who is marginalised.' I come back to this quote often. It asks us to look beyond the one visible *'inclusive'* staff member and interrogate the systems that keep relying on their unpaid emotional labour. Who is being asked to carry the weight of institutional inclusion, and why?

'Being visible can feel like a risk, not a privilege.' Visibility is complex. For some, it's empowering. For others, it's dangerous; when we choose silence in the name of neutrality, who are we really protecting? Because silence is not neutral. It can be a barrier dressed up as professionalism.

'We are tired of having to educate others.' This is a fatigue that runs deep. Before we ask a colleague or client to explain their identity or struggle, we must ask: is this something I could be learning independently? Inclusion starts with the willingness to do the work ourselves, not outsourcing it to those most affected.

'Not being able to see anyone like me in leadership.' Representation is not a luxury – it's a signal of what's possible; ask: How am I building pathways to leadership that reflect the diversity of those we serve? Inclusion doesn't end at access – it must reach all the way to influence and decision-making.

'I often choose jobs based on where I'll feel safest, not where I'll thrive.' That quote haunts me. It tells us everything about the compromises people make just to exist in a workplace. How do we shift careers support away from mere risk avoidance and towards meaningful possibility-building?

'There's a difference between feeling welcomed and feeling like you belong.' This quote should be a litmus test for our practice. Are we creating spaces of true belonging, or simply conditional acceptance? Because token welcome is not the same as cultural safety.

You don't need to answer all of these today. But let them sit with you. Let them shape the questions you ask, the silence you break, and the feedback you offer. Reflection isn't the opposite of action – it's the foundation of it. In this work, neutrality isn't fairness. It's erasure in disguise.

Too often, we conflate professionalism with sameness. We treat conformity as a sign of readiness. But for queer and trans clients – and practitioners – every act of disclosure, every choice to be seen, carries an emotional tax. I've listened to clients delay their dreams because the cost of being visible felt too high. I've sat with practitioners who didn't speak in meetings – not because they lacked ideas, but because they were gauging the safety of the room. This is the real terrain of career development, and we must stop pretending otherwise.

Saying *'bring your whole self to work'* means nothing if the environment punishes authenticity. That safety has to be built intentionally – through policy, through everyday practice, through the quiet courage of noticing and challenging what others let slide. Whether I'm consulting, teaching, or writing, one truth underpins it all: equity isn't about sameness – it's about presence, care, and response. It means tuning in to where someone is, not where we assume they should be. That's the heart of TEDI, and the thread that holds this chapter together.

This is not a call-out. It's a call-in. A call to see more, hear more, and do more – not as saviours, but as colleagues and co-creators of a better, fairer sector. Let's move beyond slogans and into substance. Let's stop asking people to hide in order to plan their futures. Everyone deserves a careers journey that honours their whole self – not just in theory but in practice.

For me, no matter the role I am in, the same truth applies – equity doesn't mean treating everyone the same. It means meeting people where they are, with the awareness, flexibility, and care their journey deserves. That is the thread that ties all my work together. Inclusion is not a checklist – it's a practice of intentional humanity. One that asks us not to fix people, but to fix the systems that were never built with them in mind. This chapter is a call-in, not a call-out. A chance to step into discomfort, and from there, into something more just. Let's build careers services that honour the full range of human experience – not in theory, but in practice. Everyone deserves to plan their future without hiding who they are.

Chapter 9
Disability in career development

Chapter roadmap

Disability is not a niche concern – it's a central equity issue. Yet across the careers sector, it remains underexplored, underrepresented, and often misunderstood. We talk about inclusion, but who are we still designing out? Who's missing when systems default to the non-disabled norm? This chapter brings disability into focus, not as an afterthought but as a lens through which to rethink practice, policy, and perception. You'll hear directly from practitioners with lived experience – whose insights challenge the status quo and demand deeper accountability. These aren't side stories. They are the story.

This chapter:

- Opens with an author's voice on why we need to name disability clearly – and why silence is never neutral;
- Defines disability through legal, medical, and social models, unpacking how language and framing shape our actions;
- Explores how ableism shows up in everyday careers practice – from inaccessible services to disclosure fears;
- Centres the lived experiences of disabled practitioners navigating the sector first-hand;
- Identifies the key barriers – structural, cultural, and systemic – that hold back true disability equity;
- Offers examples of what helps, spotlighting enablers and promising practices already happening on the ground;
- Provides a practical Practitioner Toolkit for embedding disability-inclusive approaches in everyday work;
- Lays out an Organisational Toolkit to support systems-level change – from policy to pipeline;
- Includes a reflective task using practitioners' quotes to prompt personal and team learning.

Author's voice

Disability is still treated as a specialist issue – something 'other', something we only make space for when someone discloses or when it's convenient. But disability cuts across every identity. It's visible and invisible. It's shaped by policy and culture. It's still deeply misunderstood. If we're serious about inclusion in the careers sector, we can't wait to be prompted. Access needs to be built in from the start. This chapter isn't just about compliance – it's about culture, power, and visibility. It's about not asking disabled people to do all the heavy lifting themselves.

Silence around disability isn't neutral. It never was. It protects organisational comfort while leaving disabled people to work twice as hard just to get to the starting line. Allyship isn't passive. If we're not actively challenging ableism, we're enabling it. This isn't work that can or should fall solely on those navigating disability. Those of us who are non-disabled – or temporarily able-bodied – need to step up. Not out of guilt, but because equity demands a redistribution of voice, access, and power.

Language matters. I want to be explicit: I do not use or endorse the term *'Special Educational Needs and Disabilities'*. There is nothing 'special' about needing access. There is nothing 'extra' about being included. Needs are needs. If a label must be used, let it be 'additional needs' – not to marginalise, but to name what systems must provide if they claim to be inclusive.

Disabled people do not need saving. They need equity. That starts by dismantling the culture of exceptionalism that treats their inclusion as optional, costly, or conditional. This chapter will not present disability as a heroic journey. It will not frame accessibility as a favour. What it will do is centre voices, name the gaps, and offer tools – because careers work that excludes disabled people isn't careers work. It's gatekeeping. It's time we called that what it is.

What do we mean by disability?

To me, disability means a need that society isn't currently set up to meet. It's not about someone's body or brain being broken – it's about systems being unwilling or unable to accommodate difference. When access is built in from the start, *'disability'* often disappears. But when the world is designed around an imagined 'norm', that's when disability shows up – not because of the person, but because of the environment. The way we define disability matters – definition shapes policy. Policy shapes practice. Practice shapes whether someone feels seen or sidelined the moment they walk into the room.

Under the Equality Act 2010, a person is considered disabled if they have a physical or mental impairment that has a *'substantial'* and *'long-term'* negative effect on their ability to do normal daily activities. But definitions like this, while legally useful, still frame disability as a problem within the person. That's the medical model of disability – the idea that the issue lies in the body, and that the 'solution' is fixing the individual. The social model flips that. It says: no, the problem is society. The problem is environments that don't flex. Jobs that reward sameness. Workplaces that design for one way of thinking, moving, communicating, and being. The problem is systemic, not personal. This shift – from individual deficit to structural barrier – is the starting point for equity. If we stay in the medical model, the work will always be about 'supporting' disabled people to fit in, rather than changing the structures that exclude them in the first place.

And disability isn't one thing. It's not one story, one identity, or one label. It's a spectrum: visible and invisible, temporary and lifelong, static and fluctuating. It includes physical impairments, chronic illness, mental health conditions, sensory differences, and neurodivergence. But more than that – it intersects with everything else. Disability is racialised. It's gendered. It's classed. It's shaped by how safe someone feels disclosing, and who they believe will listen if they do.

Disability isn't always visible. For those with visible disabilities – like mobility aids, facial differences, or chronic conditions that alter movement or speech – the challenge is often immediate visibility. Assumptions are made before a word is spoken. The risk is over-scrutiny, patronisation, or being treated as fragile rather than capable. People are either spoken down to or spoken about – but rarely spoken with. Invisible disabilities come with a different set of barriers. Mental health conditions, chronic pain, neurodivergence, sensory sensitivities – these don't always show up in a way the outside world can see. Which means people are constantly expected to explain, justify, or *'prove'* their need. When you don't *'look'* disabled, people assume you're fine. Or worse – they think you're making it up. You're either too visible, or not visible enough. Both can be exhausting. Both can be disempowering.

And this is where the system often fails – because it still relies on visibility to trigger support. If we can see it, we believe it. If we can't, we wait for a label. But real inclusion doesn't require a diagnosis. It requires trust, flexibility, and design that doesn't punish people for needing something different, whether someone discloses or not, whether their needs are visible or not. Our job is the same: to create a culture where support isn't conditional – and where people don't have to fight just to access what should already be theirs.

That's why language matters. As one practitioner said: *'Being mindful of different people's abilities – adjusting your practice and terminology.'* Because how we speak shapes how people are seen. Too often, the words we choose reveal the discomfort we've never dealt with. So, what do we mean by disability? We mean a mismatch between how someone functions and how the system expects them to. The answer isn't just awareness. It's redesign. Redesigning society and expectations to meet the needs of others around us.

Understanding disability in the careers sector

Let's start with the facts: over 14.6 million people in the UK are disabled – that's around 22% of the population. But you wouldn't know that by looking around most careers services. Not at the staff, not at the systems, and certainly not at the spaces we create. Career guidance is still too often designed around a fictional 'default client': someone able-bodied, neurotypical, confident, literate, and available. Anything outside of that is treated as an exception. Which means, by design, we're already excluding a significant portion of the population before they've even entered the room.

This is why the work of practitioners like Jules Benton and Chris Targett is so important. Their 2024 book, *Career Development and Inclusive Practice*, brings visibility to the systemic exclusions faced by disabled clients and offers grounded, practical strategies to reframe guidance through a genuinely inclusive lens. It doesn't just talk about disability as a policy concern – it centres it as a critical part of ethical, human careers work.

Disability doesn't show up in just one way. Some disabilities are visible, many are not. But the barriers faced aren't simply physical – they're structural, cultural, and bureaucratic. They live in our timelines, our platforms, and our assumptions. They surface when a client is expected to speak fluently in a noisy room, when they're asked to *'just fill in the form'*, or when basic adjustments are framed as discretionary favours instead of legal rights. The issue of labels runs deep. For some, a formal diagnosis can be validating and offer a pathway to support. But for others, it's a source of stigma or a battle they've had to fight through disbelief, dismissal, or a lack of access. Some will never receive a diagnosis at all – because it's too expensive, too culturally out of reach, or sits within systems that question their legitimacy – where does that leave them? In too many cases, without support.

Support plans and workplace adjustments are meant to bridge this gap, but they're only as effective as the culture that surrounds them. I've seen this up close – working in a setting where, even with a documented back injury, I wasn't given a chair that met basic ergonomic standards. Not because it wasn't possible, but because the system wasn't designed to act until damage was already done. That's not support – that's neglect wrapped in policy. While the government may offer schemes like Access to Work or the legal right, according to the 2010 Equality Act, to reasonable adjustments, the reality is often far more frustrating. Delays, administrative hurdles, and a reactive mindset make it more about shielding institutions from risk than safeguarding individuals from harm. Clients often choose not to disclose their disability – and frankly, who can blame them? Disclosure is a risk, not a guarantee. Too often, it results in increased paperwork or no action at all. Worse still, it can lead to being treated differently, judged, or even overlooked. The truth is, we haven't yet built the trust required for people to feel safe enough to be honest. If we haven't created the conditions for disclosure to lead to better outcomes, we need to ask ourselves why we keep expecting it. Practitioners, too, are often underprepared – not because they don't care, but because the training isn't there. Without that training, conversations about disability become awkward, surface-level, or skipped altogether. One practitioner put it plainly, summarising the issue as *'Misunderstandings and a skills gap'*. That gap is systemic, not personal. We have to stop placing the responsibility for filling it on individual goodwill.

Despite all of this, we continue to design services without embedding disabled voices at the centre. Not just as feedback, not as box-ticking consultation – but as co-creators, as leaders, as people whose lived knowledge should be foundational, not optional. As another practitioner said, *'It's important to integrate the voice of those with disabilities in service delivery'*. Because when those voices aren't present in the room, the services we build are not neutral – they are exclusionary by default. Disability in the careers sector doesn't need more motivational stories. It needs structural honesty. It needs us to ask, plainly and repeatedly: Who's not in the room – and what are we doing to change that?

Practitioner lived experiences

One of the most important things I've learned in this work – through research, consultancy, teaching, and simply listening – is that disability isn't the problem. The problem is the way we respond to it. Or rather, the way we don't; much of what disabled practitioners experience isn't down to their impairment. It's down to poor design, performative allyship, and systems that claim to support inclusion while actively exhausting the people they're supposed to be including.

Time and time again, practitioners shared how the careers sector often assumes it's inclusive – until someone actually needs something different. One practitioner wrote, *'Never make assumptions about the abilities or needs of others'*. But that's exactly what we do. We assume if someone hasn't disclosed, they're fine. We assume that disability always looks a certain way. We assume we'll be told if there's a problem, rather than asking what's needed from the outset. That assumption? It's not neutral. It's a barrier. Several practitioners spoke to the emotional toll of constantly navigating systems not designed with them in mind. *'Supporting clients in overcoming barriers and taking time to understand them'* sounds simple enough – but it often means working twice as hard, with half the recognition, just to make a basic level of service possible. When that labour is invisible, it goes unacknowledged. When it's acknowledged, it's often romanticised – turned into a resilience story, a sign of strength, rather than a symptom of injustice.

What struck me most was the theme of constant adjustment. One practitioner reflected on *'being mindful of different people's abilities – adjusting your practice and terminology'*, and that's it, really. That's the work. Not asking everyone to fit one mould, but shifting our own practice, our own assumptions, our own language. But this kind of reflexive work isn't always rewarded. It's emotional labour. Quiet labour. The kind that keeps everything running but rarely gets named. Others reflected on the theories we use in guidance – and whether they truly serve all clients. *'Assess own practice – when using career theories with clients, is it fit for the client's needs?'* That level of critical self-questioning is rare in day-to-day careers work, where many are pressured to use one-size-fits-all tools, timelines, and assessments. But it's crucial that not every client will thrive in a system built on linear progression, fixed goals, or verbal fluency. Let's be honest – disabled practitioners are often expected to do all the work. One quote simply read, *'Becomes agent of change'*. But at what cost? At what point do we stop expecting the people experiencing inequity to be the ones fixing it?

There's also the reality of needing to code-switch within the profession – knowing when to disclose, how to mask, which environments are *'safe'*, and which ones are going to drain your energy just getting through the door. Some practitioners shared how they've learned to overcompensate, showing up with more qualifications, more emotional intelligence, more resilience, just to be taken seriously. It's not that they're incapable – it's that they're navigating environments that make basic participation a battle. For some practitioners, disability isn't the only lens – they're also navigating racism, classism, misogyny, or all of the above. In those cases, disclosure becomes even riskier. Who is believed? Who gets accommodated without resistance? Who gets labelled as 'difficult' for asking more than the default?

Others spoke of the joy of sessions like EDI webinars – *'Engage with sessions like this :D'* – where, finally, there's permission to speak freely, to not feel like a burden for simply needing the conversation to be different. All of this tells us something we can't ignore: inclusion isn't a checklist. It's a practice. One that requires discomfort, unlearning, and active redistribution of voice and space. If disabled practitioners are constantly having to do that work alone – while navigating systems that routinely overlook them – then we need to stop calling the profession inclusive until their experience shapes how we train, recruit, support, and lead; we're just putting better language on top of the same barriers. What's missing from most strategic meetings, CPD agendas, or leadership development programmes? The lived expertise of disabled practitioners. Not as case studies. Not as inspirational speakers. But as decision-makers. Until we embed that, we're still designing systems that talk about inclusion while practising exclusion.

Barriers to inclusion

Inclusion doesn't happen just because we value it. It requires deliberate, often uncomfortable, systemic work. When it comes to disability, the barriers are almost never the bodies or minds of those navigating exclusion – they are the systems, assumptions, and silences that have been allowed to settle as norms. The careers sector is no exception. Too much of its infrastructure – its platforms, procedures, and service delivery models – has been built around a presumed default. That default assumes people can hear, speak, read, move, and process information in one standardised way. Anyone who doesn't fit that mould is viewed as a 'challenge', when in reality, it's the mould that's broken. Accessibility is still positioned as an add-on, something 'accommodated' rather than embedded. Making career appointments accessible shouldn't be revolutionary – it should be routine. Accessibility itself isn't just physical. It's also cultural, emotional, and linguistic. It's about whether disabled people feel safe enough to disclose without fear of being pathologised, whether access needs are acknowledged without delay or excessive paperwork, and whether there is confidence – not just intent – among professionals to meet those needs with care and competence. Yet, this is still not our default.

One of the most frequently raised concerns is the training gap. Many practitioners have shared that they feel underprepared to work confidently with disabled clients. That isn't a reflection of individual shortcomings – it is a systemic failure. *'Misunderstandings and a skills gap.'* That quote encapsulates the problem. As long as disability remains absent from mainstream CPD and initial training frameworks, it will continue to be treated as a niche concern – something to respond to reactively rather than proactively building it into our foundational approach. Beyond the gap lies fear. Fear of saying the wrong thing, fear of offending, fear of getting it wrong. But fear silences action. It allows inaccessible systems to persist unchallenged. But there's another gap we need to name – one that often gets overlooked entirely.

Some disabled practitioners physically *can't* attend in-person training or conferences. Chronic illness, pain, or the inaccessibility of travel and venues means that entire swathes of the profession are excluded by design. It's not that they aren't interested – it's that the spaces themselves haven't been built to include them. Will Donald speaks powerfully about this – how the assumption that *'being present'* always means *'being in the room'* erases those whose presence is already stretched thin by navigating inaccessible systems daily. It's a vital reminder: inclusion isn't just about inviting people in – it's about changing the room. Making space isn't enough if people can't reach it in the first place.

Beyond the gap lies fear. Fear of saying the wrong thing, fear of offending, fear of getting it wrong. But fear silences action. It allows inaccessible systems to persist unchallenged. If we are serious about equity, then we must challenge not just who is in the room – but *who the room is built for*. I remember walking with a disabled woman across a university campus during a training day. The building we were in had no lift access between levels, so in order to travel one floor up, she had to take a long, winding route around the outside of the building, then through a service entrance at the back. It was cold, the ground was uneven, and it took us over fifteen minutes. She turned to me and said quietly, *'This is always the case'*. Not just that day – *every* day. Every campus, every event, every time. And the worst part is that nobody notices. Because unless you're the one taking the detour, the route looks accessible enough. That's the illusion of inclusion – when access is technically possible, but structurally exhausting.

There is also an administrative burden that consistently falls on disabled clients and staff. Self-advocacy becomes a full-time job. It's the repetition of forms, the lengthy waits, the fragmented responses, and the constant emotional labour of having to prove and re-prove one's need for something others are handed without question. Bureaucracy becomes a barrier in itself – and it erodes trust, energy, and wellbeing over time. Leadership isn't immune to these failures either. Disabled professionals remain significantly underrepresented at senior levels across the careers landscape. That absence is telling. It sends a message – spoken or unspoken – that disabled people are welcome to contribute, but not to lead. That isn't inclusion. That's tokenism. As one practitioner reflected, *'Role models are needed'*. But these can't just be symbolic. They need to be people with power to shape the structure, not just endure it.

The disparities are more than symbolic – they're material. There remains a substantial wage gap affecting disabled people in the sector (a *'Huge wage gap for the disability group'*, as one respondent put it). That's not just about earnings – it's about investment. About who is seen as worth promoting, developing, and retaining. When adjustments are viewed as impediments to productivity rather than fundamental rights, disabled professionals are too often passed over, written off, or quietly excluded. Cultural inclusion is still lagging:

'Lack of cultural competency.'

'Open conversation with stakeholders.'

These are more than observations – they are indictments. When inclusion is dependent on individual goodwill rather than embedded in organisational systems, it becomes inconsistent at best – and dangerous at worst. Table 15 highlights key structural and cultural barriers shared by practitioners. But it is not exhaustive; if organisations aren't regularly engaging disabled staff and clients in open, meaningful conversations about what isn't working, then they're simply not seeing the full picture.

Table 15 Barriers and implications

Barrier	Quote	Implication
Assumptions about ability	'Never make assumptions about the abilities or needs of others.'	Reinforces bias and invisibility
Inaccessible systems and services	'Making career appointments accessible . . .'	Excludes people from engaging with services
Lack of representation	'Role models are needed.'	Reinforces the idea that disability means limitation
Limited understanding or training	'Misunderstandings and a skills gap.'	Equity depends on individual goodwill, not systems
Lack of cultural inclusion	'Lack of cultural competency.'	Intersectional needs are overlooked or misunderstood

Enablers

Naming the barriers is only half the work. The other half is showing what change actually looks like – without dressing it in hollow policy jargon or pretending it's simple. Inclusion isn't about nice words or goodwill. It's about infrastructure. It's about culture. It's about mindset. Above all, it's about the willingness to shift power. Practitioners made it clear: we don't need more pledges sitting on websites or performative diversity statements. What we need is action that dismantles exclusion from the inside out – actions that are embedded, lived, and sustained. Let's start with training – but not the kind that ticks a CPD box and leaves attitudes untouched. Not a basic 'Disability 101' that runs through adjustments in theory but ignores the complexity of real-world need. We need meaningful, ongoing development that challenges internalised bias, unpacks deeply held assumptions, and helps professionals feel confident engaging with difference rather than afraid of it. *'It is important to provide training and education to colleagues on disability-related issues.'* That was the call – and rightly so; you cannot support what you do not understand. You cannot understand what you are too afraid to talk about.

But awareness alone doesn't create equity. It has to be backed by structure. *'Being familiar with equality law and terms'* is the foundation – but it cannot end there. If policies exist but are never implemented, they are meaningless. If schemes like Access to Work technically exist but are labyrinthine to navigate, then the system is still failing. If someone is forced to 'prove' they deserve adjustments every time, then equity isn't what we've built – we've built barriers dressed up as processes. What actually works? Representation. Not tokenistic, not decorative, but structural. Representation in leadership, in governance, in the places where decisions are made. It's not about pointing to the 'one' and saying, *'Look, we have one'*. It's about asking why more haven't made it – and what we're going to do about that. *'Diversifying the workforce is a must'* wasn't just a practitioner's observation – it was a challenge; if our staff don't reflect our clients, our assumptions – and our delivery – are already off course.

And language matters. Not just the words we say but how we say them. *'Allies – using appropriate language and terminology to provide appropriate support.'* This isn't about being overly cautious or politically correct for the sake of it. It's about creating spaces where people feel safe. Language is one of the first signals of whether someone belongs or whether they'll need to mask, shrink, or walk away. Inclusive language helps people choose to disclose. Exclusionary language makes them choose to leave. Then there's culture. *'Create an inclusive culture.'* That's not a line for a poster – it's the daily work. It's what happens when someone says something ableist in a meeting and it doesn't slide. It's about not defaulting to disabled staff as the 'educator' every time access needs come up. It's about refusing to be silent when we know systems are actively harming the very people they claim to support. Practical access needs to be non-negotiable. Whether it's offering accessible appointment formats, understanding tactile British Sign Language (BSL), or simply knowing which tools exist for clients with visual disabilities – like screen readers – this shouldn't be exceptional knowledge. If these resources exist but aren't used, or practitioners don't know how or when to offer them, then we've missed the point. We've identified the gaps – so now, what does better actually look like?

The most powerful answer came from one practitioner who said: *'Important to integrate the voice of those with disabilities in service delivery.'* Not feedback. Not permission. Integration. That's the real benchmark; if disabled people aren't shaping the system, then the system was never built with them in mind – it was built to manage them. This isn't about additional effort. It's about better effort. Smarter effort. More human effort. The kind of effort that doesn't ask someone to fight for inclusion, because that space has already been created – for them, with them, and by them.

Practitioner toolkit: Disability-inclusive practice

If you're reading this and wondering what practical steps you can take – good. That's the whole point. Equity doesn't begin with perfection; it begins with accountability. With the willingness to unlearn, rethink, and shift practice. This isn't a checklist to tick through and move on. It's a mindset shift. A recalibration of how we show up for disabled clients and colleagues – not just once, but consistently.

Start here: assume nothing. Don't assume a client will disclose. Don't assume a colleague feels safe enough to ask for adjustments. Don't assume your default way of working is accessible, just because it's familiar. *'Being mindful of different people's abilities – adjusting your practice and terminology'*, as one practitioner put it, is the beginning. But awareness isn't enough. Good intentions don't translate into inclusion without action.

So pause, and ask yourself honestly: What assumptions do I hold about disability and professionalism? Am I expecting clients to 'fit in' to my style, or am I prepared to flex and meet them where they are? Have I ever avoided conversations about access out of fear of saying the wrong thing? Do I know how to use inclusive formats or assistive technologies? When was the last time I updated my approach based on something I've learned from a disabled person's lived experience?

There are actions you can take now. Start by letting go of the need for proof. If someone says they're struggling, that's enough. Ask every client proactively: *'Is there anything I can do to make this session more accessible for you?'* Offer materials in multiple formats – large print, audio, Easy Read, colour-contrasted, digital. Don't wait for someone to ask for a break – build it in as standard. Get familiar with tools like screen readers, captioning software, and dyslexia-friendly fonts. When using career theory or models, question whether they serve your client – or just your structure.

And if you're still not sure what to do? Ask. With humility. *'I want to make sure this works for you – what would help?'* That one sentence can be the difference between discomfort and trust. It's not about getting it all right – it's about building relationships where people don't have to mask or minimise their needs.

Inclusion in action looks like this: an organisation I worked with redesigned their recruitment process with accessibility as the foundation – not an afterthought. They reviewed job descriptions for ableist language, allowed video or audio applications, and shared interview questions in advance. Every candidate was asked what adjustments they needed at every stage. The result? Not only did they get more disabled applicants – but they also got better ones as the process was human-centred. Another organisation reimagined their entire performance review process. Instead of rigid tick-box forms, they introduced reflective conversations led by the employee. They asked: What are your strengths? What barriers are we missing? What do you need to thrive? The review became a space for growth, not pressure. Yes, it took more time – but it worked.

Inclusion isn't about certainty or control. It's about creating space for the unexpected answer – for different ways of being, communicating, working. *'Reflexive practice'* isn't about sitting with theory. It's about acting differently because of what we've reflected on. Build that rhythm into your practice. Reflect. Act. Repeat. You won't get it perfect. But you do have to stop pretending inclusion is someone else's responsibility; if not you – then who?

Organisational toolkit: Structural change

You can have the most well-meaning practitioners in the world, but if the organisation they work for isn't structurally accessible, all that intent just sits there – unused, frustrated, and eventually burned out. Disability equity doesn't come from one 'inclusion lead' or a single CPD session. It comes from a culture where systems are designed to flex, where access is routine, and where disabled clients and staff don't have to work twice as hard just to exist. Organisations need to stop asking, *'What do we do if someone discloses?'* and start asking, *'Why do we still need people to disclose in order for them to be supported?'*

Start by auditing the default. Review your entire service journey – from first contact to final outcome. Where is inaccessibility baked into the process? Where are you unconsciously assuming literacy, energy, vision, speech, or time? Don't just rely on theory – ask disabled clients and staff directly. Where are the drop-off points? What have they learned to work around, and what have they quietly given up on? Every assumption you surface is an opportunity to redesign.

Next, embed disability into every policy – not just the ones labelled *'health and safety'* or *'wellbeing'*. If a policy governs access, behaviour, or performance, then it is a disability policy. Don't wait for a complaint to take action. Accessibility isn't a bolt-on – it's a baseline; treat it that way. Stop siloing disability and start treating it as a leadership, strategy, and design issue. Make access routine. Provide captions on all videos. Offer BSL if requested. Ensure your PDFs are screen reader-friendly as standard, not as an afterthought. Look at your recruitment process – do people have to ask for adjustments, or are they proactively offered? Think about your physical environments too – are they sensory-friendly, trauma-informed, and genuinely navigable?

Redesign what performance and progression mean in your context. Revisit your definitions of 'professionalism'. Are you rewarding speed over clarity, output over process? Have you conflated confidence with ability or resilience with silence? These are not just abstract concepts – they are real barriers. If disabled staff aren't progressing, it's not because they lack talent. It's because the system isn't built to recognise or nurture it.

Representation, too, is non-negotiable. *'Role models are needed'* – not only at the front line but in the rooms where decisions are made. Representation isn't just about who's visible in your brochure – it's about who's heard, who's believed, and who gets to shape the future. Build advisory groups. Pay disabled consultants. Don't just invite feedback – act on it. Make sure the voices you're claiming to amplify are actually being listened to.

And be transparent about the gaps. Publish your disability pay gap. Track who's applying, who's getting hired, who's progressing, and who's leaving – and why. Report not just on the policies you've written but on the adjustments you've actually made. Create accountability loops that reach beyond HR and into every team, every level of leadership. Equity isn't a buzzword. It's an audit trail. It's data. It's power. It's design. If your systems aren't working for disabled people, then they're not working. If that feels uncomfortable – good. Sit with that. Then do something about it.

Thinking grid: Audit your practice

This isn't just a reflective grid – it's a necessary pause. A space to step back and ask: Who is this really working for? If disabled clients and colleagues are still having to work harder just to access the basics, then something's off. Auditing your practice isn't about ticking boxes – it's about catching what you've normalised, questioning what's been left unchallenged, and making space for equity by design. Use Table 16, overleaf, not just to reflect but to shift something. If inclusion isn't built in from the start, it's already broken.

Table 16 Thinking grid: Audit your practice

Category	Current reality	What needs to shift?	First step	Map your own organisation here
Leadership	Who's at the table? Who's shaping strategy?	Disabled people are rarely in visible or decision-making roles.	Map your current leadership demographics. Set a target.	
CPD	What training is offered – and who delivers it?	Disability training is often one-off, surface-level, or optional.	Invest in practitioner-led, scenario-based CPD.	
Recruitment	How accessible is your process from start to finish?	Candidates often have to request adjustments reactively.	Build access into every stage. Offer adjustments up front.	
Perception	How is disability spoken about (or not) in your setting?	Seen as medical, individualised, or avoided altogether.	Start a conversation. Make it visible in staff discussions.	
Pay/ progression	Are disabled staff progressing?	Wage gaps persist. Leadership progression is rare.	Audit internal data. Identify and remove progression barriers.	
Culture	How do people talk, joke, and lead?	Avoidance, fear, or fragility around disability remains common.	Build inclusion into supervision, not just training.	
Client work	Who is the *'default'* client your service is designed for?	Neurotypical, verbal, literate, non-disabled assumptions prevail.	Redesign materials, language, and timelines. Ask, don't assume.	

Reflective task: Unpacking disability quotes

This section isn't just a reading exercise – it's designed to help you reflect on your own practice. A slow-down. A challenge. Each quote below was shared by a real practitioner navigating real barriers in real time. These are not soundbites. They are truths. They cut through the noise.

Take your time with them. Don't rush. Don't skip ahead. Read each quote. Sit with it. Then answer the prompts – honestly, quietly, without performative reflection. No one's collecting your answers. But your practice will either shift because of them, or it won't.

'Role models are needed.'

Who do clients see when they engage with your service? Who do new professionals see when they enter the field? Who's missing from the leadership table, and why?

- What message does our current workforce send about who belongs?
- In my setting, are we showing up as representation or tokenism?
- What can I do to ensure this gap isn't sustained under my watch?

'Never make assumptions about the abilities or needs of others.'

But we do. Constantly. Often without realising it. We assume access, understanding, literacy, and emotional bandwidth. We make those assumptions because they've always been the default.

- Where in my current practice do I assume ability?
- What could I ask differently, offer up front, or design more openly?
- Who might be excluded by the *'way we've always done things'*?

'Important to integrate voice of those with disabilities in service delivery.'

Not consult. Integrate. Design with, not for. Deliver with, not to.

- Where are disabled voices shaping – not just feeding back on – what we do?
- Who do we call on to speak, teach, advise . . . and do we pay them?
- What would meaningful integration look like in my context?

'Lack of cultural competency.'

Disability doesn't show up in isolation. It intersects with race, religion, class, migration, and more. If we're only offering one-size-fits-all support, we're not supporting – we're erasing.

- Where might our well-intentioned support be missing the mark culturally?
- What do I need to learn about how disability is expressed across different communities?
- Whose ways of being are silently excluded from our *'standard'* models?

'Misunderstandings and a skills gap.'

No shame in not knowing – unless we stay there. This is an invitation to do better, not a condemnation.

- What am I still uncomfortable talking about when it comes to disability?
- What training have I had – and what training do I need?
- How can I build confidence without waiting for someone else to push it?

This isn't about being *'woke'*. It's about being ready. To unlearn. To adapt. To stop designing services around what's easiest and start designing them around what's equitable. Someone else's access shouldn't depend on your awareness. It should depend on the structure already in place.

You've made it this far – you've read the chapter, listened to the voices, named the barriers, explored the tools, and mapped your own practice. But if it stays on the page, it doesn't count. Equity doesn't show up by accident, and inclusion doesn't grow just because we care. It takes structure. Intention. Discomfort. The willingness to redesign what's familiar and to move even when the system stays still. This isn't the end of the neurodiversity conversation – it's a beginning. If disability has taught us anything, it's that 'neutrality' is often just exclusion with better branding. Ask yourself: What will I stop excusing? What will I start building? And who will I bring with me? You don't have to do everything at once. But you do need to begin. Without structure, equity is just a slogan – and without inclusion, careers work becomes just another gatekeeper.

Chapter 10
Neurodiversity in career development

Chapter roadmap

This chapter challenges the idea that equity can be achieved without redesigning the systems that erase difference. Neurodivergent practitioners and clients are navigating careers spaces that weren't built with them in mind. This isn't a call for *'awareness'* – it's a call to rebuild. You'll find lived experience, structural critique, and tools to support meaningful change.

This chapter:

- Explores why neurodiversity matters in careers work – and why neurodivergent inclusion isn't a niche concern – it's foundational to ethical, effective practice;
- Defines neurodiversity and dismantles ableist assumptions – by uncovering how dominant norms and language fuel exclusion;
- Examines neurodivergence in careers guidance – to expose misalignments and why many clients and practitioners feel unseen;
- Shares practitioner perspectives – on burnout, masking, and the lack of meaningful support for neurodivergent professionals;
- Centres client experiences – of navigating careers support with dignity and dissonance, and how reframing potential can shift the journey;
- Identifies barriers to inclusion – including systemic, cultural, and practice-based challenges that are too often left unspoken;
- Highlights enablers of inclusion – showing how inclusive models and even small shifts can create a lasting impact;
- Offers tools for neurodivergent-friendly practice – which are practical, adaptable, and grounded in real situations – not just theory;
- Includes an organisational audit tool – to support deep reflection on how services centre (or exclude) neurodivergent clients and staff;

- Presents a reflective quote section – titled *'Unpacking Assumptions'* to challenge thinking and prompt honest introspection;
- Closes with a call for systems change – not people change – urging us to stop asking neurodivergent people to adapt and start adapting the structures around them.

Author's voice

We talk a lot about inclusion in the careers sector – but too often, it stops short of challenging the deep structures that privilege neurotypical ways of thinking, working, and performing.. The pressure to conform to unwritten rules of eye contact, tone, pace, and even body language is relentless. Neurodivergent clients and practitioners alike are left adapting, masking, or burning out – not because they aren't capable, but because the systems weren't built with them in mind. This chapter hits home in a deeply personal way. I was diagnosed with ADHD while already well into my academic and professional journey – right at the start of my PhD. Up until that point, I had lived with the highs and lows of a brain that could hyperfocus for ten hours straight and then suddenly shut down with no warning. I had always sensed that I experienced time, urgency, and motivation differently – but it took that diagnosis to finally make sense of why I worked the way I did. Why I could have bursts of extreme productivity followed by deep inertia. Why deadlines were both lifelines and landmines. Knowing I had ADHD didn't change who I was – it explained it. It validated all the ways I had previously blamed myself for not fitting a neurotypical mould. But the real issue wasn't my brain. It was the systems and environments I had been asked to navigate without a map.

Although the workshops didn't explicitly explore neurodiversity due to time constraints, it was clear from the conversations that this absence needed addressing. Neurodivergent voices – practitioners, clients, colleagues – were present throughout, even if not always named. That gap wasn't just about time. It was a reflection of the wider systemic oversight that continues to silence or sideline difference; this chapter is a necessary corrective. It creates space for the perspectives that too often go unheard, misunderstood, or labelled as *'difficult'* or *'unprofessional'*.

I needed this chapter to exist because neurodiversity is still framed through a deficit lens in many careers settings. Our sector claims to be person-centred, but how person-centred are we really if we dismiss or unintentionally stigmatise difference whenever it challenges our expectations? This isn't about making small adjustments for a few clients with specific conditions. It's about fundamentally rethinking how we define communication, competence, and professionalism. If we're serious about equity, then inviting neurodivergent people into the room isn't enough – we have to reshape the room itself.

This chapter is about that shift. A shift towards curiosity, towards humility, and towards practice that doesn't just accommodate neurodivergence but genuinely values it.

What do we mean by neurodiversity?

Neurodiversity is a term that challenges the idea that there's one *'normal'* way for a brain to work. It describes the natural variation in human cognitive functioning – how we think, learn, process information, communicate, and experience the world. The neurodiversity paradigm stands in contrast to the medical model, which tends to view conditions like autism, ADHD, and dyslexia as deficits to be treated or corrected. Instead, the neurodiversity movement reframes these differences as part of human diversity – not deviations from it, and certainly not flaws.

Common neurotypes include autism, ADHD, dyslexia, dyspraxia, dyscalculia, Tourette's syndrome, sensory processing differences, OCD, and some anxiety-related profiles. Each neurotype brings its own unique patterns of perception, strengths, and challenges. But this isn't about putting people into boxes. As one practitioner put it: *'I'm not broken – I'm wired differently.'* That line stays with me. It captures something many of us have spent a lifetime trying to explain: the problem isn't the way we think – it's the way we're treated for thinking differently.

Neurodiversity isn't about labels. It's about rights. It's about dignity. It's about acknowledging how society disables people by refusing to accommodate different ways of being. That refusal shows up all the time in careers guidance, where expectations around productivity, attention, and communication are still shaped around neurotypical norms. Even when people try to be inclusive, it can slip into the superficial. Another voice said it best: *'Don't call it a superpower if you won't change the system.'* Celebrating our strengths means little if the environments we work in still burn us out.

From a legal standpoint, many neurodivergent conditions are recognised under the Equality Act 2010. This legislation protects individuals from discrimination, harassment, and victimisation on the basis of protected characteristics, including disability. A person is considered disabled under the Act if they have a physical or mental impairment that has a substantial and long-term adverse effect on their ability to carry out normal day-to-day activities. Many neurodivergent people fall within this scope – even if their conditions aren't always visible or formally diagnosed.

But let's be honest: the law isn't enough. The Act doesn't name *'neurodivergence'* as a standalone category, and that silence says a lot. The Act would apply to those whose neurological presentation deviates from the norm. Legal protections might exist on paper, but cultural understanding and day-to-day practice often lag behind. That gap between law and lived experience is exactly where exclusion and discrimination hide; as practitioners, it's not enough to just be legally compliant. We have to be culturally competent too.

Understanding the realities of neurodivergence – and designing services that honour those realities – is part of our responsibility. Inclusion isn't passive. It has to be active, informed, and intentional. Dismantling ableist assumptions starts by naming them. It means interrogating the quiet norms that shape who is seen as professional, capable, or employable. That work doesn't just sit in other people's practice – it starts in our own frameworks, our language, and our habits. When we default to one way of planning, presenting, or communicating, we reinforce the idea that anything else is wrong. But neurodivergence doesn't need fixing. What needs fixing are the systems that punish people for being different. Dismantling ableism means listening differently, designing differently, and believing people when they tell you what they need. Until we stop treating *'normal'* as neutral, we'll keep building services that exclude by default.

Neurodivergence in careers guidance

Careers guidance, as it currently operates, often isn't hostile to neurodivergence – it's indifferent. That indifference can be just as excluding. The systems, assumptions, and practices that shape our profession tend to reward certain traits: verbal fluency, forward planning, goal orientation, reflective clarity, and emotional regulation. But these are not neutral indicators of readiness or potential. They are deeply rooted in neurotypical expectations of what a *'prepared'* client or a *'competent'* practitioner looks like. This creates a fundamental misalignment between the structures of guidance and the realities of many neurodivergent clients. A client with ADHD might struggle to articulate long-term goals or remember to follow up on agreed actions – not because they lack ambition or motivation, but because executive function challenges are part of their everyday life. An autistic client might offer precise, factual answers without embellishment or eye contact – but instead of being seen as focused or honest, they are too often perceived as disengaged or disinterested. As one participant put it: *'The recruitment process has so many hoops to jump through . . . ATS, CVs, interviews . . . they may not come across well in a screening stage or be phased by the complexities of it.'*

Even the core tools of the careers profession – career action plans, psychometric tests, personal statements, CV reviews – are rarely designed with neurodivergent processing in mind. They demand a level of cognitive organisation, self-translation, and often literal masking that places neurodivergent clients at a disadvantage from the start. Yet, when those clients *'don't engage'* or *'drop off'*, we're more likely to label them hard to reach than to question the reach itself. *'I get overwhelmed by too much info in one go'*, one practitioner noted – yet we continue to deliver support in dense formats, fast-paced group sessions, or written-heavy communications with little reflection on access needs.

This isn't just about tools. It's also about presence – or the lack of it. Neurodivergent practitioners are still underrepresented, under-supported, and in many cases, invisible in our professional spaces. Their ways of working may be misunderstood, their disclosure met with discomfort or awkwardness, and their needs dismissed as personal rather than structural. One quote from the Padlet cuts to the core: *'I spent more energy appearing "fine" than actually doing the job.'* That sentence alone says everything about the emotional labour that comes with being neurodivergent in a system that sees difference as disruption. It doesn't help when those tasked with supporting others haven't received support themselves. *'As career advisers we don't have training in disability. It can quickly go away from employability topics to medical/support that is outside the scope of our work.'* This lack of training leaves practitioners unsure, hesitant, and at times complicit in systems that exclude. *'Training and access to service users with disabilities is lacking. CPD and ongoing updates are needed. Who gives that training?'* These aren't rhetorical questions – they're urgent gaps.

Neurodivergence is not a barrier to careers guidance. But the current model of careers guidance can be a barrier to neurodivergent people. Until we redesign our approach with flexibility, trauma-informed understanding, and cognitive accessibility at its heart, we will continue to exclude the very people we claim to serve. As one quote reminds us, *'People need to understand the impact of disabilities on the ability to maintain work – not just get into it'*. The same can be said of guidance – it's not just about access; it's about sustainability. It's not enough to make room. We need to redesign the room entirely.

Practitioner lived experience

Across the Padlet responses, one theme echoed again and again – the emotional and cognitive toll of working in systems that do not accommodate neurodivergence. Practitioners described not only what was missing in terms of support but also what was actively harmful. I know I've already quoted this line earlier, but it bears repeating – because the weight of it doesn't lessen with familiarity: *'I spent more energy appearing "fine" than actually doing the job.'* That line cut through everything. It spoke to the quiet burden of masking, of compensating, of having to self-regulate in spaces that failed to meet basic accessibility needs. It's repeated here not by accident, but by design – because that is the reality for many neurodivergent practitioners: living in loops, experiencing the same barriers across contexts, with little meaningful change in sight. When a single quote keeps surfacing, it's usually because it says what so many are thinking but haven't had the space to name out loud. That's the power of lived experience – not in how many times it's said, but in the truth it holds every time it's repeated.

Masking was a recurring pressure, described by several practitioners who reflected on how much energy was spent hiding traits or overcorrecting behaviour to appear *'professional'*. This invisible labour is rarely accounted for in workload models, supervision, or line management. It is assumed, absorbed, and rarely spoken about. One person described *'burnout cycles every few months'* directly linked to the lack of understanding or flexibility in their working environment.

Training gaps were another repeated issue. *'As career advisers, we don't have training in disability'*, one respondent admitted. *'It can quickly go away from employability topics to medical/support that is outside the scope of our work.'* This recognition was paired with frustration. The lack of training not only affected practitioner confidence, but it also left neurodivergent clients vulnerable to inconsistent support. One person asked plainly, *'Who gives that training?'* – a question that remains unanswered in many organisations.

There were also reflections on how neurodivergence intersects with expectations around performance and leadership. *'I'm seen as unreliable if I need different timelines or structures'*, someone shared. Another said, *'Leadership still looks like loud, fast, polished. I'm none of those, so I get overlooked'*. These insights highlight the cost of equating extroversion and speed with competence, and how these assumptions continue to shape progression routes across the sector.

Several practitioners also flagged the problem with disclosure. For some, the risk felt too high. *'I can't tell my manager – they wouldn't get it. I'd rather just struggle than be labelled.'* For others, even when disclosure occurred, the response was underwhelming. *'I told HR I had ADHD – they said I seemed fine, so it wasn't noted.'* These experiences reflect the structural nature of the issue – the system requires disclosure in order to offer support but punishes people for disclosing in subtle and overt ways.

Practitioners also emphasised the importance of role modelling and community. *'Seeing someone like me in this field would've made such a difference.'* There was a hunger for visibility, for validation, for spaces where neurodivergent ways of working were not just tolerated but valued. It was not about asking for sympathy – it was about wanting to show up to work without hiding, without fear, and without having to shrink to fit someone else's idea of what 'professional' looks like.

Client perspectives

When careers guidance is described as 'client-centred', it's worth asking: which clients, and whose centre? While that approach may serve some well, it can inadvertently sideline others – especially neurodivergent clients – when the structures, tools, and expectations aren't built with them in mind. Several practitioners have shared how standard practice can feel overwhelming, inaccessible, or misaligned with their ways of processing.

Take, for example, a typical session structure: open-ended questions, psychometric tools, and follow-up emails full of jargon and linear action plans. For some, that's manageable. But for others – especially those navigating sensory sensitivities, executive dysfunction, or social anxiety – it can be an exercise in overload. As one practitioner shared: *'I get overwhelmed by too much info in one go.'* It's not that the guidance is intentionally exclusionary – but when it's designed around assumed norms of communication and cognition, accessibility becomes an afterthought. In those cases, the idea of *'informed choice'* risks becoming more symbolic than real – not because the intent is lacking, but because the format itself hasn't been questioned. It's worth pausing and asking: *What assumptions might I be making about how clients receive and process information?* If we want guidance to be genuinely client-centred, we have to be willing to expand our definition of the centre – and rebuild professional practices around it.

Clients who don't align with expected norms – such as making small talk, sustaining eye contact, or setting neat, linear goals – are too often interpreted as disengaged or *'not ready'*. But these interpretations reflect the frameworks in place more than the clients themselves. As one person explained, *'I can't do small talk – that doesn't mean I'm not engaged.'* Communication differences are frequently misread as disinterest, leading to breakdowns in rapport, missed opportunities, and misunderstandings that place the burden of adjustment on the client rather than the service.

The recruitment process adds further layers of exclusion. Clients are encouraged to navigate a landscape filled with application tracking systems, CV screenings, and interviews – none of which are typically designed with neurodivergence in mind. As one person observed, *'The recruitment process has so many hoops to jump through . . . ATS, CVs, interviews . . . they may not come across well in a screening stage or be phased by the complexities of it'*. Another described the additional barriers: *'Not confident asking for reasonable adjustments or can't find contact details for recruitment-related queries.'* These systems continue to reward fluency in normative behaviour, often valuing presentation over potential and conformity over capability.

Education, too, plays a role in entrenching exclusion. It is often the site where neurodivergent learners first encounter the message that they are 'less than'. As one quote pointed out, *'The education system was created for a particular type of learner/achiever. There are many who do not fit into the education system and struggle through it.'* By the time neurodivergent young people encounter careers services, their confidence may already be eroded by years of being misunderstood or unsupported. For those outside traditional pathways, the options can be extremely limited: *'Limited opportunities for young people not able to get GCSEs even if capable in those areas (e.g. media) – the education system fails them as there may belimited non-GCSE based pathways.'* This narrowing of options begins early and compounds over time.

Many clients internalise this exclusion. They begin to believe they are the problem – that their thinking, communication, or pacing is incompatible with success. But neurodivergence itself is not the barrier. It's the rigidity of systems that refuse to accommodate it. As one person stated: *'People need to understand the impact of disabilities on the ability to maintain work – not just get into it.'* This distinction is crucial. Inclusion must be ongoing, not one-off.

There is a need to rethink what is meant by 'readiness'. It should not be defined by how well someone mimics professional norms or delivers a polished CV. Readiness should reflect whether a client has been met with respect, flexibility, and belief in their potential. Neurodivergent individuals don't need to be changed to access careers support – they need the support to change.

Barriers

Despite good intentions, many aspects of career development practice continue to exclude neurodivergent clients and professionals – not through overt prejudice, but through the quiet enforcement of unspoken norms, inaccessible processes, and unquestioned assumptions. These barriers are rarely dramatic. They are often subtle, systemic, and cumulative. Yet their impact is deeply felt. The profession still upholds a particular model of what *'professionalism'* looks and sounds like. Behaviours such as small talk, eye contact, and polished articulation are often treated as indicators of readiness or engagement. But these expectations are deeply neurotypical. One practitioner shared, *'I failed the mock interview for being "too blunt"'.* Their honesty – direct and unfiltered – was penalised because it did not conform to the expected emotional tone. Another reflected, *'I can't do small talk – that doesn't mean I'm not engaged'.* This misreading of authenticity as rudeness, or clarity as disinterest, reveals a wider issue: that neurodivergent communication styles are too often pathologised instead of understood.

The issue extends to the very resources and materials we use. Many are text-heavy, jargon-laden, or delivered in cognitively overwhelming formats. One practitioner explained, *'I get overwhelmed by too much info in one go'*, while another noted, *'It's important to have information in multiple formats – videos, bullet points, visuals, not just long paragraphs of text'*. These statements speak to a reality that many careers resources still presume uniform literacy, stamina, and processing ability. For those with executive functioning differences or sensory sensitivities, this assumption becomes exclusionary. The pace and format of delivery – especially in group settings or written-heavy interactions – often leave clients behind before they have even had a chance to begin.

The internal burden of masking remains one of the most invisible yet exhausting aspects of navigating professional environments. A practitioner shared, *'I spent more energy appearing "fine" than actually doing the job'*. Another reflected, *'I'm exhausted before I even start work.'* These are not just passing comments – they reveal how emotional labour becomes a full-time task, especially in spaces that do not acknowledge neurodivergent traits as valid or normal. The effort to 'pass' as neurotypical drains the energy that could otherwise be used for creativity, innovation, or meaningful engagement. When this becomes the unspoken price of employment or acceptance, it is no wonder that disclosure rates remain low, and burnout remains high.

The lack of training and confidence across the sector continues to widen the gap between intention and impact. Several practitioners echoed a similar concern: that they had received little to no formal training in disability and often felt underprepared to support clients whose needs extended beyond narrowly defined 'employability' concerns. For some, there was anxiety about crossing into areas perceived as medical or outside their remit; for others, a sense of frustration that the systems around them offered no clear routes to upskill. The message was consistent: there is a training void, and it's leaving practitioners hesitant to engage in conversations they fear they're not qualified to have. But that hesitation – though entirely understandable – can be experienced as dismissal. One comment captured this tension succinctly: *'Who gives that training?'* The rhetorical weight of that question lingers. It points not just to a lack of provision but to a broader absence of structural commitment to inclusive, informed practice.

Wider structural barriers persist across systems. Recruitment processes still centre neurotypical standards of presentation and performance. This is where exclusion happens quietly – in the details, in the assumed familiarity with systems, in the absence of visible flexibility. Even once in work, the barriers remain. One practitioner commented, *'The impact of having to work to targets – it affects wellbeing'*. High-pressure environments, rigid expectations, and one-size-fits-all policies leave neurodivergent professionals constantly adapting or opting out. The space to thrive rarely exists. When disclosure is linked with risk – risk of being misunderstood, sidelined, or seen as a problem – it becomes safer to remain silent. As one voice captured, *'Disclosure implies disability is a dirty little secret'*.

None of these barriers exist in isolation. They are cultural, professional, and institutional. They shape who feels welcome, who is seen as capable, and who is allowed to belong without apology. Neurodivergent clients and practitioners are not struggling because they are unfit for the work. They are struggling because the environments have not been designed with them in mind. Until we shift our frameworks, review our tools, and challenge our assumptions, careers guidance will continue to fall short of true inclusion. The sector does not need more performative statements. It needs structural change, cultural humility, and honest conversations about where the real work begins.

Enablers

If barriers block access, enablers are what open the door – quietly, consistently, or through deliberate redesign. They are not grand gestures, but everyday acts rooted in empathy, adjustments grounded in equity, and practices born from listening. When implemented thoughtfully, they do not just support neurodivergent people – they make the entire environment more inclusive, more flexible, and more human. Several practitioners emphasised that inclusion does not need to be complicated or expensive. One shared, *'Training employers that reasonable adjustments don't necessarily mean costly equipment or large-scale changes – but minimal, cost-free changes that benefit everybody'*. This captures the essence of universal design: creating systems with difference in mind from the start, rather than retrofitting inclusion after exclusion has already occurred. By embedding flexibility at the foundation, the need for case-by-case exceptions begins to fade.

Ordinariness came through as a quiet revolution. One practitioner remarked, *'Normalising disability in the workplace. Not token disabled people – but everyday activities where reasonable adjustments are seen and accepted without question.'* It is this shift from exception to expectation that enables true belonging. Inclusion becomes less about accommodating 'others' and more about removing the idea that there is only one right way to be. Genuine inclusion is not performance – it is culture. For some, that culture must be backed by knowledge. Calls for consistent professional development were strong: *'Bitesize refresher training and CPD on specific topics – as there is so much to learn and take in.'* Inclusion is not a single-day induction session. It is a long-term learning process, one that requires revisiting, reflection, and updates informed by lived experience.

Workplaces themselves must be interrogated – not just in theory but in process. From recruitment to appraisal, systems need to ask hard questions: Are we rewarding productivity or just neurotypical expressions of it? Are we measuring communication through confidence and charisma, or are we recognising clarity in different forms? Is the space safe for someone who processes slowly, who avoids eye contact, or who contributes best asynchronously? Enabling change means reimagining the very systems that often pride themselves on neutrality, yet in reality are structured around a narrow template of success.

For neurodivergent professionals, sometimes the most transformative act is simply not having to mask. Being able to work without the emotional labour of pretending, adjusting, or apologising for how one processes information or engages with tasks is powerful. As many shared across the Padlet and beyond, a supportive colleague, an understanding line manager, a flexible policy, or a physical space that does not overstimulate can make the difference between surviving and thriving. Inclusion is not about inviting neurodivergent people into fixed spaces and asking them to fit in. It is about questioning the rigidity of those spaces and asking how they can stretch. As one practitioner rightly pointed out, *'We need to shift our thinking from "How can they fit our model?" to "How can our model shift to include them?"'*

Ultimately, enabling inclusion is not about fixing neurodivergent people. It is about fixing the systems that were never built with them in mind. It is about moving from tolerance to transformation – from individual effort to structural accountability. The tools are already here. The ideas have already been voiced. The question now is not what we need to do, but whether we are ready to do it.

Reflective quotes

Sometimes the most powerful learning does not come from a model or framework – it comes from a sentence that refuses to leave you. These quotes were not shared for effect. They emerged from lived experience and honest conversations – quiet truths that speak louder than policies. Use them in supervision, team CPD, journalling, or moments of pause. Let them interrupt your thinking. Let them shift what you have come to accept as standard.

'Don't call it a superpower if you won't change the system.' The temptation to rebrand neurodivergence as a gift often masks the deeper issue. If the system remains unchanged – rigid, inaccessible, exclusive – then no amount of positive language will undo the harm. Are we celebrating difference while still requiring assimilation? Are we offering real change – or simply rewording the same barriers?

'Disclosure implies disability is like a dirty little secret.' This forces us to consider how we frame disclosure. Are our processes creating safety – or signalling risk? When clients share neurodivergence, do they experience it as empowerment or exposure? We must examine how our forms, conversations, and expectations shape this dynamic.

'I can't do small talk – that doesn't mean I'm not engaged.' Neurodivergence often shows up in communication styles that challenge professional norms. Are we equating confidence with competence? Are we misreading silence as disengagement, or directness as rudeness? This quote reminds us that inclusion is not just about who is in the room – but how they are understood once they arrive.

'We don't get taught how to support neurodiverse clients.' This speaks directly to the professional gap. If training fails to prepare us to meet neurodivergent needs, we are not practising inclusion – we are hoping for tolerance. Whose needs are we trained to recognise instinctively, and whose remain invisible unless declared?

'What helps you feel safe, seen, and supported?' This should be asked more often. Of clients. Of colleagues. Of ourselves. Inclusion cannot be assumed. It must be invited, co-created, and sustained.

I would suggest you explore one of these questions each week, either as a team or individually, reflecting on where this showed up in your own practice. These aren't quotes to decorate a wall with – they are prompts to redesign the room itself.

This marks the final intersection in the book – but it is by no means the end of the conversation. Diversity is vast. It stretches beyond any framework, beyond any chapter, beyond the boundaries of what has been covered here. We have explored key intersections, but there are still many others – age, migration status, literacy level, care experience, to name just a few – that deserve the same level of attention, reflection, and systemic reimagining.

The careers sector talks a lot about inclusion. But inclusion without structural change is just assimilation. It's the quiet expectation that neurodivergent people – and others – shape-shift into systems never built with them in mind, and that when they do, we call it resilience.

That is not equity. Neurodivergent people, and all those whose identities challenge dominant norms, don't need inspirational slogans or awareness days. We need policies that reflect lived experience. We need environments that take sensory needs seriously. We need flexible timelines, accessible processes, and a culture where saying *'I need...'* is met with solutions, not suspicion.

This chapter, and this book, are not about perfection. They are about possibility. The insights are already here. The voices have spoken. The real question now is whether we are ready to listen – and to act. If we are serious about equity, we cannot keep tweaking the edges. We need to shift the core.

Let that be where the real work begins.

Tools for practice

Inclusion can feel abstract until it becomes embedded in the tools we actually use. It is easy to assume we are being inclusive if we have the right intentions, but unless those intentions are backed by adjusted tools and methods, the impact will not follow. The practices below are simple, low-cost, and designed to bring neurodivergent inclusion into real-world guidance settings. They are not exhaustive. They are a starting point.

Sensory environment checklist

Neurodivergent clients and practitioners are often affected by sensory triggers in ways that others may not notice. This tool helps you audit a physical or virtual space for:

- Lighting – Is it harsh, flickering, or overly bright?
- Noise – Are there background sounds that could overwhelm?
- Movement – Are there distractions in the room or on screen?
- Smells – Is there strong perfume, food, or cleaning products in use?

Why it matters: Sensory discomfort can cause anxiety or shutdown before a session even begins.

Accessible planning template

Many clients benefit from structure, but not everyone processes it in the same way. This template supports clients to:

- Break tasks into visual steps;
- Estimate time realistically;
- Track progress without overwhelm.

Why it matters: Executive function differences mean that long-term planning or sequencing can be difficult – this makes it doable.

Inclusive communication guide

Often, it's not what we say – it's how we say it. This guide helps practitioners:

- Give instructions in multiple formats (verbal and written);
- Avoid idioms, metaphors, or sarcasm unless explained;
- Build in time for processing and repetition.

Why it matters: Neurodivergent clients may interpret language literally or need extra time to respond fully.

Neurodiversity reflection prompts for clients

Neurodivergent clients may have been taught to suppress their preferences in the name of *'fitting in'*. These prompts centre on their needs instead:

- *'What environments help you feel focused and safe?'*
- *'How do you like to receive information?'*
- *'What drains your energy and what restores it?'*

Why it matters: These questions invite clients to reframe their needs as valid, not inconvenient.

Practitioner self-check

Inclusion starts with us. Use this prompt regularly:

- *'Am I expecting clients to adapt to me, or am I adapting to them?'*

Why it matters: This question disrupts default thinking and keeps equity at the centre of your practice.

These tools won't change the system on their own – but they're a step. A way to signal to neurodivergent clients and colleagues: I see you, I've thought about you, and I'm trying to meet you where you are.

Practice reflection: Identifying barriers in your context

Use Table 17 to begin identifying and addressing barriers within your own practice or organisation. Reflect honestly, involve others, and consider the lived experiences that may be missing from your design processes.

Table 17 Practice reflection: Identifying barriers in your context

Area of practice	Potential barrier	Evidence or observation	Action needed
Client communication			
Careers resources/tools			
Staff training and CPD			
Workplace culture			
Recruitment or onboarding			
Disclosure processes			
Environment and accessibility			

This tool isn't about blame – it's about building awareness and taking responsibility. Inclusion doesn't happen by default. It happens by design.

Organisational audit

Inclusion isn't just about what individual practitioners do – it's about how our organisations are structured. Policies, processes, and cultures all send messages about who belongs, whose needs are anticipated, and whose realities are overlooked. This audit tool helps teams take a systemic look at neurodivergent inclusion across their organisation – not as a one-off exercise, but as an ongoing commitment to equity.

Use Table 18 to review what's in place, identify gaps, and create space for lived experience to shape change.

Table 18 Organisational audit

Area	What to look for	Current status	Actions needed
Physical/sensory environment	Is there control over lighting, noise, movement? Are quiet spaces available?		
Digital accessibility	Are websites, forms, and portals compatible with assistive tech? Easy to navigate?		
Communication and language	Is information available in plain English and multiple formats?		
Staff training and CPD	Is there regular training on neurodiversity, led or co-designed by neurodiverse voices?		
Policies and procedures	Are reasonable adjustments clearly defined and easy to request?		
Supervision and line management	Do neurodiverse staff feel safe disclosing and supported post-disclosure?		
Recruitment and progression	Are neurodiverse candidates supported during recruitment? Are progression routes inclusive?		
Representation and lived experience	Are neurodiverse people involved in co-designing services, not just consulting on them?		
Feedback and accountability	Do you collect feedback from neurodiverse clients/staff and act on it transparently?		

This isn't a tool for shaming. It's a tool for surfacing what's often invisible. It encourages us to ask: Who are we building for? And who's still being asked to squeeze themselves into systems that weren't made with them in mind?

When inclusion becomes embedded in the infrastructure – not just in the personality of the most empathetic practitioner – that's when transformation becomes possible.

Chapter 11
Socio-economic status in the careers sector

Chapter roadmap

Socio-economic status shapes so much of what is possible – from access to education and stable housing to confidence, networks, and cultural capital. Yet it often remains the least discussed axis of equity in careers work. This chapter invites us to sit with the realities of class and economic inequality – not as background noise, but as central forces that shape the careers landscape for both clients and practitioners.

This chapter:

- Shares why I centre class and economic equity in my careers work;
- Unpacks what socio-economic status (SES) means and how it intersects with education, race, gender, and geography;
- Highlights how class-based disadvantage shows up systemically, not just individually;
- Brings in lived experiences from both clients and practitioners navigating classed spaces;
- Identifies barriers and enablers specific to SES within career development;
- Offers practical tools and reflective prompts to challenge assumptions and shift practice;
- Ends with a call to reimagine careers work through a socio-economic justice lens.

Author's voice

I come from an area of Derby which is inner city, and for me, this has always prompted my commitment to social justice. Growing up in a deprived community meant seeing the realities of systemic inequality up close – but also witnessing strength, resilience, and potential that was too often overlooked by institutions. People are often scared to go for it in areas like mine, even though we lived there, and it was fine. The fear didn't come from the community – it came from the way society framed us. When I worked as a Careers Coordinator for Learn by Design; I excelled in that role not in spite of my background – but because of it, who I am, where I come from, and the insight that gives me. I understood the barriers, the silences, and the coded expectations in ways that made me better at connecting with the young people I worked with. That's why SES isn't just a label or statistic – it's a lived experience that can be leveraged to support others, rather than used to hold them back.

This chapter matters to me deeply because I've lived what it means to be underestimated, misread, or made to feel out of place. Socio-economic status, unlike some other dimensions of identity, is often invisible – until it's not. Until someone makes a comment about how you speak, what you wear, or where you studied. *'Professionalism'* in our sector often operates as a coded reference to middle-class norms – language, presentation, behaviour – and that leaves many of us editing ourselves just to be seen as competent. I've seen first-hand how SES is one of the most stubborn drivers of inequality across education and employment. It's persistent. Structural. It affects everything – from aspirations and access to outcomes and confidence. Perhaps what isn't spoken about enough is the emotional cost: the shame, the weight of not having, of not knowing, of feeling like you don't belong. Shame holds you back in ways data can't quantify. It seeps into your self-perception, your voice, and your sense of place.

There's also the loss of a place to belong – that lingering ache when you move between social classes and no longer quite fit where you started, but aren't fully accepted where you've landed either. That feeling is real, and it echoes across the journeys of so many of us doing this work. In this chapter, I want to unpick how socio-economic status plays out in career development. The goal isn't to diagnose or label – but to explore, reflect, and push for a sector that doesn't assume a single starting point. Equity in careers work starts with acknowledging that not everyone begins from the same place – and that matters.

Socio-economic status definition

Socio-economic status (SES) is not a single data point – it's a web of interlinked factors that shape life chances from early childhood to the labour market. It typically refers to indicators such as household income, parental occupation, level of education, housing quality, postcode, food insecurity, and access to technology. In the UK, government measures often use eligibility for Free School Meals (FSM), Pupil Premium (PP) status, or Index of Multiple Deprivation (IMD) data as proxies for economic disadvantage. These indicators influence targeted support in schools, university widening participation schemes, and access to funding – but they do not tell the full story. SES is more than a funding metric – it's a lived experience. It's growing up in overcrowded housing with no quiet space to study. It's walking to school because the bus fare isn't an option. It's choosing between heating or eating during exam season. It's watching your peers join clubs and go on residentials while you stay back, not because you don't want to – but because you can't afford to. Critically, SES intersects – deeply – with other forms of disadvantage. Being working-class and Black, or working-class and disabled, or working-class and care-experienced compounds barriers in ways that cannot be addressed in isolation. As one practitioner noted,

'These experiences are often reduced to demographic tick-boxes. Do you remember being asked if your parents went to university? What jobs they do? Whether you were eligible for free school meals? These aren't just benign questions – they are coded measures of class. I've been asked them more times than I can count. They are usually framed as helpful context, a means to identify who might need extra support. But that support rarely materialises in ways that disrupt systemic inequality. These questions reveal that our institutions already know SES matters. Yet instead of changing the conditions that shape disadvantage, the data is often used to monitor rather than mend.'

This is where the myth of meritocracy becomes most dangerous. The narrative that if you work hard, you will succeed sounds empowering – until you realise that success often depends on unpaid internships, parental networks, or the cultural capital to walk into a room and feel like you belong. In careers work, this shows up in how we frame resilience. We celebrate young people from low-income backgrounds for *'overcoming adversity'*, but rarely interrogate why they had to overcome so much in the first place. As one Padlet practitioner reflected,

'The trauma of poverty isn't just about material lack – it's about shame, silence, and constantly feeling like you're out of place. Even when you "make it," the class codes don't disappear. You carry them. You adapt. You code-switch. You navigate two different worlds and belong fully in neither. That tension lingers, shaping how you speak, dress, connect, and lead. That is why careers guidance cannot afford to treat SES as an afterthought. It's not a background characteristic – it's the water so many of our clients are swimming in. If we want to deliver careers guidance that is genuinely equitable, we need to go beyond surface-level recognition. We must redesign our practice so that it honours, reflects, and advocates for the realities of working-class lives – not just those who survive them, but those who are still trying to be seen.'

Understanding SES in careers work

There's a moment I'll never forget. I was in a careers outreach session in a secondary school, and the classroom was filled with Southeast Asian students from an inner-city area – similar to the one I grew up in. When we asked the students what they wanted to do when they were older, many said things like, *'Own a takeaway'*, or *'Drive taxis, like my dad'*. There was no hesitation, just quiet certainty. They weren't joking. They weren't unsure. That was what they had seen, and so that was what they could imagine. Later, I questioned the school staff about it – why weren't we expanding their aspirations? One teacher shrugged and said, *'Well, that's all they know . . . they probably won't have the right connections anyway'*. It was said gently, even sympathetically. But what it really revealed was how low the expectations were – not of the young people, but of what they could be. That comment has stayed with me for years; it wasn't just about this one group of students. It was about how careers guidance often reinforces the very limitations it claims to challenge.

There's a kind of soft bigotry in the system – coated in politeness, wrapped in good intentions – that quietly boxes young people in. We say we want to inspire, but then offer advice based on postcode, accent, family background, or what we assume someone's *'realistic'* options are. When students from more affluent areas say they want to be lawyers or engineers, we applaud their ambition. When students from deprived communities say the same, we nudge them towards something *'more practical'*.

What made that session so powerful – and so painful – was that I saw a mirror of my own community. I recognised the kids who were written off before they even opened their mouths. I recognised the silence that comes with internalised limitation – the kind where you don't even know what else is possible because no one's ever shown you. Careers work should be about possibility, not prediction. It should be about naming the systems that shape your vision of the future – and then helping you challenge them. When we only see what we've always seen, we don't just limit aspiration – we reproduce inequality. That's the uncomfortable truth we have to face in this profession. We can't face it unless we name it.

Careers advice often assumes you have the financial, emotional, and social resources to pursue your goals. That you can do unpaid placements. That your parents will drive you to an interview. That you have Wi-Fi at home and a quiet space to prepare. But those of us who've grown up with none of that know that advice like *'just network'* or *'dress to impress'* lands differently when you don't have the right shoes, let alone a blazer.

The careers sector still subtly codes class into its expectations. It shows up in mock interviews that reward confidence over content, in CV templates that assume access to extracurriculars and Duke of Edinburgh awards, and in feedback like *'you come across as too casual'*, when what they really mean is: you don't speak the middle-class script. As one Padlet practitioner put it: *'Accent, way we speak, engage.'* We rarely name linguistic bias for what it is – tone policing rooted in class.

I've sat in rooms where candidates were ruled out because they didn't shake hands firmly enough, or because they didn't have the 'right' university on their CV. The unwritten rules of employability are saturated in middle-class values – and they're often enforced by people who don't even realise they're doing it. It's why some young people from working-class backgrounds describe job interviews as a performance where they play a role that isn't theirs.

And all of this is happening while the world of work itself is changing rapidly. As one participant noted, *'Jobs that are falling away/new jobs . . . several careers in a lifespan'*. For young people without a financial safety net, the pressure to get it right the first time is immense. They can't afford to 'fail fast' or 'pivot' when rent is due. Flexibility and instability aren't trendy – they're terrifying.

Careers work, if it's going to be meaningful, has to do more than offer advice. It has to interrogate the structures it operates within. It has to question whose norms we're reinforcing, whose language we're privileging, and whose realities we're ignoring. For too long, careers work has claimed to empower – while quietly rewarding those who already know the rules.

Lived experience and professional blind spots

Although I am not a Career Development Professional (CDP) myself, I am a researcher in this field – and in developing the EDI strategy, I've spoken to countless CDPs across the UK. What I've seen, again and again, from the sidelines and through deep listening, is a sector that talks equity but struggles to name class. What's said in closed rooms isn't always what's felt on the ground. Those from working-class backgrounds – whether clients or practitioners – are often expected to adapt, decode, and translate. Working in the careers sector as someone from a working-class background is like having a foot in two worlds – both familiar, and neither quite your own. You know what it feels like to be on the receiving end of assumptions. Now, as a practitioner, you see those same assumptions being made – sometimes gently, sometimes unconsciously, but always with consequence.

Early in their careers, several CDPs told me they sat in meetings where everyone just seemed to know when to speak, what tone to take, which acronyms to use. They didn't. Not because they lacked understanding, but because they hadn't grown up speaking the same professional dialect. One Padlet practitioner captured this perfectly: *'Not being able to communicate in meetings in the same way.'* That's it. Not about skill – about translation. You learn to decode. You learn to mimic. But it takes energy to show up as someone you're not, just to be heard. There's an emotional labour to being the one who 'gets it' – not just because of training, but because you've lived it. You hear *'hard to reach'* and you flinch. You hear *'low aspiration'*, and you remember how often that was said about people like you. As one reflection put it: *'Discussion often lacks an understanding of the lived reality of working-class families.'* That gap – the one between what the policy says and what the community knows – that's the space so many of us inhabit in silence. This silence can feel like erasure. Especially when class isn't named. Not in recruitment. Not in progression. Not in CPD. As another practitioner wrote: *'Not really fitting into a new environment but losing a sense of belonging with family background.'* That stayed with me; it's not just about breaking into the profession – it's about what you have to leave behind to stay in it. The code-switching. The softening of the accent. The careful editing of experience. Yet, people keep showing up. They do this work because they see the students who remind them of themselves – quiet voices in loud classrooms, those who apologise for not knowing, who shrink their dreams before they've even tried. They know what it means to not just offer guidance, but dignity. The careers sector likes to position itself as aspirational. But aspiration without structural critique isn't equity – it's performance. If we really want to reflect the communities we claim to serve, then we need to talk about class – not as a box to tick, but as a lens to see more clearly. Those from working-class backgrounds don't just bring perspective. They bring truth. They bring context. They bring the clarity this profession so often lacks.

Client perspectives

I've been a career mentor to many young people over the years, and I've had countless conversations where the core issue wasn't ability – it was access. It was the invisible wall of cultural capital. The unspoken knowledge that some young people are handed without asking – how to shake hands, how to structure an email, how to talk about a gap year without sounding *'unserious'*. These things are rarely taught. They're assumed. If you haven't absorbed them through your environment, you're already a step behind, even when you're more than capable. Cultural capital isn't just about museums and music preferences. It's about knowing how to navigate systems that weren't built with you in mind. Pierre Bourdieu's theory reminds us that this form of capital – social habits, linguistic patterns, even aesthetic preferences – can be just as important as economic wealth when it comes to social mobility. In the careers world, this plays out in real, material ways. Who gets picked for the student council? Who gets fast-tracked for leadership schemes? Who feels comfortable in a room full of professionals because it mirrors their dinner table at home?

I've lost count of how many young people I've spoken to who believed they couldn't even apply for their dream job – because of a bus fare. Or because they didn't have the right clothes. Or because they weren't sure what an application form was actually asking. Not because they didn't have potential – but because the system is full of silent requirements that no one names. In one case, a young woman told me she wanted to apply for a trainee legal position but didn't go through with it. When I asked why, she said, *'I didn't have anything smart to wear, and it was in a different city – I didn't even know how I'd get there'*. That sentence has stayed with me. Not because it shocked me, but because it was so common. In careers guidance, we talk about *'confidence'* and *'readiness'*, but we often ignore the structural conditions that strip both away before someone's even started.

One practitioner put it plainly: *'Young people from lower socio-economic backgrounds may not be able to participate in extracurricular activities.'* And what matters – those unpaid placements, school trips, music lessons, or DofE awards? They fill out UCAS forms. They sit on CVs. They build the kind of social capital that the middle-class system is quietly calibrated to reward. It's not just about money. It's about networks. *'Access to networks, role models'*, one practitioner shared. We can't keep telling young people to *'be what they can't see'*. Role models aren't just motivational – they're mirrors. Without those mirrors, ambition starts to shrink to fit the limits of proximity.

Then there's the narrative. Too many clients have internalised the idea that their ambition makes them unrealistic. They're told – sometimes directly, more often subtly – that certain careers *'aren't for people like them'*. Or they compare themselves to peers who've had tutoring, parent-led internships, family-run businesses – and they assume they're already behind. One Padlet voice said: *'There's a perception that if you don't have connections, you're not worth the investment.'* Careers guidance, if it's not careful, risks reinforcing this. The sector still leans into meritocracy myths and *'resilience'* stories. But if we praise young people for surviving the system, we must also ask: Why are we letting that system stay broken? Clients are not under-ambitious – they are under-resourced. They are not disengaged – they are overwhelmed by barriers. It's our job, not to simply prepare them for that reality but to challenge it – every time we step into a room, hold a conversation, or design a programme. The message shouldn't be work harder. It should be you deserve better.

Barriers

We talk a lot about opportunity in the careers sector, but opportunity doesn't mean much when the starting line isn't the same. For so many working-class clients, the barriers aren't dramatic or headline-grabbing – they're subtle, constant, and cumulative. They begin early and compound over time. Often invisible to the system, they show up in every application not submitted, every interview not attended, every opportunity silently passed by. If we don't name these barriers and challenge the conditions that create them, we risk upholding the very inequalities we claim to address. Application processes, for instance, appear fair – same form, same instructions – but they reward those fluent in the unspoken rules: tone, phrasing, structure, self-promotion. One practitioner summed it up: *'Application processes are a barrier – could be simplified, fit for the role?'* These forms don't just assess competence – they reflect how well someone fits a professional mould shaped by middle-class norms.

That mould also shows up in how we interpret language, accents, and communication. *'Accent, way we speak, engage'* – that quote cuts deep. Regional and working-class accents, even when articulating clearly and confidently, are often judged as less professional or less intelligent. These biases are rarely acknowledged, but they linger in hiring rooms, shape mentoring dynamics, and influence whose voices are perceived as credible. Add to this the assumption of unlimited availability – another invisible standard baked into the way careers advice is delivered. Caring responsibilities, usually gendered and frequently hidden, are barely considered. When a client can't attend a morning session or travel for an unpaid placement because they're parenting, supporting a sibling, or looking after a parent, they're often read as disengaged. The reality is they're doing double shifts – juggling futures while shouldering responsibilities most professionals never have to consider when designing their offer.

Digital exclusion is another barrier we've normalised. Access to a device is not the same as access to opportunity. Without stable Wi-Fi, digital literacy, a quiet place to work, or confidence to navigate online systems, clients are excluded from virtual interviews, job applications, and online learning. One practitioner said it plainly: *'Technology – lack of access due to poverty leads to narrowing of opportunities.'* We've designed services that assume digital access is a given, not a privilege – and when people don't engage, we interpret it as a lack of motivation rather than a lack of infrastructure. The same goes for unpaid work placements and enrichment activities. These so-called *'open opportunities'* often rely on someone being able to work for free, travel, and buy appropriate clothing. One Padlet voice put it perfectly: *'Young people don't have the chance to get the CV that others have through unpaid placements.'* That doesn't mean they lack ambition – it means they've been priced out of access.

Then there's the most insidious barrier of all: shame. *'Shame holds you back.'* It's not loud. It creeps. It sits in silence, convincing people not to speak, not to apply, not to believe they deserve to be seen. Shame teaches self-doubt before the system ever has to. It shapes posture in interviews, apology in tone, and an invisible script that says, *'Don't take up too much space'*. This emotional cost – so rarely measured – is one of the most significant impacts of socio-economic inequality. It leads people to opt out long before they're given the chance to be counted in.

Even the basics – transport and childcare – can quietly but completely rule people out. *'If you don't have transport or childcare, it can rule you out before you've even applied.'* These aren't excuses; they are real logistical barriers. Yet flexibility is still treated as a luxury, not a right. When people miss sessions, we question their commitment rather than interrogating our own assumptions. Who decided that success meant showing up in a particular way, at a particular time, in a particular format?

Another barrier is the network gap – the unspoken key to access. *'Access to networks, role models.'* That quiet truth reverberates across our sector. Success still depends heavily on who knows you, who advocates for you, who shares their insider knowledge. Careers guidance continues to frame networking as a neutral skill, yet it fails to reckon with the fact that most working-class communities haven't had access to those circles in the first place. I've seen people lean into their communities, turning to aunties, cousins, and neighbours for guidance. These informal support systems matter deeply – but they can only offer what they've had access to themselves. If opportunity hasn't passed through the door, no one inside knows to point towards it. There's also the myth that once you've made it, you can just reach back and pull others through. But the truth is, unless you hold institutional power – over hiring, policy, or funding – the path behind you remains just as overgrown. You can tell someone what helped you, but the gatekeeping remains. Knowing someone might help you be seen, but it doesn't always help you get through. The careers sector often tells young people to *'network'*, yet if the only people you know are navigating the same barriers, what exactly are you supposed to leverage?

We cannot keep romanticising resilience and resourcefulness as solutions to structural problems. Personal effort will never be enough to offset systemic design flaws. Until we address the actual conditions – childcare, transport, digital access, scheduling, funding, cultural norms – we will continue to offer opportunities that are *'open to all'* but accessible to few. None of these barriers are accidental. They are the result of design choices made without working-class lives in mind. Awareness is not enough. We must interrogate and redesign our services with an honest lens. Otherwise, we will continue to mislabel systemic exclusion as individual deficit – and people will keep falling through the cracks of a system that was never built to hold them.

Enablers

If barriers are what block access, enablers are what build bridges. They don't just remove obstacles – they create something new. In this section, I want to focus on what's already working, what could work better, and what's still missing. These aren't just examples of *'good practice'* – they represent structural interventions that actively invite working-class clients to belong on their own terms. Enablers shift the lens. They don't ask, *'Why didn't you do this?'* but rather, *'What conditions were in place – and how can we change them?'*

Mentoring was stated as an enabler across all workshops. Time and again, practitioners suggested: *'The CDI could help to develop mentoring and networking programmes to help individuals from lower socio-economic backgrounds connect with professionals.'* That insight is more than a suggestion – it's a call to action. Mentoring by someone who shares not only professional insight but also lived class experience creates a different kind of connection. It brings relatability, honesty, and realism. I've seen mentoring work. I've been on both ends of that exchange. When someone sits across from you and says, *'I've been there'*, it cuts through abstract motivation and replaces it with grounded belief – belief that feels reachable. But mentoring alone can't do all the heavy lifting unless it's paired with resources that reflect people's real lives. Career tools need to centre cultural context and financial realities, not just showcase glossy futures that feel so far out of reach they might as well be fiction. One Padlet comment named this clearly: *'Careers education often assumes access to resources, and those from low-income backgrounds are made to feel behind before they've started.'* That starting line isn't just about financial capital – it's about feeling seen, respected, and set up to succeed on your own terms. This is where enablers can transform the conversation. They help us ask different questions. Not *'what's wrong with the client?'* but *'what assumptions are we making – and who are we leaving out in the process?'*

Apprenticeships offer one of the clearest opportunities to challenge these assumptions. Too often they're framed as the second-best option, pushed towards some students with little agency and treated as a fallback instead of a first choice. That's a missed opportunity. When promoted with equal status, transparency, and parity of esteem, apprenticeships become powerful routes that combine income, qualification, and real-world experience. For many working-class clients, they're not a compromise – they're the smartest, most strategic path forward. We need to shift how we talk about them – not as a last resort, but as a deliberate, valued choice. During this work, one model that stood out was the NHS four-week job trial scheme. Clients are paid to explore a variety of healthcare roles before committing to applications. It's simple but effective. It removes risk, builds confidence, and gives people the freedom to test things out without pressure or fear of failure. One practitioner said, *'Trying things out in real environments helps reduce fear and shows them they belong'.* That sense of belonging can't be overstated. We need more initiatives like this – programmes that provide exposure not as a privilege, but as a foundation.

Some enablers don't need complex funding or revolutionary innovation – they require a shift in mindset. One practitioner shared: *'Training employers that reasonable adjustments don't necessarily mean costly equipment or large-scale changes – but minimal, cost-free changes that benefit everybody.'* That's the principle of universal design: embed accessibility from the outset, rather than retrofit inclusion later. This means offering flexible interview times, hybrid engagement options, simplified application forms, and genuine recognition of lived experience as valuable expertise. When systems start by asking what would make participation easier, they become more humane. Another practitioner offered a powerful reflection: *'Normalising socio-economic diversity in the workplace – not tokenising people, but creating a culture where difference isn't a burden.'* That's the crux. The goal isn't just to open the door – it's to make sure people feel welcome once they're inside. Do they feel safe to speak in their own accent? Do they feel respected for their different journey? Or are they made to perform a version of professionalism that erases who they are? Inclusion doesn't start and end with access – it lives in the culture we create.

Enablers do not need to be extraordinary – they need to be intentional. Whether it's providing childcare support, travel stipends, community-based career hubs, or multilingual resources, each shift brings us closer to equity. Every time we remove a barrier or meet someone where they are, we affirm their dignity. One practitioner captured this vision: *'Make inclusion ordinary – not a special programme, but standard practice.'* That is what we must strive for. Not token gestures. Not one-off projects. But embedded structural inclusion that doesn't ask working-class clients to adapt to systems but reshapes those systems to finally see them, support them, and work for them from the start.

Reflective quotes

Sometimes, the most powerful truths are not found in policies or research papers – they surface in passing comments, whispered frustrations, and lived realities. These quotes reflect the quiet resilience and invisible barriers experienced by those navigating socio-economic inequality. They are not here to inspire pity or be skimmed over. They are here to prompt reflection, to challenge assumptions, and to ask better questions in our practice.

'Parents may be unable to have meaningful career conversations with their children.' This invites us to reconsider how we involve families in careers work. Are we assuming a shared knowledge base or cultural capital that isn't there? What does support look like when families are navigating survival, language barriers, or fractured trust in the system?

'Lack of access – basics/survival needs – hand to mouth.' This isn't disengagement – it's exhaustion. When basic needs are unmet, careers guidance cannot start with personal statements or progression routes. It must begin with compassion, pacing, and support structures that honour the reality of scarcity. *'Loss of a place to belong.'* Belonging isn't a bonus – it's foundational. If clients have to shed parts of themselves – accents, histories, postcodes – just to be seen as *'professional'*, we are not building inclusive spaces. We are

reinforcing exclusion under a different name. *'It's a lot about who you know and what you know.'* Access isn't just about opportunity – it's about invitation. Who gets to be in the room? Who gets heard, referred, supported? Redistributing access means actively challenging the gatekeeping that passes as neutrality in our sector.

'Shame holds you back.' Shame doesn't show up on CVs, but it shows up in every session. How do we challenge narratives that equate poverty with failure? Are we offering validation – or asking clients to 'fix' their confidence before we take them seriously? *'Young people don't have the chance to get the CV that others have through unpaid placements.'* When we equate value with visibility, we erase so much. What if care responsibilities, part-time work, or navigating benefits were seen as legitimate evidence of resilience and skill? Do we only validate experience when it mirrors privilege? *'Career advisers often lack understanding of what it means to live in poverty.'* This one cuts deep. It's a reminder that no amount of qualification replaces lived empathy. What have we internalised about merit, professionalism, or aspiration? What do we need to unlearn?

These reflections are not just for wall displays or staff training slides. They are for the heart of our work. Use them in team discussions, reflective journals, or client work. Let them become anchors – not to hold us back but to ground us in what matters. Equity in the careers sector doesn't start with strategy – it starts with listening.

We need to stop measuring success by how well someone contorts themselves to fit a system never built for them. The careers sector has long rewarded those who already speak the right language, wear the right clothes, know the right codes. But what happens when we stop mistaking confidence for competence, or polish for potential? What do we uncover when we see resilience not as a badge of honour but as a survival strategy? It's time to challenge the myth of meritocracy. The *'pull yourself up by the bootstraps'* narrative assumes people have boots to begin with. It turns systemic inequality into individual failure. That's not just inaccurate – it's deeply damaging. We cannot call ourselves inclusive while upholding the same narrow definitions of success, effort, and credibility.

Reframing equity means challenging our own frameworks. It means seeing ambition in places others overlook. It means recognising that silence might be fear, not disinterest; that late might mean overwhelmed, not lazy; that presence itself is a form of persistence. Equity in careers work means starting from where people are – not from where we expect them to be. It means responding to people with humanity, designing support with dignity, and holding an unwavering belief that every person deserves more than the system has offered them so far.

Although this is the final intersection explored in the book, it is not the end of the conversation. Diversity stretches far beyond what has been captured here. From language, age, and immigration status to interfaith experiences, regional identity, and beyond – every identity holds nuance. What matters is not how many intersections we can list, but how willing we are to unlearn, to listen, and to build careers work that acknowledges the full, complicated, beautiful breadth of human experience. This work does not end at the final chapter or the closing of this book – it begins with you, the reader.

Tools for practice

We talk a lot about theory, policy, and frameworks – but sometimes, it's the everyday tools that make the biggest difference. What we ask, what we assume, what we offer – all of it can either build trust or quietly reinforce exclusion. These tools aren't about reinventing careers work – they're about embedding equity into what we already do (see Table 19).

Table 19 Tools for practice

Tool	Description
Socio-economic lens audit	A reflective checklist for practitioners and organisations to assess class-based assumptions that often go unnoticed. For example: Do you assume clients have access to a quiet study space at home? Are your events scheduled during typical working hours, excluding those in shift-based or precarious employment? Do you consider the costs of travel, uniforms, or work experience placements? *Do you expect parents or carers to attend careers meetings?* While this may be uncommon for many, in some contexts, such as clients with additional needs who consent to parent/carer being present, it could be assumed as the norm. This tool doesn't prescribe a single approach – it invites us to notice what we take for granted and to think more intentionally about access, time, cost, and power.
Inclusive application toolkit	Plain-language CV and application templates that are clear, accessible, and adaptable. Includes examples from diverse experiences (e.g. care work, community roles) to validate the lived skills that traditional templates ignore.
Financial barriers checklist	A structured prompt sheet to identify the hidden costs in different career paths – travel, uniforms, course fees, devices, or lunch. Helps clients and practitioners plan realistically and pushes services to consider funding support or alternative options.
Cultural capital conversation cards	A set of client-facing prompts that help make the invisible visible. They invite reflection on knowledge, norms, values, and networks – and help clients reframe their stories not as lacking, but as shaped by a different set of strengths. Example prompt: 'What skills have you developed from responsibilities at home?'

These tools aren't just paperwork – they're signals. They say: We've thought about your context. We expect difference. We're ready to adapt. They make room for people to show up as they are – without apology and without needing to prove they belong.

Organisational audit table

This tool isn't about blame – it's about clarity; many exclusionary practices happen not through intent, but through habit. This audit (Table 20) invites your team to pause, reflect, and reset. Change isn't just about big statements – it's in the everyday decisions, partnerships, and assumptions we make.

Table 20 Organisational audit

Area	Current practice	What needs attention?	Actions
Outreach	Focus on high-performing schools	Misses many low-income, underserved communities	Broaden outreach criteria. Build local partnerships.
Staff diversity	Team lacks working-class voices	Creates blind spots in decision-making and policy	Review hiring practices. Recruit inclusively.
Advisory input	Advisory boards made up of senior professionals	Lacks lived experience of socio-economic disadvantage	Include voices with real community insight.
Programme design	Assumes access to tech, time, and travel	Excludes those facing digital or logistical barriers	Co-design services with clients. Offer flexible options.
Progression routes	Heavy emphasis on university pathways	Reinforces prestige bias and ignores local labour realities	Showcase apprenticeships and community-based routes equally.
Language and tone	Uses corporate or academic language	Alienates clients unfamiliar with sector jargon	Use plain language in all materials. Test with real users.

You can add to this audit as needed – and you should. Inclusion is not a one-time workshop or a comms campaign. It's an ongoing practice of asking, 'Who's not in the room, and why?'

PART THREE
IMPLEMENTATION
AND ACTION

This final section of the book brings everything together – moving from insight to action. While Parts One and Two build foundational understanding and deepen awareness across diversity intersections, Part Three is unapologetically practical. It's where EDI becomes more than intention and starts to take root through implementation.

You'll move through the following chapters:

- Chapter 12 – Creating inclusive career guidance practices – explores what it means to embed EDI across everyday guidance delivery, including how inclusive practice can be meaningfully measured, communicated, and sustained.
- Chapter 13 – Transforming practice through inclusion – offers a forward-facing vision for change, inviting the reader to become an active part of reshaping the careers sector. This includes reflections on leadership, systems change, and lifelong learning as core elements of inclusive careers work.

These chapters are grounded in the principle that change is a practice, not a destination. You'll find tools, templates, and frameworks you can use, adapt, and return to in your professional journey – whether you're a careers adviser, educator, policymaker, or EDI lead.

This section is your call to action. It's an invitation to take the insights from earlier chapters and apply them with care, courage, and clarity – because equity in career development is not a one-off intervention but a lifelong commitment. It needs to be embedded within everything we do; it is not an optional add-on.

Chapter 12
Creating inclusive career guidance practices

Why implementation matters now

After exploring the intersecting barriers experienced by clients and practitioners in Part Two, this chapter marks a deliberate shift – from analysis to action. As someone who has been living and breathing EDI for many years, I've seen first-hand how often inclusive intentions get lost in operational realities. This chapter is written for the career practitioners who care deeply about equity but feel unsure where to begin. It's also for services that are ready to move beyond tokenism and towards equity that is embedded – not simply promised. My aim here is not to overwhelm you with jargon or unattainable ideals, but to offer tools, reflections, and lived examples that make inclusion tangible and doable in the real world of careers work.

One thing I hear often – whether I'm leading a workshop, speaking at a conference, or working with leadership teams – is: *'Ifza, you just get how to implement this stuff, but we don't.'* That statement, though often well-meaning, is telling. It reveals something about where the work is being placed and the assumptions that underpin it. It implies that EDI is somehow instinctive, innate, or only doable by certain 'types' of people. But I want to say this clearly: inclusive practice is not magic. It's method. It's clarity, care, and commitment – repeated over time. You don't need to have lived every identity or experienced every form of marginalisation to create inclusive environments. You need the willingness to listen, to reflect, and to rework how your systems operate. This chapter is my answer to those who feel stuck, overwhelmed, or hesitant. You don't need to be perfect. You just need to begin – honestly, humbly, and with a readiness to learn and unlearn.

The reason I've written this book – and particularly this chapter – is that so many organisations say they want inclusion, but few are genuinely ready to invest in the ongoing consultancy, capacity-building, or structural redesign required to do it meaningfully. Sometimes it's about limited budgets. Other times, it's a case of *'we know it matters, but we're not sure what to do'*. Either way, this is my offering – my way of giving you access to my expertise, strategies, and voice, especially for those of you who won't necessarily have a consultant walking the journey with you. This chapter is not just another guide. It's a blueprint born from lived experience and organisational learning. My hope is that it becomes something you return to – not because you have to, but because you want to get this right. Equity isn't a side dish or an add-on. It's the way we futureproof careers work, so it serves everyone, not just the most resourced or recognised.

So let's be honest about the context we're operating in. We are living through a time where *'EDI must die'* campaigns, anti-wokeness rhetoric, and performative backlash are becoming louder. Inclusion is being politicised, ridiculed, and in some cases, actively defunded. That makes this work not just relevant – it makes it resistance. There has never been a more urgent time to embed EDI properly. Not as a reaction to hashtags or funding cycles, but as a principled, ethical stance. We cannot afford to dilute this work to appease discomfort. This chapter is written as a quiet refusal of that dilution. A refusal to step back, to minimise, or to de-centre equity for the sake of convenience or controversy when inclusion is under attack, clarity and conviction become our most powerful tools.

This is not about being performative. It's about being prepared. Being strategic. Being rooted in the unwavering belief that we all deserve access to safe, affirming, and equitable careers work – regardless of who we are, where we come from, or what barriers we face.

Principles of inclusive guidance

Equity-focused guidance is grounded in four foundational principles: belonging, voice, flexibility, and accountability. These aren't abstract ideals to strive towards – they're the essential architecture of any service that claims to centre inclusion. Too often, we hear the phrase everyone is welcome here, but when you dig deeper, there's little evidence that the welcome extends beyond surface-level gestures. A poster on the wall or a tagline on the website is not enough if your systems, language, and expectations still signal that clients need to assimilate in order to succeed. Inclusion means designing services in ways that enable people to actually show up, be seen, and feel safe. It demands that we build environments where difference isn't simply tolerated but expected and planned for. Without that structural commitment, inclusion remains a concept, not a practice.

This is where the TEDI framework – Transformative Equity, Diversity, and Inclusion – moves us from ideas to action. TEDI is not another tick-box initiative. It's not about performative allyship or one-off workshops. It's a whole-system approach that embeds EDI at every level of service design and delivery. TEDI encourages us to move beyond awareness and into redesign. It challenges us to critically examine our assumptions about what 'good practice' looks like and asks: Who does your service really work for? Who does it unconsciously exclude? Drawing on the four TEDI principles, we begin to see how belonging, voice, flexibility, and accountability are not standalone values – they're interconnected levers for system change.

Take belonging, for instance. It's not about whether someone subjectively feels welcome. It's about whether your systems actively signal that they belong. That includes visual representation, accessible spaces, inclusive language, and meaningful cultural safety. If a queer Muslim client walks into your centre and is asked to tick *'other'* when stating their identity, that moment communicates something about for whom the system was built. TEDI teaches us that belonging must be engineered. It's not accidental. It needs to be embedded in how we design waiting rooms, write intake forms, run sessions, and communicate expectations. Likewise, voice is not just about collecting feedback – it's about disrupting power hierarchies. Inclusive services do not merely consult clients; they involve them in co-creation. A TEDI approach repositions clients as co-designers and experts in their own experiences. It asks: Whose voice is shaping this work? Whose knowledge do we privilege when making decisions? If feedback mechanisms are tokenistic or inaccessible, then voice is performative. True voice means that marginalised perspectives shape strategy, delivery, and evaluation. That might look like client advisory groups, staff feedback loops, or anonymous platforms that enable people to speak truth without fear of consequence.

Flexibility is often where services say they struggle. But in reality, rigidity is a choice – one that privileges efficiency over equity. TEDI pushes us to reimagine flexibility as a requirement, not a luxury. Can we offer career guidance through different formats – video, phone, text, in-person? Can we accommodate trauma histories, neurodivergence, or energy limitations by building more adaptive systems? If not, who are we leaving out? Flexibility, done right, doesn't mean compromising standards; it means expanding what support can look like so that more people can access it. It challenges us to shift from *'how we've always done things'* to *'what do people actually need?'*

Accountability, the final TEDI principle, is perhaps the most uncomfortable – and the most necessary. It asks us to get honest about what happens after the good intentions, after the training sessions, after the strategy documents are published. Are we changing anything in practice? Are we measuring outcomes through the lens of inclusion, or simply collecting diversity stats with no real follow-up? Accountability means setting benchmarks, inviting critique, and being prepared to act on what we hear. It's about building internal mechanisms that ensure equity work doesn't fall off the agenda when leadership changes or when budgets tighten. Inclusive guidance also requires us to challenge unspoken expectations around 'professionalism', ambition, and success. Too often, we ask clients to conform to dominant norms – white, middle-class, neurotypical, English-speaking – without questioning where those norms came from. If a neurodivergent young person pauses between thoughts, do we wait patiently or rush them? If a client wears cultural dress or brings faith into their career planning, do we lean in or silently bypass? If we're asking people to show up authentically while punishing anything outside of the mainstream, we're not being inclusive – we're being conditional. That's not good enough.

We must ask ourselves, as practitioners, what norms are we upholding without realising? How have we built systems that work brilliantly for some but require others to contort themselves just to participate? Who gets to feel at ease in our spaces, and who has to constantly scan for safety? These aren't rhetorical questions – they are diagnostic tools. They sit at the heart of TEDI; if we don't ask these questions, we end up building services that replicate the very inequalities we claim to dismantle.

Reflective prompts:

- In what ways has your service been unintentionally designed around dominant cultural norms?
- How could you reframe belonging as something structural, not emotional?
- What would it look like to genuinely redistribute power to clients and communities?
- Where could your service become more flexible, and who might that enable to participate more fully?
- How are you tracking your progress on inclusion – and are you willing to act on what's revealed?

Inclusive guidance is not a destination – it's a daily decision. The TEDI framework offers a map, but it's our responsibility to walk the path, even when it's difficult. Especially when it's difficult, anything less than that is not equity. It's maintenance of the status quo. We owe our clients more than that.

Building inclusive environments using the TEDI framework

Inclusive careers work can't be retrofitted – it has to be intentionally built from the ground up. You can't sprinkle in inclusion after the fact and hope it sticks. It must be in the blueprint. The TEDI framework helps us do exactly that. It doesn't simply ask us to consider identity or fairness in the abstract – it offers a structured, systemic approach that embeds equity into the very foundations of how we design and deliver services. TEDI isn't just a reflective tool – it's a radical shift in how we understand and operationalise inclusion. At its core, it moves us away from *'add diversity and stir'* models, and towards a way of working that recognises equity as a deliberate and ongoing commitment. It challenges the comfort of status quo systems that claim to be neutral but in fact reproduce deep inequalities, because they were never built with everyone in mind.

This framework begins with a truth many organisations still struggle to name. Equity isn't about treating everyone the same. It's about understanding what different people need, what barriers they face, and designing services that don't just tolerate those differences but actively work to accommodate and affirm them. That means interrogating the assumptions embedded in our work – why our intake forms look the way they do, how our success metrics are defined, which languages and cultural norms are privileged in guidance conversations, and whether our teams reflect the communities we serve. TEDI invites us to ask hard questions about power: who holds it, how it shows up in policy and practice, and how we can redistribute it more fairly.

But TEDI doesn't just diagnose – it's also deeply practical. It provides a roadmap for redesigning environments in ways that are sustainable, flexible, and rooted in real-world application. It pushes us to build trust with communities that have historically been underserved or excluded, not through performative gestures but through consistent, embedded change. TEDI is grounded in four tenets – belonging, voice, flexibility, and accountability – each of which interlocks to create a framework that is both challenging and actionable. These aren't abstract values – they're mechanisms for change. Through them, we can begin to repair fractured relationships between services and service users, move from superficial representation to meaningful inclusion, and design with – not just for – the people most impacted.

Importantly, TEDI also recognises that each organisation is different. The pressures, the constraints, the context – it all matters. That's why this framework is deliberately adaptive. It offers a set of principles to guide your work, but it's not prescriptive. You are invited to use it as a compass rather than a checklist, because true inclusion won't come from copying someone else's strategy. It has to grow from within. TEDI helps you centre your context, listen to your people, and build something real – something that outlasts policy cycles, staff turnover, or shifting political winds.

And that matters more now than ever. With growing backlash against EDI – *'anti-woke'* rhetoric, funding cuts, performative allyship – it's easy to retreat into silence or stagnation. But that's precisely why we need TEDI; inclusion can't be conditional. It must be structural, intentional, and brave. We owe it to our clients – and to ourselves – to do better than perform. TEDI gives us the tools to start.

From principles to practice

Turning the TEDI principles into practice cannot fall on frontline staff alone. Equity isn't something we delegate – it's something we embed. That requires leadership to do more than sign off on strategy documents or send supportive emails during Black History Month. Real transformation only happens when there is alignment between those delivering the service and those designing it. We need a dual commitment: top-down support and bottom-up momentum. TEDI is not about 'doing EDI work on the side' – it's about leadership recognising that inclusion is central to mission, culture, and service excellence.

I've seen too many EDI strategies fail because they lived in a Word document rather than in the daily rhythms of the organisation. You can't just appoint an EDI lead or commission a training session and expect the culture to shift. Embedding TEDI means restructuring systems – not just tweaking practice. It means redistributing power, not just consulting once. It means funding real change, not relying on passion projects from marginalised staff. The truth is, when inclusion is only driven by those with lived experience, without structural reinforcement from leadership, burnout is inevitable, and progress stalls.

Leadership buy-in isn't about saying the right things in public – it's about doing the difficult things in private. It requires an ongoing commitment to curiosity, accountability, and courage. It means being willing to reflect on your own biases, listen without defensiveness, and put budget behind your beliefs. TEDI invites leadership teams to move beyond reactive responses and instead ask the deeper, systemic questions: Who is thriving in our service? Who is missing from our leadership tables? Whose perspectives shape our policies? And how might we be unintentionally upholding systems of exclusion even when we intend to do good?

The TEDI framework can offer leaders practical prompts for systemic reflection. Under the tenet of belonging, they might ask: *How do our organisational spaces signal inclusion – from our meeting rooms to our websites? Whose identities are reflected in our communications, and who is invisible?* Under voice, they might examine: *Where are decisions made, and who has the power to shape them? Are feedback mechanisms safe, accessible, and meaningful? Do we act on what people tell us, or simply collect data for appearances' sake?*

When it comes to flexibility, leadership should question what norms are treated as fixed – and who those norms serve. For example: *Are our recruitment processes inclusive of neurodivergent applicants? Are we open to different ways of delivering guidance services, or do we default to the way it's always been done?* Finally, with accountability, leaders must consider: *What metrics do we use to measure inclusion? Are there consequences when progress stalls – or do we just repackage the same pledges with different branding?*

True TEDI implementation at the leadership level is uncomfortable by design. It disrupts the illusion of neutrality. It challenges leadership to move from symbolic support to structural change. But when leadership commits – really commits – to this journey, the impact ripples outwards. Staff feel safer. Clients feel seen. Equity becomes more than a buzzword – it becomes the standard.

Common pitfalls and what to avoid

In my consultancy work, the most common barrier I've encountered isn't malice or wilful exclusion – it's fear. Fear of saying the wrong thing. Fear of being called out. Fear of getting it 'wrong' in a space where the stakes feel increasingly high. These are not imagined fears – they are deeply felt, often by practitioners and leaders who care but feel paralysed by the weight of getting it right. I've sat in rooms where staff whisper their worries after the session, not because they don't believe in inclusion, but because they don't trust themselves to speak it well. Yet, when fear breeds silence, neutrality, or avoidance, it becomes a barrier in itself. We cannot do the work of equity while staying quiet in moments that demand courage. I remember being in an EDI lunchtime session with a senior leader who shared, *'Ifza, the truth is, we want to do better – but we honestly don't know how. You make it look easy, but we don't want to get it wrong.'* That honesty struck me. It reminded me that inclusion doesn't require perfection – it requires bravery. The work isn't about never making mistakes; it's about building cultures where mistakes become opportunities for learning, not reasons to retreat. That shift – from fear to learning – is where transformation begins.

Across my work, a few consistent pitfalls have emerged. One of the most common is performative inclusion – where branding becomes the work. Rainbow logos in June, hashtags during Black History Month, and stock images of 'diverse' people scattered across promotional materials. But underneath, little has changed in recruitment practices, client engagement, or organisational culture. Representation on the surface does not equate to representation in decision-making. Clients and staff notice when the external image doesn't match the internal reality. Trust is fragile, and once lost, it takes a long time to rebuild.

Another pitfall is the assumption that everyone starts from the same place. In careers work, it's easy to unconsciously apply a middle-class, neurotypical,

English-speaking lens to the design of our services. But access is unequal. Some clients are navigating the legacy of exclusion, carrying trauma, or translating systems on behalf of their families. Others are masking neurodivergence just to stay in the room. When we treat everyone as if they've had the same runway, we miss the chance to offer support that is truly responsive.

A third trap is conditional inclusion – expecting people to disclose their identities or trauma in order to access adjustments. I've worked with services where clients only received flexibility once they 'proved' they were struggling, or where practitioners unknowingly demanded vulnerability before establishing safety. Inclusion should never hinge on disclosure. It should be embedded by default. We need to shift from 'tell me what's wrong so I can accommodate you' to 'this space is built to work for multiple ways of being, whether you name them or not'.

There is also the all-too-common confusion between equality and equity. Treating everyone the same feels fair on the surface – but it often reinforces advantage. If we give everyone the same session format, the same timeline, the same expectations, without accounting for access, capacity, or cultural relevance, we create a system that works brilliantly for some and leaves others behind. Equity is about redistribution. It's about recognising that fair does not mean identical.

Inclusion work is inherently messy. It's not a linear process or a neat checklist. It asks us to hold discomfort, reflect on our own complicity, and redesign systems that many of us were trained to maintain. It requires humility, not ego. A willingness to unlearn, not just learn. Most importantly, it calls us to shift from aspiration to action.

Reflective prompts:

- Where in your service are you choosing safety (silence, neutrality) over transformation?
- Are there moments when fear is stopping your team from naming or addressing inequity?
- How do you ensure inclusion is embedded in practice – not just visible in branding?
- In what ways might your systems rely on disclosure instead of proactively designing for variation?
- Are you applying equality (treating everyone the same) where equity (meeting different needs) is needed instead?

Inclusion isn't about getting it perfect – it's about committing to getting it better. I always say forward is forward; being scared or stagnant means nothing changes.

Case studies in inclusive practice

Before we move into the case studies, I want to invite you to pause – not just to read but to reflect. Each of the examples that follows offers a real-world snapshot of inclusion-in-action. These are not perfect case studies, nor are they meant to be replicated wholesale. They are illustrations of what becomes possible when equity isn't an afterthought but a design principle. Each example offers different entry points: from reimagining how we engage underrepresented learners, to building community trust, to embedding inclusive principles into leadership and service delivery.

As you read, ask yourself: What resonates with your own context? What assumptions do these examples challenge? What might be transferable – and what might need to look different in your setting? These aren't models to copy and paste. They're provocations, reminders, and conversation starters. They show that inclusive guidance is not only possible – it's already happening.

But inclusive practice isn't just about learning from others. It's also about turning the mirror inward. So, with each case, I encourage you to reflect:

- What would this look like in my service?
- What conditions made this work?
- What got in the way – and what changed to make it possible?
- Who benefited most – and who might still be left out?

Inclusion, after all, is not about ticking off a checklist. It's about cultivating the kind of culture where these case studies are not the exception, but the expectation.

Case Study 1: Menopause webinar – The power of shared understanding

During one of the EDI lunchtime webinars I facilitated on menopause in the workplace, something unexpectedly profound happened. A male participant – visibly moved – said, *'Ahh, I get it now'*. That moment of realisation, live in the chat, stood out not because it was performative, but because it was honest. He wasn't minimising the issue. He was recognising a gap in his understanding and closing it.

Why it worked: The webinar created a psychologically safe space. We didn't overcomplicate. We spoke plainly about real experiences. We gave room for people to listen without judgement and ask questions without fear. The result? A shift in mindset, not just a transfer of knowledge.

Reflective prompts:

- Where are you creating low-stakes spaces for learning and unlearning?
- How do you invite emotional connection – not just policy awareness?

Case study 2: Confidential listening at board level

During my time as a Board Member of a national organisation, I initiated a series of confidential listening conversations – across all levels of the organisation. I sat with staff across job roles and pay grades, creating private, off-record spaces to share what wasn't being said in meetings. Patterns began to emerge: microaggressions, access barriers, unspoken burnout. I fed these insights directly into strategy conversations with senior leadership – connecting lived experience to structural change.

Why it worked: Trust. People knew their words would be carried forward ethically, not extracted or exposed. The leadership was prepared to listen and act, even when what they heard was uncomfortable. This wasn't a diversity survey; it was equity in action.

Reflective prompts:

- Are you collecting feedback that can't be easily anonymised or safely shared?
- How do you bridge the gap between frontline voices and strategic decisions?

Case study 3: The CDI's Transformative EDI Strategy

At the Career Development Institute (CDI), I helped co-create our Transformative EDI Strategy – a bottom-up, practitioner-led approach rooted in the TEDI framework. We didn't just write a strategy and leave it on a shelf. We piloted it, reviewed it, adapted it. We held open lunchtime sessions, gathered feedback through Padlets, and brought intersectional voices to the forefront. Over time, we moved from a checklist to a culture – where EDI is not a standalone task, but a lens applied to everything we do.

Why it worked: Because it wasn't a top-down mandate. It was built with practitioners, for practitioners. It evolved through feedback. It prioritised transparency and reflexivity.

Reflective prompts:

- Is your EDI strategy being lived or just referenced?
- What mechanisms exist in your organisation for adjusting the course when needed?

Practitioner reflection prompts:

- How does your identity shape your approach to guidance?
- Where do your values align – or conflict – with your organisational culture?
- Whose voice is missing from your service design, evaluation, or feedback loops?
- When have you stayed silent – and why?
- How might your fears around getting it *'wrong'* be holding you back from trying?

A step-by-step guide to embedding TEDI in careers work

Turning intention into infrastructure

So much of EDI work gets stuck at the level of intention. We want to be inclusive; we want our clients to feel seen – but without structure, intention alone can fall flat. That's why this next section exists. It's not about ticking boxes or offering a universal formula. It's about showing you how to take the TEDI principles – transformative equity, diversity, and inclusion – and root them into the everyday design of your careers work. I often get asked, *'Where do we start?'* And the truth is, there isn't one starting point. Different services will need different entry routes. What matters is that you begin, and that you begin with purpose. The prompts that follow are designed to help you look at your service through an equity lens – not just in theory but in tangible, observable practice. These steps don't require perfection. They require honesty. They also require courage once you've seen the gaps – the assumptions in your forms, the rigidity in your delivery, the silence in your feedback loops – you can't unsee them. But that's the work. That's where TEDI lives. In the micro-decisions, the redesigns, the uncomfortable moments of change. This is your space to reflect and reimagine: How might you redesign for inclusion, not just respond to exclusion? Where can your service shift from default settings to deliberate, equity-focused practices? And most importantly – what do your clients need from you that they haven't yet had the language or safety to say?

Embedding equity into careers work is not a one-off intervention or a rebranded CPD session – it's a conscious, continuous practice. This step-by-step guide offers a TEDI-aligned approach to shifting not just what we do, but how we do it. Each section acts as both a prompt and a provocation. It asks you to look at the systems you've built, the assumptions you may have internalised, and the changes you're ready to make. This is not about wholesale reinvention overnight. It's about building muscle memory for inclusion – small, strategic shifts that compound into cultural change. Use these steps as a scaffold, not a script. Adapt them to your setting, your communities, and your capacity – but stay honest. Where are you stuck? What have you avoided? Who has been left out? The aim is to move from aspiration to application. TEDI isn't just something you implement. It's something you become, the more you practise and embed the framework into your workplace. This isn't a checklist for performative compliance. It's a diagnostic tool for radical redesign. This section isn't about offering a tick-box manual. It's about giving you tangible, real-world actions that reflect the principles of the TEDI framework – Transformative Equity, Diversity and Inclusion – and help you build inclusion into your service design from the inside out. Each step below is grounded in practice, not just theory, and serves as an invitation to critically reflect on your own systems and how they might be reimagined through a TEDI lens. Think of this as a conversation starter with your service, your team, and yourself.

Environment and language audit

Look around your space – both physical and digital. What story does it tell about who belongs there? A TEDI approach begins with the premise that environments shape experience. From the moment someone enters your website or waiting room, they're scanning for cues of safety, recognition, and dignity. Are there ramps, quiet rooms, gender-neutral toilets? Do your visuals reflect the race, age, faith, disability, and gender diversity of your client base – or of who you wish to serve? Is your language plain, welcoming, and affirming of multiple identities and access needs? Your forms matter too. If pronouns, caring responsibilities, access needs, and self-descriptions are missing from your intake processes, you're asking people to edit themselves before they've even spoken. Systems must be designed for how people actually live – not how we assume they do. Inclusion is not about accommodation. It's about anticipation.

Reflect:

- Who is visible in your space?
- What identities are centred in your communications?
- Where might someone feel erased or tokenised?

Inclusive intake and data collection

Too often, intake is transactional: *'What job do you want?' 'What's your CV like?'* TEDI challenges us to go deeper. Our initial conversations set the tone – are they extractive, or are they relationship-building? Are we allowing people to share their story on their terms, or rushing them to fit into ours?

We need to reframe intake as a trust-building opportunity. Ask questions like:

- 'What's your story?'
- 'What are your values?'
- 'Where do you feel most yourself?'

These are not fluffy or off-topic – they're fundamental to understanding a person's career journey in context. Data collection also needs to shift. Don't just track outcomes. Track access, inclusion, and attrition. Who's coming? Who's staying? Who's leaving – and why? Disaggregate your data. Only then will you see the equity gaps hiding in plain sight.

Reflect:

- Are you hearing clients' full stories?
- What data are you not collecting?
- How do you close the loop once data is gathered?

Flexible delivery models

Inclusion doesn't always mean doing more – it often means doing things differently. Flexibility isn't a bonus; it's an equity tool. Offering career guidance through a variety of formats – phone, video, face-to-face, email, or even asynchronous written summaries – helps ensure that people with varying needs, schedules, and energy levels can still engage. This is especially vital for disabled clients, neurodivergent individuals, carers, or those navigating trauma. One size never fits all, and if your service is rigid, it will always favour those already best equipped to engage. Instead, consider drop-in options, shorter sessions, or flexible booking systems. Let people access your support in the way that best fits their life. That's not lowering standards; it's raising access.

Can you work in a more accommodating, flexible manner? More importantly, will you work flexibly? Flexibility is not about convenience – it's about justice. It acknowledges trauma, neurodivergence, chronic illness, caring duties, and more. This might mean offering:

- Drop-ins for those with fluctuating schedules;
- Written summaries for neurodivergent clients;
- Multiple modalities (video, voice, message) for accessing guidance.

If your model only works for people who are already well, well-resourced, and well-supported, then it isn't inclusive. It's exclusive by design.

Reflect:

- Where could your system flex?
- Who is currently being left out due to rigidity?
- How could you pilot new models without overhauling everything?

Ongoing feedback and accountability

Feedback should not be a box-ticking survey at the end. TEDI sees it as a dynamic, ongoing conversation. Build mechanisms that centre client voice – especially from those who are minoritised or underserved. Use anonymous feedback loops, advisory groups, and co-designed evaluation tools. Make feedback part of strategic decision-making, not just an afterthought. Act on what you hear. Publish your learning. Name your gaps. Show that feedback leads to change. If you collect insight but never shift practice, you break trust. Accountability also means tracking progress. Are you meeting your equity goals? Are you applying TEDI consistently across teams? Who holds the mirror up? Set benchmarks, review regularly, and make inclusion non-negotiable – even when funding or leadership changes.

Reflect:

- What happens to feedback once it's collected?
- How are clients and staff involved in shaping change?
- Where does accountability for inclusion sit in your structure?

Mini toolkit for embedding equity

To support these four steps, I've included some practical prompts and tools that you can use immediately:

- **Equity session checklist**
  Ask yourself: Have I checked for access needs? Have I used visuals and examples that reflect diverse lived experiences? Have I offered more than one way to engage?
- **Inclusive group-work planning tool**
  Who feels safe enough to speak in your sessions? Are you assuming everyone will contribute verbally, or are you building in alternatives like writing, drawing, or small group sharing?

Sample questions for inclusive 1:1s

'What do you want your work to feel like?'

'Is there anything about you that you'd like me to be aware of as we work together?'

'Have you ever felt the need to hide parts of yourself in past educational or work settings?'

These steps aren't a tick-box exercise or list to be completed once. They're an evolving practice – rooted in the TEDI values of belonging, voice, flexibility, and accountability. Start small if you need to, but start with intention. The most inclusive services aren't the ones with the most diverse posters – they're the ones that do the hard work of redesigning systems so that difference doesn't just fit in but thrives within the culture of true transformative equity, diversity, and inclusion.

From checklist to culture

Inclusion doesn't live in a policy document or a one-off training session. It lives in the daily choices we make as practitioners, leaders, and teams. It's how we show up, how we listen, how we design spaces, and how we respond when harm is named. A checklist is a starting point – but if we stop there, we reduce equity to a tick-box exercise, not a transformative process. What we're striving for is a shift in culture – a move from compliance to conviction.

Practitioners often ask me, *'Am I doing this right?'* But inclusion isn't about always getting it right. It's about staying curious, being honest, and choosing bravery over comfort when the system defaults to silence. This is where the real work begins: in the questions we ask of ourselves, in the feedback we're willing to receive, and in the spaces we create for discomfort to be held, not avoided.

Culture change happens when we normalise reflective conversations, when feedback is welcomed without defensiveness, and when equity is embedded into how decisions are made – not just who is in the room. It requires leaders who model vulnerability, not just authority, and practitioners who feel safe enough to challenge upwards as well as support outwards.

Let's ask ourselves:

- Do we treat inclusion as everyone's responsibility – or as one person's job?
- Do our systems reward conformity or enable authenticity?
- Are we brave enough to name the harm – even when it implicates the structures we're part of?

Inclusion is not an end state. It's a muscle, a mindset, and a commitment to do better, be better, and design better – every single day.

Reflective practice grid

Inclusion isn't a destination – it's a direction. Reflection is how we stay aligned on the path. This grid invites you to pause, assess, and consider where you truly are in your EDI journey – not where your policies say you are, or where you hope to be seen, but where your actual practice sits.

Use this tool (Table 21) individually or as a team to spark honest dialogue. It's not about shame or blame. It's about recognising the gap between intention and action – and choosing to close it. Every organisation, and every practitioner, sits somewhere on the spectrum between compliance and conviction. What matters is the willingness to shift.

This isn't a one-off exercise. Revisit the grid regularly. Challenge each other. Reflect on how your practice has evolved – and where it's still coasting on performative gestures. Ask yourself: Am I doing this work because I have to, or because I believe in it? And what would it look like if I did both – with integrity? Moving from compliance to conviction isn't just a personal shift. It's a cultural one. It starts with honest, grounded reflection.

Table 21 Reflective practice grid

Area of practice	Compliance (box-ticking)	Conviction (culture-shifting)	Where are we?	Next step
Language use	Using inclusive terms when prompted or trained	Proactively adapting language to affirm identity		
Client relationships	Offering support if identity is disclosed	Creating space for identity to be expressed safely		
Team discussions	Avoiding *'sensitive'* topics to keep harmony	Making space for hard conversations, even when messy		
Policy and documentation	Updating documents to meet minimum standards	Co-creating policies with marginalised voices at the centre		
Feedback culture	Inviting feedback occasionally	Embedding feedback loops into everyday practice		
Learning and development	Attending mandatory EDI training	Embedding learning into ongoing CPD and supervision		
Leadership	Speaking about inclusion during awareness weeks	Demonstrating equity through resourcing, decision-making, accountability		

TEDI culture audit tool

Culture is not defined by what we declare in our policies – it is shaped by what we normalise, what we prioritise, and what we allow to remain unexamined. It is the silent language of an organisation – the daily habits, unspoken rules, and embedded values that determine whose presence is affirmed, whose voice is centred, and whose identity must be adapted to fit in. This TEDI-aligned culture audit invites you to pause and interrogate the cultural foundations of your service with honesty and depth. TEDI is not about ticking boxes. It is about fundamentally rethinking how we build and sustain environments that truly honour equity, diversity, and inclusion – not in theory but in practice. The TEDI framework offers four pillars to guide this reflection: Transformative Practice, Equitable Policies, Diverse Culture, and Inclusive Practices. Together, these pillars act as levers for change, encouraging us to move from performative commitments to systemic redesign. This audit is not about self-congratulation or surface-level gestures – it is a tool to uncover misalignment between values and reality. Whether used in leadership retreats, supervision meetings, or team development spaces, it provides a mirror. What we do with the reflection is what matters most.

Transformative practice

Services rooted in transformative practice recognise that today's inequalities are not accidental – they are historically produced and structurally maintained. Transformation requires us to acknowledge the roots of exclusion, power, and access in the careers sector. Are we openly discussing how history has shaped present-day disparities in opportunity? Are we recognising how gatekeeping, credentialism, and dominant norms have limited entry and progression for certain communities? Transformative practice demands truth-telling. It asks us to go beyond *'raising awareness'* and instead situate our work within broader socio-political realities that have long marginalised ethnically diverse and underserved groups.

- Do we talk about the histories of inequality that shape clients' access to careers?
- Are we aware of how our own sector has excluded or gatekept certain groups?
- How do we honour lived experience alongside data in our decision-making?

☐ Rarely ☐ Sometimes ☐ Often ☐ Always

Equitable policies: Identity, power, and organisational norms

Equity cannot thrive in a system that treats everyone the same despite vastly different starting points. Equitable policies acknowledge the complexity of people's lives, identities, and access needs. They dismantle assumptions baked into definitions of professionalism, success, and suitability. Equity asks: Do our policies embed fairness beyond formal equality? Do they proactively dismantle barriers to inclusion, progression, and voice? Are our systems designed for dominant identities – or are they adaptable, reflective, and grounded in justice? The work of equitable policy is never neutral. It demands intention, responsiveness, and courage.

- Do we make space for clients and staff to express their identities without fear of judgement or consequence?
- Do our definitions of professionalism and readiness accommodate cultural and cognitive variation?
- Are our policies explicitly designed to address historical and structural disadvantage?

☐ Rarely   ☐ Sometimes   ☐ Often   ☐ Always

Diverse culture: Representation, safety, and challenge

A truly diverse culture is not just one that includes different faces – it is one that affirms different truths. Culture is made visible through representation, but it is sustained through psychological safety and organisational self-awareness. Whose stories are told in your materials? Whose knowledge is treated as valid? Who feels safe enough to challenge the norm without fear of penalty? A TEDI-aligned diverse culture goes beyond inclusion as image. It embeds difference as strength and treats dissent not as disruption but as data. A diverse culture does not wait for harm to occur before taking action – it builds safety in from the start.

- Are minoritised clients and staff represented meaningfully, not in a tokenistic way for show?
- Do team members feel safe to speak up about exclusionary dynamics?
- Are cultural knowledge systems beyond the white, Western canon legitimised in your guidance work?

☐ Rarely   ☐ Sometimes   ☐ Often   ☐ Always

Inclusive practices: Everyday access and accountability

Inclusive practice is the everyday expression of equity. It's the decision to offer multiple formats for engagement, to embed access without requiring disclosure, and to treat flexibility as a design principle rather than an optional extra. Inclusive practice is not about accommodating those who ask – it's about anticipating the full range of human variation in how we plan, deliver, and evaluate our work. TEDI reminds us that inclusion must be measurable, maintained, and made real through structures – not only feelings. Are your systems actively enabling participation, or are they quietly reproducing exclusion through default norms? Are you tracking what works – and changing what doesn't?

- Do our day-to-day practices anticipate difference or only respond to it once raised?
- Are accessibility, flexibility, and trauma-informed delivery part of our standard offer?
- Is there a clear process for acting on feedback and measuring progress on inclusion?

☐ Rarely   ☐ Sometimes   ☐ Often   ☐ Always

Next steps reflection

This audit is not about appearance – it is about alignment. Once completed, take time to collectively reflect. Where are you moving with clarity, and where are you coasting on habit? Use the TEDI pillars to structure your next steps:

- Which TEDI pillar do we need to focus on over the next quarter?
- What is one actionable shift we can embed this month that would create the conditions for greater equity?
- Who needs to be part of this conversation – and how are we centring those most impacted?

Transformation is not a single leap – it's a series of deliberate steps taken in the direction of justice. TEDI offers the framework. This audit helps you see where you truly stand.

Chapter 13
Transforming practice through inclusion

Author's voice

We've made it to the end of the book, but this is not the end. This is a loop, a cycle, a rhythm that continues far beyond these pages. When I think about EDI, I often picture the scene from *The Lion King* – Mufasa's voice echoing to Simba, reminding him of the Circle of Life. That's how I've always understood this work. Equity, diversity, and inclusion is not a checklist you complete or a finish line you cross. It is an ongoing, dynamic process – a cycle that keeps turning, re-evaluating, growing, shedding, and beginning again. It is transformative because it demands constant return – to ourselves, to our policies, to our behaviours, to the lived experiences around us. It is not linear. It loops. It widens. It deepens. We look at organisations from the top-down, the bottom-up, sideways, and diagonally. We zoom in on the micro-moments in one-to-one interactions, and we zoom out to the wider systems of harm, privilege, and access. Equity can't be inserted as a bolt-on. It must be embedded. This work is not the remit of one EDI lead or a single role on a staff chart.

Too often, EDI is siloed, handed to one person who becomes a figurehead – frequently someone already from a marginalised background. This model isolates and tokenises. If inclusion is to be real, it must be everybody's work. Every line manager. Every practitioner. Every leader. Every admin team. Every governing board. Inclusion is organisational, cultural, and structural. It is everyone's responsibility because diversity isn't rare – it's universal. In every webinar I deliver, in every consultancy session, and in every conversation where someone asks what EDI has to do with them, I offer this reminder: Every single person has some angle of diversity. Every single one of us carries a story, an identity, a set of experiences that shapes how we walk through the world. Diversity is not what separates us – it is what makes us human. Recognising and valuing that diversity, however, is what builds cultures of safety, dignity, and belonging. We return to the beginning, but differently. With more awareness. With sharper tools. With clearer vision. Inclusion is not the end point of this book. It is the ongoing centre.

I went back and forth for quite some time on whether to end this book with three distinct chapters – one to answer *why EDI*, another to explore what tools we can use, and a final one to imagine what the future could look like. There was a case for each of them standing on their own. There's a lot to unpack in each. But the more I reflected, the more it felt artificial to separate them. In practice, they are deeply interconnected; instead, I chose to weave them together into one concluding chapter – a space where we centre purpose, equip ourselves for the work ahead, and pause to dream. This is the point of EDI: it isn't a fixed destination or a checklist of compliance – it's a way of thinking, acting, and relating that shapes both the present and the future. This final chapter brings that full circle.

Why is EDI important?

After exploring the intersecting inequalities that shape career development across sectors, this chapter marks a turning point. We now move from reflection to action – from diagnosing exclusion to actively reshaping practice. This chapter is not about ticking off tasks on a diversity agenda. It is about rooting equity in the everyday – embedding it where careers work actually happens, not just where strategies are written. If you've made it this far into the book, I want to begin by saying this: I see you. You are still here, still reading, still invested. That matters. The work of equity is not performative. It is not a badge. It is daily, iterative, and uncomfortable. It is also liberating.

When I first began this work, I too wondered whether anything could really change. Policies often felt like they were designed to maintain the status quo, not shift it. Careers guidance sometimes felt disconnected from people's lived realities. This disconnect must now be challenged. As career practitioners, we sit at a critical intersection of people's journeys. Our interactions can either reinforce exclusion or disrupt it. That's the power we hold – not just in what we say but in what we choose to centre, question, or ignore. This chapter is written for those of us who feel the weight of that responsibility and want to carry it with care.

So how do we transform practice? Clarity must come first. We must define what we mean by inclusion. This is not a buzzword, but a commitment to shifting structures. Inclusion means thinking about who our services are built for – who they are built without. It requires us to ask: Whose stories have we made room for? Whose ambitions are recognised as valid? Who must leave parts of themselves at the door in order to be seen as equals ? This is where the TEDI framework becomes not just useful, but necessary. TEDI grounds our work in four pillars – Transformative Practice, Equitable

Policies, Diverse Culture, and Inclusive Practice. These are not theoretical. They are practical guides to realigning our practice with justice.

TEDI framework

Transformative practice

This pillar takes us deeper than intent. Naming what often goes unspoken is essential to transformative practice. We must examine how power operates in our sessions, systems, and selves. Wanting to be inclusive is not enough. Assumptions, habits, and expectations need scrutiny. Consider the questions asked during a careers meeting. Are they open, or loaded with cultural assumptions? Do we expect a particular communication style? Is there a default vision of success? When someone doesn't fit the mould, do we adapt or expect them to conform?

Transformative practice begins when uncomfortable questions are asked. Who benefits from current session structures? Who is quietly opting out? Who isn't accessing support at all? These questions are not here to shame. They exist to sharpen. Inclusion begins when we notice the gap between values and impact.

Equitable policies

Policies often become the graveyard of good intentions. Many services claim inclusivity, yet referral forms, access criteria, and eligibility requirements often contradict this. Equitable policies address barriers proactively – not reactively. We must ask: Are we flexible for those with caring responsibilities, trauma histories, or digital exclusion? Are alternative formats available without repeated requests? Do we assume identical starting points for all?

Equality offers the same to everyone. Equity ensures everyone receives what they need. Policies reveal whether this distinction is understood. Are we penalising lateness without exploring its causes? Are we rewarding assertiveness in ways that marginalise culturally or neurologically diverse clients? Are translation services and fee waivers offered in ways that empower, not stigmatise? Designing for dignity should be the goal. Clients should not have to fight the system to benefit from it.

Diverse culture

Culture is defined by what we allow, reward, and ignore. An EDI statement cannot guarantee inclusion. Feeling invisible can still happen under a colourful banner of diversity. Representation matters, yet without belonging, it is hollow. Many practitioners have shared that they *'tone down'* their identity to fit in. Accent. Clothing. Name. Faith. Hair. Personality. Expectations around professionalism often favour a narrow aesthetic. Neutrality, in these cases, is exclusion wearing a mask.

A truly diverse culture embraces difference. It doesn't manage it, flatten it, or fear it. This kind of culture requires intentional effort. Senior leaders must model vulnerability. Brave conversations need encouragement. Poster campaigns are not enough. Listening – deep, honest listening – must become a cultural norm.

Inclusive practice

The final pillar is where the TEDI framework becomes tangible. Every interaction with a client is an opportunity to choose inclusion. It's visible in posture, pauses, and paperwork. Do we create time for reflection? Are experiences validated? Are assumptions named or unspoken? Careers guidance should hold space for the whole person – not just the CV. The effects of trauma, racism, poverty, or marginalisation may shape responses. Practitioners must avoid pathologising those responses.

An inmate once said to me, *'I didn't need anyone to fix me. I just needed the system to not make me feel broken.'* That stayed with me. Being inclusive isn't about having all the answers. It is about creating an environment where people feel seen, safe, and ready to act on their own terms.

Barriers to implementation and how to move through them

This work is not easy. Services are under pressure. Funding is scarce. Time is limited. People are tired. Resistance is real. Trauma is present. Despite this, equity remains essential. Inclusion must not be treated as an extra. Services that work for everyone cannot be built without change. Letting go of the familiar, working through fear, and accepting inevitable mistakes are part of the process.

Leadership must step up. Inclusion needs resources – time, training, investment, and accountability. The mindset must shift from *'there's no time for this'* to *'this is non-negotiable'*. Exclusion, even when unintentional, undermines the sector's purpose.

From intention to infrastructure

The careers sector prides itself on being values-led. However, values without action are empty. Inclusion must show up in systems, behaviours, and structures. This chapter does not offer a checklist. That was intentional. Instead, it offers a provocation – a call to re-examine practice with new eyes. Inclusion is not a destination. It is an orientation. A way of being, doing, and staying accountable. The process is imperfect and uncomfortable. It is also liberating and necessary. When done well, it upholds the highest purpose of careers guidance: to help people see, shape, and step into futures where they matter.

Recommendations

If I could offer one recommendation to anyone engaging with this work – regardless of role, seniority, or lived experience – it would be this: Pick up this book and read it but not in one sitting. Let it sit with you. Read slowly, one section at a time, and allow space for the ideas to settle. This isn't a manual to rush through. It's a companion to return to, again and again. As you read, think critically about other intersections of diversity that haven't been named. Think about your own work – your daily practice, your assumptions, your barriers. Ask yourself: How could this apply to neurodivergence, to migration status, to trauma, to the intersections I encounter but may not yet fully understand? Consider what tools could support you in holding space for those realities. Reflect on how TEDI could be embedded more deeply into your team, your organisation, your conversations. Don't wait for the perfect time – start now, with what you have.

Use this book not as a final answer, but as a launchpad. Run a team audit. Invite different voices into the room. Hold webinars. Set up reflection groups. Organise listening sessions. Not tokenistic ones – real ones, with intent and follow-through. Call in speakers, clients, practitioners, and community members, and actually hear what they are saying. Not everyone wants a panel seat. Not everyone wants to be made a symbol. Representation cannot mean being expected to carry the weight of an entire group. One person cannot be the voice for all Muslims, all disabled people, all trans workers, all working-class communities. The moment you begin asking one individual to speak for many, you've lost sight of equity. I say it all the time: no two fingers are the same. Even in the same family, no two siblings are the same. Everyone is shaped by different circumstances, timelines, and truths. We must stop boxing people in and meet them as they are. That's not just EDI – that's humanity.

I recommend that every organisation invests in EDI literacy. Equip yourselves with the terminology but also with the courage to sit in discomfort. Don't be afraid to say, *'We don't know enough yet, but we're here to learn'*. Host training days that aren't one-offs, but part of a long-term commitment. Explore different identities and intersections even if you don't feel ready. Especially if you don't feel ready. Inclusion doesn't arrive once you've done a checklist – it's built through relationship, accountability, and persistence. Call people in, not out. When you invite someone to lead a session, a keynote, or a consultation – pay them. Pay them for their time, their labour, their energy, their knowledge. Do not rely on volunteers to carry your strategy. Equity costs money. You cannot extract the emotional and intellectual labour of marginalised people for free and call it inclusion.

Above all, EDI must not sit with one person. It's not the responsibility of a single *'diversity lead'* or *'inclusive practice officer'*. It must live across the entire organisation – from boardroom to break room, from HR to curriculum, from reception to leadership. Everyone must carry some part of it. Inclusion is not an add-on; it must be embedded. Otherwise, the work becomes shallow, and it breaks. When leadership fails to invest, EDI becomes the first thing cut. When leadership sees it as essential – as central to quality, to growth, to care – everything changes. Leadership buy-in is the difference between success and stagnation. This work fails when it is performative. It flourishes when it is authentic, when it is resourced, when it is strategic.

In careers work, especially, the need for this is urgent. The workforce is not homogeneous. People come from every imaginable background and bring with them all the beauty, complexity, and contradiction that diversity entails. If we want guidance to be meaningful, to be ethical, and to be effective – it must honour that. EDI is not separate from careers work. It is careers work. Without it, we're simply teaching people to adapt to broken systems. With it, we're equipping people to navigate, challenge, and reshape the world around them. That's the promise of this book. That's the power of the TEDI framework. Not to offer a quick fix, but to build a way forward – together. The next section will share practical tools, frameworks, and guides to support this shift. These tools are not replacements for your values. They are companions. Inclusion is not defined by where we start. It is shaped by what we choose to do next.

Tools for transformation: Practising equity through TEDI

The last section asked you to pause. To reflect. To look not just at your work, but through it. It wasn't about guilt or perfection. It was about honesty. About seeing where power sits, whose voices shape the work, and what might need to change. This next part is where we shift from reflection to action. Not through tick-boxes or token gestures, but through intention, structure, and care. These tools are grounded in the TEDI framework, not as abstract theory, but as something to be lived – through policy, practice, culture, and conversation. Each tool comes from lived work. From real moments with clients, practitioners, and educators navigating the tensions between values and reality. They've been shaped by stories – of harm, hope, invisibility, fatigue, resilience. They're here to offer scaffolding. To help you move from where you currently are in your inclusion journey to where you wish to be. They're not perfect. They won't be right for every space. But they're a starting point.

I don't offer them as a one-size-fits-all manual. I offer them as a mirror. A way for you – and your team – to pause and ask honestly: What's really going on here? What needs to shift? And who's missing from the table when we're making those decisions?

This toolkit isn't about ticking boxes. It's about reshaping how we think, act, and embed equity in our everyday work. Below is a quick reference list of the tools included in this chapter. You don't need to use them all at once. Come back to them when you're ready – adapt them, expand them, and make them work for your context. Equity is never static. These tools shouldn't be either.

Tool Name	Purpose	Page
TEDI self-assessment grid	To benchmark where you are and identify growth areas across all pillars	191
Culture audit tool	To interrogate team norms, values, and patterns	192
Client's support and access form	To build inclusion into client engagement from the outset	192
Inclusive guidance checklist	To embed equity in client sessions and daily practice	193
Case study reflection prompts	To explore bias and intersectionality in team learning	193
TEDI implementation map	To turn equity values into trackable strategic actions	194
Leadership accountability matrix	To make equity leadership visible and accountable	194
Client voice integration tool	To centre client feedback in service development	194

If you only choose one to start with, choose the one that speaks to your current tension point – where you feel most stuck or unsure. That's often where transformation begins.

TEDI self-assessment grid

Purpose: To benchmark where you are now and identify areas for growth.

How to use: Use this tool individually, with teams, or in supervision. Revisit regularly to track change and foster collective accountability (Table 22).

Table 22 TEDI self-assessment grid

TEDI pillar	Practice statement	Red	Amber	Green	Notes/actions
Transformative practice	We regularly reflect on who benefits from our current practices.				
Equitable policies	Our policies adapt to meet the varied needs of our service users.				
Diverse culture	Staff can show up as their full selves without fear of judgement.				
Inclusive practice	Sessions validate lived experience and foster trust.				

Culture audit tool

Purpose: To examine your team/service culture with honesty and intention.

How to use: Complete as a team, reflect together, and identify patterns that need changing.

- What behaviours are consistently rewarded?
- Who holds power in conversations and decisions?
- Who doesn't hold power, and why is this?
- When someone raises an issue of exclusion, how is it received?
- What identities are centred in visual materials?
- How are cultural and religious needs acknowledged?
- What does 'professionalism' look like here, and who is excluded by that?

Client's support and access form

Purpose: To establish dignity-centred access from the outset.

How to use: Share before or during the first contact with clients.

- Name you would like us to use:
- Pronouns (if you wish to share):
- Preferred communication style (e.g. verbal, written, visual):
- Do you have any sensory sensitivities we should be aware of?
- Are there cultural, religious, or personal practices important to you?
- Do you require any support to fully take part in sessions (e.g. breaks, translation, support person present)?

Inclusive guidance checklist

Purpose: To make equity tangible in day-to-day client work.

How to use: Reflect before, during, and after sessions. Use it as a personal or team tool – not to police practice, but to deepen it (Table 23).

Table 23 Inclusive guidance checklist

Reflective prompt	Yes	No	Notes/actions
Have I made space to learn how the client defines their own identity, needs, and goals?	☐	☐	
Have I paused to examine my assumptions about the client's background or ambitions?	☐	☐	
Am I using language that invites, not excludes?	☐	☐	
Have I considered the impact of trauma, exclusion, or marginalisation in how the client engages?	☐	☐	
Is the session accessible – physically, emotionally, culturally, and practically?	☐	☐	
Have I centred the client's own definition of success?	☐	☐	
Did I validate what they shared, or did I rush to solution mode?	☐	☐	
Have I left room for silence, reflection, and cultural nuance in communication?	☐	☐	
Have I followed up with resources relevant to their context?	☐	☐	
If I made a mistake, did I name it and reflect on it?	☐	☐	
What will I do differently next time to ensure inclusion is lived, not just spoken?			

Case study reflection prompts

Purpose: To explore bias, power, and intersectionality in team learning.

How to use: Use anonymised client scenarios or create fictional ones.

Prompts:

- What assumptions were made about this client?
- How might their background affect how they present?
- Did the session centre the client's values or ours?
- What systems might be impacting their options?
- What alternative supports or referrals could be offered?

TEDI implementation map

Purpose: To turn values into a living, trackable strategy.

How to use: Set timelines, assign roles, and review quarterly (Table 24).

Table 24 TEDI implementation map

TEDI pillar	Quick wins (3 months)	Medium actions (6–12 months)	Strategic shifts (1–3 years)	Notes/lead
Transformative practice				
Equitable policies				
Diverse culture				
Inclusive practice				

Leadership accountability matrix

Purpose: To make equity leadership visible and accountable.

How to use: Use in line management, strategy reviews, and board meetings (Table 25).

Table 25 Leadership accountability matrix

Area	Evidence of action	Gaps identified	Next steps	Lead/deadline
Recruitment				
Staff development				
Policy inclusion				
Harm response and repair				

Client voice integration tool

Purpose: To centre feedback as a tool for relational change.

How to use: Offer clients multiple ways to share their experience.

Template prompts:

- What worked well for you in this session?
- Was there anything that felt uncomfortable or unclear?
- Do you feel your voice was heard and respected?
- What would you change about how we supported you?
- How can we support you better moving forward?

The ongoing TEDI journey

Every tool shared in this chapter has been carefully created, not just as a resource, but as an anchor – something to come back to when the noise gets too loud or when the intention behind the work starts to feel diluted. These aren't neat solutions or formulas to follow. These are provocations wrapped in practice. They're made to evolve, be challenged, and stretched. I don't want you to read these and put them away on a shelf. I want you to use them, question them, remix them, and make them your own. That is TEDI. That is how equity lives and breathes through practice. I always say that EDI isn't a checklist or a side project. It is the bloodline of the system – embedded into every artery of the organisation. If these tools feel clunky or cause discomfort, that's the point. Discomfort is the birthplace of growth. When something feels hard to read or apply, take a breath and sit with it. That unease is telling you something. That's data. That's where the real work begins – not on the pages, but in the room with another person, in the moment where you choose to pause instead of reacting, to reflect instead of dismissing.

These templates, audits, prompts, and grids are not here to make you feel boxed in. They're companions for the long haul. You will grow. Your practice will evolve. Your understanding will deepen. What you need today may not be what you need in a year's time. That's okay. Come back, revise, rip them up if you need to. Write new ones. Include your clients, your community, your teams. Let the tools transform with you. This whole final chapter has been structured intentionally – not to wrap up the book with a bow, but to walk you back to the roots. Why TEDI? What tools can I use? What might the future look like? These were not just editorial decisions. They came from the very heart of how I see EDI as a cycle. At one point, I thought about splitting these ideas across three separate chapters, but that didn't sit right. They are interlinked. The why leads into the how. The how shapes the future. The future reflects back on the why. It's a loop. Just like TEDI. Just like the work.

We've made it to the final section of the book, but I want to be clear: this is not an ending. This is a checkpoint. A moment to stop, reflect, breathe – and keep going. I often think of EDI as the Circle of Life. Mufasa. Simba. Legacy. Renewal. It isn't linear. It's not something you finish. It's cyclical. You start, you deepen, you pause, you pass it on. You revisit. You realign. You look at things top-down, bottom-up, sideways, inside-out. That's what TEDI asks of us – to keep returning to practice, to keep checking ourselves and our structures, to keep rebuilding. EDI must never be about a single person – an EDI officer, a tokenised leader, a poster child for representation. That model fails. Every time. This work belongs to everyone. It is organisational. It is cultural. It is human. We all carry an angle of diversity – none of us is the same. Even within the same family, the same home, the same job role. I say this all the time in my lunchtime webinars and in every conversation I have:

no two people are the same. No two siblings. No two students. No two clients. Everyone holds their own story, their own truths, their own intersections of identity and experience. To honour that, we cannot place people in boxes. We must meet them where they are.

Here is my recommendation – one I offer with care and conviction. Whether you're a senior leader, a practitioner, a student, a client, or someone trying to understand your place in all this: pick up this book. Not to race through it. Not to tick a training requirement. Read it in sections. One chapter at a time. Let it sit with you. Ask yourself, how does this apply to the intersections I haven't yet explored? Where does TEDI show up in my world? What tools do I need right now? What might I be missing? Then go deeper. Host a webinar. Open up dialogue. Create space for voices you haven't heard yet. Don't allow the same people to speak for entire communities. Don't make unfair representations of people's diversity based on what's visible or convenient. Stop pushing people into categories they never asked for.

This is the hard bit – EDI needs resourcing. The F word – funding. I say this everywhere I go – equity work needs money. You cannot create deep structural change on goodwill alone. If you're asking for change, pay people properly. Fund the work and, most importantly, respect the labour. Respect the lived experience. Respect the expertise. Get leadership buy-in. From the very top. Without it, nothing sticks. If it's tokenistic, it will collapse. This has to be genuine. Not just for compliance, but because you want your organisation to be better, more humane, and more reflective of the world it serves. Careers work is not neutral. It never has been. It's political, relational, and deeply human. The people walking through your doors are carrying their lives on their backs – race, class, trauma, ambition, hope. If you're serious about supporting them, you have to understand them. If you're serious about inclusion, then TEDI cannot be optional. It must be the foundation. I leave you with one final question: What's the one thing you will change today?

References

Chambers, N., Kashefpakdel, E. T., Rehill, J., & Percy, C. (2018). *Drawing the Future: Exploring the career aspirations of primary school children from around the world.* London: Education and Employers. https://www.educationandemployers.org/drawing-the-future/ (Accessed 13 June 2025).

Edelman, M. W. (1992). *The measure of our success: A letter to my children and yours.* Boston: Beacon Press.

Equality Act 2010. (2010). *c.15.* London: The Stationery Office. https://www.legislation.gov.uk/ukpga/2010/15/contents (Accessed 13 June 2025).

Frigerio, G., & McCash, P. (2013). *Career development learning, higher education and the capable graduate: Theory and practice.* Abingdon: Routledge.

Hambly, L. (2009). *The courage of confidence: The role of faith in career choice.* https://www.creativecareercoaching.org/wp-content/uploads/2015/02/The-Courage-Of-Confidence.pdf (Accessed 13 June 2025).

Lindqvist, A., Sendén, M. G., & Renström, E. A. (2020). What is gender, anyway: A review of the options for operationalising gender. *Psychology & Sexuality*, 12(4), 332–344. https://doi.org/10.1080/19419899.2020.1729844

Modood, T., & Ahmad, F. (2007). British Muslim perspectives on multiculturalism. *Theory, culture & society*, 24(2), 187-213.

Neary, S., Hanson, J., & Cotterill, V. (2017). *A career in career – understanding what career looks like in the career development sector.* Career Matters.

World Health Organization (WHO). (2023). *Gender and health.* https://www.who.int/health-topics/gender#tab=tab_1

Supporting resources

CDI. (2023). *Equity, diversity and inclusion strategy.*

Frigerio, G. (2017). Making sense of faith and career development: Exploring the career narratives of Christians working in education. *British Journal of Guidance & Counselling*, 45(4), 438–450. https://doi.org/10.1080/03069885.2016.1213373

Mertens, D. M. (2017). Transformative research: Personal and societal. *International Journal for Transformative Research*, 4(1), 18–24.

Neary, S. (2020). Diversifying the careers workforce: Opportunities and challenges. *Journal for Perspectives of Economic, Political and Social Integration*, 25(2), 65–81.

Neary, S., Hanson, J., & Cotterill, V. (2017). A career in career-understanding what career looks like in the career development sector. *Career Matters*, 5(3), 20–22.

OpenLearn. (n.d.). *Diversity and inclusion in the workplace.* The Open University. https://www.open.edu/openlearn/money-business/diversity-and-inclusion-the-workplace/content-section-overview (Accessed 13 June 2025).

Open University & Career Tech. (2020). *Inclusive career development reports.*

Targett, C., & Benton, J. (2024). *Career development and inclusive practice.* Basingstoke: Trotman.

The McGregor-Smith Review (Gov.uk).

Youth Futures Foundation. (2021). *Race equity in careers guidance.*

DISCOVER TROTMAN'S
CAREER DEVELOPMENT INSTITUTE
COLLECTION

The Career Professional's Guide to Research
9781911724599
By Emma Bolger

Equity, Diversity, and Inclusion in Career Development
9781911724698
By Ifza Shakoor

The Career Development Professional's AI Toolkit
9781911724650
By Michael Larbalestier and Marianne Wilson

Sustainable Careers
9781911724537
By Liz Painter

Career Coaching for Midlife and Beyond
9781911724711
By Denise Taylor

The Career Development Professional's Survival Guide
9781911724674
By Jules Benton and Chris Targett

trotman | **t** Estd. 1969

Enhance your careers library with careers essentials, free resources and expert articles

Visit www.trotman.co.uk